D0498418

A THEOLOGY OF EXILE

A THEOLOGY OF EXILE

Judgment/Deliverance in Jeremiah and Ezekiel

THOMAS M. RAITT

FORTRESS PRESS
Philadelphia

Library of Congress Catalog Card Number 76–62610
ISBN 0–8006–0497–0

6178L76 Printed in U.S.A. 1–497

for
Walter Harrelson
teacher, scholar, friend

CONTENTS

Preface		ix
Introduction		1
I	The Oracle of Judgment: Structure and Setting	15
II	Radicalization of the Judgment Message	35
III	The Rejection Motif	59
IV	Theodicy	83
V	The Shift from Doom to Salvation	106
VI	The Prophetic Oracle of Deliverance	128
VII	The Content of the Deliverance Message	174
Conclusion		223
Abbreviations		231
Select Bibliography		232
Notes		235
Index		269

PREFACE

In the summer of 1966 I began studying the prophetic Oracle of Deliverance. In some ways that was the beginning of this book. During the years that followed, I grew increasingly interested in the relationship between God's justice and his love, his punishment and his forgiveness, and in the two prophetic speech-forms which most typify each pole: the Oracle of Judgment and the Oracle of Deliverance. Paralleling this I was increasingly curious about what happened to Israel's election and covenant traditions at the time of the Exile. These lines of thought converged in the summer of 1970 when my family and I began a leave year with a summer's stay at Heidelberg University. The major part of the leave was spent at the central seminary of Reform Judaism, Hebrew Union College, in Cincinnati. One of my hopes for the book is that Jews, as well as Christians, will find a way to profit from it. What has resulted from the ensuing years of work is something which I see as an organic unit. If I may be permitted one special plea to the reader it is this: this study stands as a whole; distortions will result if some chapters are read in isolation from other chapters. I hope those who begin it will finish it.

In any study which has taken a long time to write and revise, one becomes indebted to many people. Most of all I am indebted to Walter Harrelson without whose unfailing encouragement and counsel this study would never have come to print. It is to him I gratefully dedicate what I have done. My gratitude also goes to the librarians of San Francisco Theological Seminary, Heidelberg University, Hebrew Union College, Pittsburgh Theological Seminary, the Methodist Theological School in Ohio, and my own institution, The College of Wooster. For help with difficult German passages I want to thank Frank Steiner and Barbara Green. At various critical points in the preparation of the manuscript fellow Old Testament teachers and scholars have read what I have written and made helpful comments; they include: Walter Harrelson, Walter Brueggemann, and Gene Tucker. I was assisted in improving my style of writing by Hugh King Wright and by Walter Harrelson. The major part of three drafts of the manuscript was typed by Mrs. Jo Ann Yoder. The others who helped with the typing were Mrs. Gladys Barz, Mrs. Carol Kane, Mrs. Teen Hoffman, and Mrs. Jean Shunk. For the generous leave program on which this project was begun and the subsequent grants which have enabled its completion I want to thank the officers of my college: President J. Garber Drushal, Vice President Frederick W. Cropp, and Dean Henry Copeland. Finally, for enduring the last six years with me, and for providing emotional and personal support I express gratitude to my wife and my two sons.

The reader should note that the biblical chapter and verse references are to the Revised Standard Version. The first time a work is cited the note may contain only the author and title; in those cases the remaining data will be found in the Select Bibliography. Less frequently cited works will have full bibliographical information in the first note referring to them.

INTRODUCTION

STRENGTHENING FAITH IN A TIME OF HISTORICAL REVERSAL

A. A Comparison between Israel's Situation and Our Own

Prophetic faith interprets history from a theological perspective. In 587 B.C. history dealt Israel a reversal as the last Judeans were rudely expelled from their land into an alien place where they awaited an uncertain future.[1] This kind of catastrophe was not included in the alternatives and terms by which Israel had lived out a relationship with Yahweh God since the time of Moses. In the view of the majority of the people such a calamity violated what could reasonably be expected from a "God of providence." Historical events could be made to support a certain framework of theological assumptions as long as they moved within a reasonable latitude of variables. Israel's Babylonian Exile was an unreasonable variation. How her theology attempted to cope wtih this event is the subject matter of this study.

In the last part of the twentieth century America too has begun to see the tide of history running against what have been traditionally understood to be its national goals. In spite of its awesome power, America seems to be not the beneficiary but the victim of the course of events. This has created some deep uncertainties. If it can yet be affirmed that there is a God wooing all mankind toward the fulfillment of the best that is in them, and if it can still be said that nations have distinctive roles to play in this process, how do we explain to ourselves that we in America seem to be out of any sure harmony with that supportive Benevolence which led us from our days of early settlement through the Second World War?

Early in the sixth century before Christ, Israel's faith struggled to survive and understand the challenge of events even more dismaying than we have tasted today. The special intention of this study is to throw light on this limited period in the history of Israelite faith. Our claim, implicit throughout, is that the struggle to understand certain events then provides a model pertinent to the assessment of the meaning of our own situation. Behind this is the affirmation that no satisfying understanding of the historical present is ever obtained without a critical comparison and analysis of models of comparable situations drawn from the past. We will find that the sifting of faith-traditions to find footage for saying "yes" in the face of history's "no" at the time of the Babylonian Exile is rich with latent suggestions for dealing with the problems confronting our faith in the flow of events today.

B. A Resource Neglected: The Theological Significance of the Exile

For too long Old Testament studies have stressed the faith that grew out of the Exodus from Egypt, and the faith that grew out of the end of the Babylonian Exile, best seen in the lofty theology and poetry of Isaiah chapters 40–55. But the survival of a lived faith is not so much determined by how it can build on the advantages provided by events flowing in a supportive direction; rather, the survival depends more upon whether faith can endure the worst reversals imaginable.

We have had theological reflection on Creation, the rebellion of first man, God's call and guidance of the Patriarchs, the Exodus from Egypt, the Sinai Covenant, holy wars of the Judges, kingship in the Davidic era, the eighth century prophetic conception of God and social ethics, the Messiah, Second Isaiah's theology of the end of the Exile, Daniel's apocalyptic vision. But I know of no systematic work in the last fifty years focused on the onset of the Exile. One can hardly exaggerate the challenge to Israel's faith posed by the collapse of the national state, Judah, and the removal of its survivors to captivity in a land hundreds of miles away. The rude and crushing factuality of these events *brought to an end traditions of expectation which had been developing in Israel for over six hundred years.* The one tradition which could approach making sense of this catastrophe, the prophetic assurance that the nation's sufferings would be proportionate to its sins, had to stretch itself out of reasonable proportions in order to protect God's justice in the face of these horrible reversals. And once that prophecy of judgment followed Israel to the edge of the abyss and shouted to it as it plummeted into darkness: "you deserve what you are getting," then even that resource for understanding had expended itself and had nothing more to offer. But within a few years after this, Jeremiah and Ezekiel were promising Judah a regeneration to a life beyond anything which it had known previously. These promises were unqualified and unconditional. To be sure, many writers have called attention to the juxtaposition of words of judgment with words of deliverance in the prophetic books. But no one has attempted anything approaching a systematic analysis of the tension between those two theological poles, their relationship, and their historical and theological roots in the only two prophets where one finds extensive series of judgment proclamations followed by shorter but substantial sequences of promises of salvation: Jeremiah and Ezekiel, the two prophets whose role it was to interpret the onset of the Babylonian Exile.[2]

The dimensions of the transformation in Israelite religion at the onset of the Exile have often been commented upon, but it must be said that we are still in the early stages of understanding how these changes took place and what they implied. What we are calling attention to here is a theology of disaster as probing as Job's, but on a corporate level. In the development of Israelite faith, it falls between Amos' and Hosea's interpretations of the fall of the ten northern tribes (Israel) in 722, and Daniel's handling of the Seleucid persecutions of Jews in 167 B.C. Second Isaiah (chs. 40–55), much studied, gives us the bright side of the exilic coin; Jeremiah and Ezekiel give us the darker side, and then the astonishing turn toward hope. Even though they have attracted less attention and study, the prophets of the onset of the Exile can rightfully be claimed to be as deep as Second Isaiah, if for no other reason than that they faced a harder task theologically. Jeremiah and Ezekiel went through the searchings of Job, but they had to make their answer understandable to a whole nation. Jeremiah's and Ezekiel's Oracles of Judgment were more painful to utter than even those of Amos, the most noted "prophet of doom," because Jeremiah and Ezekiel delivered their oracles in the actual existential situation of Judah's demise. Similarly, Jeremiah's and Ezekiel's Oracles of Deliverance required deeper faith and hope in the future than those enunciated by Second Isaiah, the most famous "prophet of salvation," because Jeremiah and Ezekiel promised salvation when there was as yet no historical hint that such a turn of events could become an actuality.

What Eliphaz, Bildad, and Zophar tried to do for Job, with no apparent success, Jeremiah and Ezekiel accomplished for Judah with a brilliance seldom recognized. One cannot appreciate Jeremiah's and Ezekiel's Oracles of Judgment and Oracles of Deliverance as the answers they are unless one develops a feeling for the questions which they presuppose. No less than in Job, the questions that the people were inescapably asking strain the limits of Israelite faith. More than Job, Jeremiah and Ezekiel were given the grace to answer just those poignant questions by significantly expanding the framework of Israelite faith through a rediscovery of additional foundations.

C. Onset of the Exile as a Challenge for Interpretation

It should be emphasized that the onset of the Exile was not solely a problem for Israelite faith. Some hint of the challenge of the paradigm for our own times is seen in that the Exile refuses to fit into any of the three main models used to understand how God revealed himself in and through the Old Testament. 1) The canonization of the Old Testament along with the New Testament into a book called the Holy Bible and referred to as Scripture assumes that the contents of it are a self-contained, coherent, and timelessly true Word revealed from God. If that is true, however, one would have no way of holding together how the God of Israel could make unconditional promises of punishment and extermination; then a few chapters and a few years later promise unconditionally a sweeping deliverance. Especially as we move from just before the Exile to its onset, and then to its immediacy, it appears that what is theologically true changes. Thus the traditional, theologically conservative model for understanding the inspiration and authority of the Bible is an interpretative pattern which has great difficulty dealing with the unique pressure of the Exile and the inner dynamic of the faith that responded to it.

2) Earlier in this century quite wide acceptance was given to the model of interpreting the Old Testament influenced by the theory of evolution and the form of humanism prevalent then. This position held that we find in the Old Testament a progressive revelation, or as some would put it, an evolution of man's religious insight. Thus we are led to expect Israelite faith to move from a lower level (naive, polytheistic, ethically crude) to a higher level (sophisticated, monotheistic, ethically elevated) on a fairly consistently "upward" sloping line of development. This model seems totally incapable of explaining how there can be a more dramatic transformation of Israelite faith in the twenty years between 600 and 580 than in the two hundred years between 1000 and 800. Israel's religion simply did not change or grow or mature at anything like a uniform rate, and at no point is that more obvious than in the period we now study.

3) A model of interpretation which continues to hold a dominant position in the wide central section of the Protestant theological spectrum is that God's revelation is in events rather than in words. The words of the Old Testament are said to be a witness to these God-revealing events, such as the Exodus and the Conquest of Canaan. The series of these saving events, recited in worship as Israel's own formulation of theology, has been called by the German name *Heilsgeschichte*, or history of saving events. Events of salvation give rise to words of salvation

(testimony to the events), and the Bible is related to history just as the creed of *Heilsgeschichte* is related to the actual events in which God is seen as acting redemptively. But how are we to understand the Exile under this model? It is an anti-Exodus, an event counter to *Heilsgeschichte.* The almost causal connection between saving event and saving word is destroyed, in the miracle that Israel's faith grows much stronger precisely as history threatens to destroy it.

To some extent, then, we share with Israel a feeling about the challenge of the Exile: it is a reality which faith cannot ignore, but which cannot be readily understood under the previously existing convenient frameworks of interpretation. Our understanding of events must mature. One is pushed to realize that religious belief cannot simply draw on the traditions of the past, but must be ready to resynthesize them creatively and faithfully in order to say "yes" to a present that is disturbing and a future which is problematic. Events set for theology its task and refuse to submit to any secure system of interpretation. *One cannot institutionalize as final, definitive, or normative any single perceived pattern of how God works in history.* First, the Old Testament defined itself over-against highly stylized interpretations of how God works in nature (as these were prominent in the ancient religions of Egypt, Babylon, and Canaan). Then, it developed instead a faith about history. Israel was given an identity and a cohesion by the way it remembered the Exodus and the Conquest. But, in time that led into a highly stylized interpretation of how God works in events: reward for the righteous/punishment for the wicked (best seen in Deuteronomy and in the Deuteronomic histories). Too few people understand that Israelite faith subsequently moved beyond that point. It was the devastating impact of the Babylonian Exile which first forced them out of what had become an institutionalized, orthodox view of how God acts in history. Unlike many people of today who unable to find God in history look for God in nature, Jeremiah and Ezekiel broke through to a *new* vision of God in events. In this vision God has so much freedom and institutional religion has so little claim on him that even 2,500 years later what these two prophets of the beginning of the Exile communicate is seldom understood and even more rarely accepted.

Our situation is not unprecedented when we face a theological crisis created by historical realities changing more rapidly than faith can interpret. Indeed it is encouraging to know that belief patterns in the biblical tradition can change, can adapt, can cope with most difficult reversals. Grappling with the onset of the Exile, Jeremiah and Ezekiel show us how religion redefines itself and creates structures of interpretation supportive for faith in the midst of troubled times.

A CRITICAL SURVEY OF THEORIES ON THE DOOM/SALVATION SHIFT

The heart of the issue with which we deal is the shift from a predominating message of doom to a dominant emphasis on salvation which occurs in both the Book of Jeremiah and the Book of Ezekiel. This is at once one of the most puzzling, seemingly illogical, and yet brilliant developments in the whole unfolding of Israelite religion.

In a rather general way the doom/salvation shift in prophetic literature has caught the interest of scholars from early in this century. It is not within the purposes of the present study to examine what all of the literature has said about this, but it will help us to look at some of the main patterns of interpretation.

A. A Pattern Borrowed from Other Ancient Near Eastern Religions

While some scholars were excising all promises of salvation from the authentic words of prophets from Amos to Jeremiah on grounds that true prophets were doom prophets,[3] and other scholars were anachronistically reading into every word of doom an implicit qualification that God's mercy would guarantee some form of continuity,[4] the first scholars to take *both* doom and salvation preaching seriously brought forth the unfortunate theory that these motifs *belong together naturally,* as matched halves of one whole organism.[5] They found this two-sidedness in all of the prophets, and not just in Jeremiah and Ezekiel. In their view the juxtaposition of doom motifs with salvation motifs was a definite and fixed *pattern* with a rationale of its own. They thought that this pattern was not original and indigenous to Israelite prophecy but an outgrowth of the recurrent death to rebirth, darkness to light, destruction to restoration patterns characteristic to the alternations (summer/winter) inherent in the cyclical view of time in other religions of the Ancient Near East.

Scholars suggested a doom/salvation pattern more frequently earlier in this century than they do today. Their efforts ought not to be revived. We now know that the prophetic message of doom was contained in a speech-form with quite a separate origin from the message of salvation. Sometimes the editors of the early prophetic books arranged these speeches in close juxtaposition, but in Jeremiah and Ezekiel we encounter segments many chapters in length proclaiming doom followed by substantial blocks of separate salvation oracles. Thus there is no intrinsic off/on, off/on light pattern in the two prophets of the beginning of the Exile. It is predominantly darkness (doom) followed by consistent light (salvation) with only one turning point. In what follows we will argue that each phase has a separate ideology and that the turning point is as much determined by historical as by conceptual factors. Whatever explanation is offered for the alleged pattern in Amos, Hosea, Micah, and Isaiah must be seriously questioned as providing an appropriate model for understanding the doom/salvation shift in Jeremiah and Ezekiel. Their blocks of doom oracles can be fairly confidently dated to before the fall of Jerusalem in 587, and their blocks of salvation oracles during and after that traumatic event.[6]

B. Doom and Salvation Operating on Separate Levels

If some scholars have overstated the unity of the doom and salvation motifs, depriving each theme of much of its meaning by making both subservient to an overarching, unifying, timeless structure, other scholars have pushed these motifs too far apart. They have done this not by separating the phases in time or literary development, but by opening a theological cleavage which has doom and salvation operating on entirely different levels, so that the salvation never attempts to *reconstruct* what the doom *destroys.* Two scholars have envisioned the promise of salvation being offered to a historical-theological entity distinctly different from the intended audience of the terrible promises of doom.[7] They have seen the tension between doom and salvation being resolved by having each message addressed to different groups: doom was preached to the decadent *community* Israel, while salvation was offered to the repentant *individual* Jew.[8]

Some problems with this view are that a meta-historical meaning is attached to the oracles of doom, and a precedent for God's rejection of Judaism in favor of the Church is set up, if the interpreter is not very careful to stipulate that it was merely the Israel of 722 or 587 which God rejected, and that only temporarily. The problem appears in those passages where the Dutch scholar H. Renckens thinks of the new form of Israel "not as a state, but almost as a church,"[9] or where he speaks of "the universal church of the Jews."[10] As Jews understand "Israel" it always meant, at a minimum, a religious-cultural community of Jews which one enters by birth. The Church, on the other hand, is strictly a religious institution which one enters by individual conversion. It is thus both a Christian value judgment and an anachronizing misinterpretation of the prophets' meaning to have their oracles of salvation create a proto-church, rather than a new Israel within Jewish terms of understanding. In fact, these promises are addressed to a corporate body of Jews, not to individuals, and promise the restoration of a religious-cultural community.

C. Rooting the Shift in a Dichotomy in God's Nature

In the scholarship of Johannes Lindblom we find what is probably the best modern analysis of the problematic relationship between doom preaching and salvation preaching in Israel's prophets. It is difficult to give full attention and consideration to the two contrasting motifs at the same time, but Lindblom determinedly holds onto this tension.

However, instead of discussing the prophets' interpreting the alternate possibilities of punishment and forgiveness in terms of the rationale embodied in a plan for history revealed by God, Lindblom stresses their taking their clue from whichever disposition at the poles of the divine nature was then expressing God's intent. He says that "a tension ensued between Yahweh's love and Yahweh's wrath"[11] when the people whom God had elected out of love became unfaithful to him and violated his commandments. Looking for a historical basis for the tension, Lindblom suggests, "The idea of Yahweh's mercy was as much a part of the religious tradition of Israel as was the idea of the punitive God."[12] But this excellent generalization loses its strength when Lindblom fails to back it up with a discussion of particulars. The historical frame of reference fades out of view as Lindblom then articulates the position that "in the pre-exilic prophets Yahweh's wrath . . . was the anti-thesis of His love."[13] This position reaches its climax in the following statement:

> What is the relation between Yahweh's love and Yahweh's wrath in the preaching of the pre-exilic prophets? According to the view of history represented by these prophets, two parallel lines ran through the history of the Israelite people, one determined by love, the other determined by wrath. There was a course of events which served to demonstrate how Yahweh worked for His people's good and for the fulfillment of their election. There was another course of historical occurrences, of which the sole aim was the victory of Yahweh's punitive will and the satisfaction of His wrath. There is no real organic connection between the two. They represent two different sides in Yahweh, both equally proper to His divine nature.[14]

I see two main problems in this position. The suggestion that God's wrath sends promises of doom and God's love offers assurances of salvation works too zealously to eliminate what must have been an authentic tension by nearly dividing the divine nature into two parts. We rightly ask, Is God's love conscious and functioning when wrath is sending judgment? And is wrath conscious and functioning when love is sending salvation? Is the God of Amos the same as the God of Second Isaiah? Does God change halfway through the Book of Ezekiel? To ask these questions is to suggest an answer: The issue cannot be resolved by theories concerning the inner workings of the divine nature. Lindblom raises the issue of the doom/salvation shift as a problem in the history of Israelite religion. But he does not resolve it within that same frame of reference. He resolves it by becoming a theologian, by turning adjectives for God into attributes of God. He begins by trying to understand the rationale for God's actions in history, and ends with subtle theological reflections over God's *nature*.

While some scholars have taken the doom/salvation reversal seriously, although interpreting it in an unsatisfactory way, they have more often overlooked it or dealt with it all too briefly and simplistically.[15] Working through the relevant literature, I have found no satisfactory treatment of the whole problematic shift from a message of doom to a message of salvation in the course of the prophetic ministries of Jeremiah and Ezekiel, related in one way or another to the onset of the Babylonian Exile.

ISSUES AND THESES WHICH DEFINE THE DIRECTION OF THIS STUDY

To anticipate what will come later, I would suggest that there have been three basic problem areas in moving toward a better understanding of the doom/salvation shift which constitutes the heart of the theology of the onset of the Babylonian Exile. 1) Perhaps many people look at the polarities the way one of my students did in an examination question asking her to analyze the judgment/deliverance tension in the prophets. She used a model of an old style scale, or balance for weights. She said that on this scale justice was very heavy in Amos and mercy very light; then it went through various adaptations in the following prophets; finally, in Second Isaiah there was a real shift to mercy as much heavier than justice. The problem with this view is that it treats "justice, wrath, judgment" as one type of entity or reality, and "mercy, love, deliverance" as an entity or reality of a totally different sort. In themselves each is static, and only the external proportions between their weights (thrust toward actualization) is dynamic. But as the present study has progressed, I have gradually come to see judgment and deliverance in creative interaction. Each acts on the other, affects the other; each has an element of the other in it. They are not totally separate entities: ultimately they come from the same source and center. They are bound together in the unity of the divine will and the unity of the Divine Person. They stand in a quite variable, but always creative, tension with one another. *It is precisely the latent or residual presence of justice and will toward judgment in the midst of unconditional deliverance which differentiates the epoch of salvation from the shallow grace of false prophecy.* And in the most severe judgment pronouncements of Amos, Hosea, Jeremiah, and Ezekiel, mercy and deliverance are residually and latently present. It is this which exempts Yahweh from charges of monomaniachal fury and makes him the same God found later in the deliverance passages, in the Talmud, and in the New Testament.

2) There has been a series of rather successful efforts to deal with the onset of the Exile on a historical level, and there has been a series of attempts to deal with the doom/salvation revolution on a theological level. But I know of no study which really tries to put the two of these together in the times to which Jeremiah and Ezekiel had to speak. It is both difficult and precarious to try to see how faith and events work on one another. In this study we consider it very important to make that effort and to run that risk.

3) The author of a recent survey on prophetic speech-forms said: "The similarity in structure of the prophecies of salvation and disaster suggests a *Sitz* ["setting in life"] common to both should be sought."[16] This scholar is certainly not alone in that opinion. Such luminaries in the form-critical study of the prophets as H. W. Wolff, H. G. Reventlow, and K. Koch have

expressed the same conviction.[17] But, as we shall see, they are in error. *Perhaps the most fundamental point of this study is that the message of doom and the message of salvation are carried by distinct, and totally different, speech-forms.*[18] These forms (genres) are quite different in structure, and they are equally divergent in setting. Any modern study of the relationship between doom and salvation in the prophets is necessarily a study of these two speech-forms. *We ask not merely how does God move from wrath to love, but how do the prophets move from the Oracle of Judgment to the Oracle of Deliverance?* What does the structure of each speech-form say about the rationale, content, and ideational center of this type of message? What do the themes and theological motifs of each genre say about the structure? What is the tradition-historical line of development of each speech-form? What sort of transition in the understanding of God's will and plan for history is involved in moving from the one genre to the other? Are the ground rules, assumptions, and institutions which are operative during the articulation of the Oracle of Judgment operative during the articulation of the Oracle of Deliverance? *The failure to deal with the issue in these terms is the basis of the failure of all heretofore existing attempts to explain the doom/salvation shift in the prophets.*[19]

One of the distinctions of the present study is that it is the first attempt to deal with *both* the Oracle of Judgment (as a genre and in light of its content), *and* the Oracle of Deliverance (as a genre and in light of its content) as these shed light on the theological shift which took place when Judah went into Babylonian Exile, and as they illuminate the doom/salvation switch in at least this part of the prophetic literature.[20] Furthermore, this study asks the crucial questions: Is there any continuity between Jeremiah's and Ezekiel's use of the Oracle of Judgment and the Oracle of Deliverance? Does their use of the Oracle of Deliverance stand in any kind of theological integrity with their use of the Oracle of Judgment? What we offer is not primarily a form-critical study, but an inquiry which uses form-critical methodology to understand more adequately a limited but crucial period in the history of Israelite religion. The use of this methodology pulls our attention into a quite specific focus upon identifiable patterns of speech, thereby avoiding the abstractions and generalizations which have no direct relation to the real situation in which the prophets addressed now one and now another type of message to the people. What we learn by form criticism about this segment of the development of Israelite religion we believe will have rich implications for theological understanding in our own time.

Chapter I

THE ORACLE OF JUDGMENT: STRUCTURE AND SETTING

STRUCTURE

Most of the prophetic judgment preaching is contained in a form of speech which I will call the Oracle of Judgment.[1] This is by far the most common speech-form employed by the prophets from Amos to Jeremiah, and it dominates the first half of Ezekiel. The Oracle of Judgment has been thoroughly and competently analyzed, while investigation of the Oracle of Deliverance[2] has been so much less adequate that we will need to devote a major chapter to it in a later part of this study.

Although seventy years of research on the Oracle of Judgment have not resolved all of the problems, there has emerged from this effort a clear and generally accepted understanding of the structure of the Oracle of Judgment. And at least most of the plausible lines for explaining its setting have been explored. Therefore it is not our purpose to attempt a new study of the structure of this form. What we say about setting will be an attempt to support the more convincing lines of research, and to suggest some new perspectives on this speech-genre especially as we look at it through our two prophets who stand late in the tradition of its employment.

One of the watersheds in the study of the prophetic judgment speech was crossed in 1934 with the publication of H. W. Wolff's article "The Bases of the Prophetic Speeches of Salvation and Disaster."[3] Prior to Wolff the dominant tendency had been to deal with judgment preaching as contained in two separate speech-forms, "Reproach" and "Threat," although a few scholars had suggested that these motifs belong together.[4] Wolff convincingly demonstrates that the prophetic Oracle of Judgment is by nature a two-part speech: the "Reason" (Accusation) segment tells why a future action of God's judgment is about to come; the "Future-Instruction" (Proclamation) segment shows its rootage in the "Reason" and comes as its consequence.[5] The "Reason" describes the people's sin in such a way as to convince them of their guilt and to make it understandable to them that God's action of judgment is not arbitrary, but fully justified.[6] Wolff sees this as a "pastoral" dimension of the prophet's role both in his desire that the people accept God's punishment in faith, and also in his unspoken hope that the people "would yet repent before it is too late."[7] Using an illustration from Hosea —"they sow the wind, and they shall reap the whirlwind" (8:7) —Wolff speaks of the "knotting together" of "Reason" and "Future-Instruction."[8] "As the harvest corresponds to the sowing, so of natural necessity must the judgment come."[9] The essential unity of the two parts of the Oracle of Judgment is rooted in the justice of God.[10] These components stand together in a cause and effect relationship; the transition from the accusation of sin to the proclamation of God's judgment is usually marked by a connecting word like "therefore," "because," or "behold."[11] Within the integral relation of the two parts, Wolff sees considerable flexibility for sequence and arrangement. With "a" standing for "Future-Instruction" and "b" for "Reason," he finds the following sequences in descending order of frequency: b-a, a-b, a-b-a, and b-a-b.[12]

Subsequent scholarship on the structure of the Oracle of Judgment has sometimes found a place for subdivisions within the two basic components which Wolff sees in this genre,[13] or found reason to add an additional component,[14] but scholars never omit as central to the genre a part which describes how the people have committed wrongs against the Lord ("Reason" = Accusation) and a part which proclaims how the Lord will punish them for these wrongs ("Future-Instruction" = Proclamation). Furthermore, subsequent scholarship never agrees in disagreeing with Wolff; so, no new consensus has arisen. The other side of this fact is that a growing number of scholars appear to have accepted the Accusation-Proclamation structure as describing what they actually find in prophetic texts in which God is going to enact judgment.[15]

As the reader has anticipated, this is how I would designate the structure:

Oracle of Judgment:	Accusation Proclamation

This structure is probably more readily seen in the eighth century prophecy than in the sixth century prophecy (Westermann gives as some of his primary examples Amos 4:1–2; Hos. 2:5–7; Isa. 8:6–8; 30:12–14; Mic. 3:1–2, 4),[16] but we can find it many times in Jeremiah and Ezekiel. In Jer. 5:1–5 we see the Accusation, followed by the Proclamation in 5:6. Other examples are: 5:7–13 Acc./5:14–17 Proc.; 6:9–10 Acc./6:11–12 Proc.; 8:4–9 Acc./8:10 Proc.; 9:4–6 Acc./9:7–9 Proc.; 13:20–23 Acc./13:24–26 Proc.; 14:10a Acc./14:10b Proc. There are many other texts we could cite. Jeremiah is very creative in the variations he works on this structure. In his identification with the people addressed, Jeremiah sometimes precedes the Accusation with a lament; sometimes he alternates the Accusation and Proclamation as a kind of dialogue, brooding over Judah's fate. Ezekiel is even further from a strict use of the genre, and yet it is presupposed in much of the early part of his book. The litany in chapter 20 and the symbolic story in chapter 16 both contain Accusation (of sin) and Proclamation (of judgment) as fundamental themes, interwoven and stated repeatedly. The genre as such is found in Ezek. 5:5–12; 6:11–14; 7:1–4, 5–9, 10–13, 23–27, among other places. The latter four passages all put the Proclamation first. This may be partly because Ezekiel prophesies *after* the catastrophe of 597, so that there is some immediacy to his explaining and justifying that event. Also because the theophanic element and theme of God's self-vindication are more prominent in Ezekiel than in Jeremiah, it follows that those themes would flow more into the Proclamation section than into the Accusation.[17]

SETTING

A. Options for Understanding the Setting of This Genre

This is a particularly difficult time to say something meaningful about the spheres of influence out of which the prophetic Oracle of Judgment arose, and the life situations in which it was most naturally used. Even though a great deal of work has been done on the setting of this genre of speech, the most recent survey of the history of prophetic form criticism concludes that "no definition of the *Sitz im Leben* [setting in life] for the prophecy of disaster has yet won general agreement."[18] Complicating matters further, in recent months there have been several suggestions that the basic methodological assumptions prevailing since the time of Gunkel about the relationship between setting, and the structure, content, and intention of a genre are based on false notions. Entirely new ways of understanding setting are currently being suggested. We may be led to deal with multiple "matrices," instead of one assured setting in Israel's society.[19] We may have to learn to think of setting as something which arises from the nature of language itself, or from the mood of an age, or from the "typical operations of man's mind."[20] Once the newly opened methodological issues are resolved, a new round of efforts to find the settings or matrices of the Oracle of Judgment can begin. We need not remain silent in the meantime. Within what will have to be a tentative position, we can point to some lines of influence and frames of reference which add a great deal to the understanding of the Oracle of Judgment.

Even in the most traditional sense of setting, I would question whether the prophetic Oracle of Judgment originally was spoken, in anything resembling the form as we now have it, inside any social institution like the secular law court, the cult, or the covenant—to name the three spheres of origin most often suggested. The genre draws on a number of lines of tradition and is created as a new thing from those, but without the kind of deterministic sociological influence once commonly envisioned by many scholars.

The Oracle of Judgment as "Messenger Speech" is a case in point. C. Westermann throws very helpful light on the prophet's role as messenger, and what it meant in relation to earlier Israelite and the Ancient Near Eastern background to speak as God's messenger.[21] But he overworks his point. The prophet plays many roles in addition to the messenger role. And the "Messenger Formula" ("Thus says the Lord . . .") is found sufficiently often in other genres, like the Summons to Repentance and the Oracle of Deliverance, that it is not definitive of what is unique to this genre. This is why I would *not* include the Messenger Formula as part of the description of the genre structure (compare my structure near the top of page 17 with Westermann's structure in footnote 13). We understand better the source of the authority with which the prophet speaks in the Oracle of Judgment if we take seriously the prominent use of the Messenger Formula in this genre. But that supplies only one (minor) part in the constellation of factors and influences which make up the Oracle of Judgment. It does not, for example, tell us anything about the rationale by which the whole people could be brought to accusation.

To take another example, it is useful to be reminded that there are resemblances between parts of the prophetic Oracle of Judgment and elements of speech in the secular law court.[22] This seemingly supports the studies on the *rîb* or controversy pattern,[23] from which it has been claimed that there was such a thing as a "covenant lawsuit" which supplies the immediate background to the Oracle of Judgment.[24] But the secular juridical practice, taken in itself, is only a limited help in understanding what is going on when one hears the prophet speak an Oracle of Judgment to the people. The institution of secular law has no precedent for God's bringing his whole people under accusation, or for God's playing the roles of prosecuting attorney, judge, and executioner . . . all at once. A different framework is needed to understand that.[25]

Perhaps I have understood setting in a different way from those who now attack it. I think of it more as the ideological home of the genre than the institutional home. I think of it as supplying the frame of reference in relation to which and from which this speech has moved. I think of it as supplying the unspoken thing that is shared between the speaker and his audience in the particular category of communication, so that the audience knows what kind of rationale is assumed.

The position I propose is that the Oracle of Judgment has two levels of setting, or two matrices. First of all it takes its frame of reference from the Mosaic Covenant tradition. Secondly, and most obviously in sixth century prophecy, its setting is the developed tradition of Israelite prophecy as that has synthesized and applied beliefs to actual events from the Mosaic Covenant and related sources.

B. The Mosaic Covenant as a Setting

1. The Basic Question of Accountability

The prophets were not teachers. It would have been an impossible task to convince the people of the validity of a fundamental tenant of faith just introduced to them, and then immediately accuse them of violating its requirements and call down judgment on them for that violation. With their short, emphatic, orally delivered forms of speech, the prophets of necessity worked within already widely known traditions. There is nothing in the cult, as such, or in secular law court procedure to provide a basis for the view that the nation as a whole was accountable to Yahweh. Speaking in reference to the Oracle of Judgment, E. Würthwein has said: "Only where an obligation exists can an accusation be raised. This obligation, presupposed by the prophets, is defined through the covenant relationship between Yahweh and Israel."[26]

One of the great hindrances to a more ready and universal acceptance of the covenantal background of classical Israelite reforming prophecy is the relative absence of the technical word for "covenant," *b*ᵉ*rît,* in eighth century prophecy. George

Mendenhall, who is one of the leaders in the modern study of the covenant, has weighed this matter and concluded:

> Whether or not the prophets of the eighth century were completely aware of the nature of the Mosaic covenant . . . it is certainly true that their messages are completely in harmony with its basic structure. Their messages are in the nature of and indictment for breach of covenant, but they had to use every other figure and device to convey their message than that to which their message really related.[27]

Where is it set forth that the whole people of Israel are specifically obligated to God in such a structured way that they could understand and accept the claim that the source of Israel's election could become its accuser? If there is no answer to this question, then the people would not have taken the prophets' words seriously. But there is an answer to the question. The ideological framework necessary to understand the prophetic Oracles of Judgment is the covenant tradition associated with Moses.

2. The Conditional Covenant

It is important to realize that Israel had a variety of covenant and election traditions in which one stands apart from the others. In God's election of Abraham (Gen. 12:1–3), as in the old narrative source of the covenant with him (15:17ff.—"J"),[28] there are divine promises given without qualifications on the continuity of God's favor, without preconditions in the form of laws or terms which Abraham and his successors must meet to sustain their privileged position.[29] Similarly, in the election of David (2 Sam. 7:8ff.; Ps. 89) there are no conditions, no qualifications; it is purely God's promise to David and his house, with an emphasis on the eternal validity of these promises (2 Sam. 7:16; Ps. 89:4, 20, 28, 29, 36, 37). So also in God's election of Zion (compare 2 Sam. 6; Pss. 78:67ff., 132).[30]

Quite in contrast, in the beginning of the covenant through Moses God says:

> Thus you shall say to the house of Jacob . . .: You have seen what I did to the Egyptians, and how I bore you on eagles'

> wings and brought you to myself. Now therefore, *if* you will obey my voice and keep my covenant, you shall be my own possession among all the peoples. . . . (Exod. 19:3–5)

The underlined "if" supplies the condition; it constitutes the theological pivot of this covenant. *If* the people will obey God, he will hold them in a favored relationship, and they will receive many blessings. But *if* the people do not obey, then their relationship with God is jeopardized, and they can count on every misfortune enunciated in the curses coming upon them. It is generally agreed that the covenant found in Exodus 19–20, Joshua 24, and in the whole of Deuteronomy has the following structure:

a. *Preamble* (Yahweh introduces himself as the initiator of the covenant. He stands both inside and above the covenant structure.)

b. *Historical Prologue* (The Exodus or other acts of deliverance are recounted to show that God has given the people a basis for trust in him.)

c. *The Stipulations* (This came to be the normative setting for Israelite law.)

d. *The Oath* (Israel formally obligates itself to the terms of the covenant offered by Yahweh.)

e. *The Blessings and Curses* (God promises that good fortune will come to Israel if it is faithful to the terms of the covenant; but if it is unfaithful, every conceivable disaster will descend upon it.)

The *if* of Exod. 19:5 develops within this structure into several dimensions of interlocking jeopardy and conditionality. The law provides specific terms to which Israel is sworn, while the curses reinforce the expectations of that commitment. Quite in contrast to the other three election and covenant traditions *there is,* within the Mosaic Covenant tradition, *an obvious basis for the prophetic Oracle of Judgment.* The Accusation would indict the people for breaking the terms of the covenant, and the Proclamation would declare the enactment of the curses.

3. Textual Evidence for the Role of Covenant in Eighth Century Prophecy

It is not generally doubted that the Mosaic Covenant tradition was known and served as a basis for the preaching of the sixth century prophets. Even the scholars who are most reserved on this matter acknowledge that the Mosaic Covenant is at the heart of the Book of Deuteronomy, which when it was found in 621 sparked King Josiah's reform (see 2 Kgs. 22–23).[31] The issue which I want to advocate is not that Jeremiah and Ezekiel introduced a covenantal dimension into the Oracle of Judgment, but that they inherited the Oracle of Judgment with a covenantal frame of reference from the eighth century prophets (and then increasingly worked changes and innovations into that matrix).

Therefore we may ask: what are the indications of the presence of a structured conditional relationship between God and Israel in eighth century prophecy? Taking Hosea alone as our example, we can summarize the evidence. 1) He uses the technical word *b^erît* in the sense of the Mosaic Covenant in 2:18; 6:7; and 8:1. 2) The "Covenant Formula" appears in 1:9 and 2:23.[32] 3) The use of "know," *yāda',* in the technical sense in which it means to recognize covenant stipulations as binding, appears in Hos. 2:20; 4:1, 6; 5:4; 8:2; 13:4.[33] 4) The connecting of imagery from the Exodus experience with statements of Israel's accountability to God can be seen in Hos. 2:15; 8:13; 9:10ff.; 11:1ff.; 12:13–14; 13:4–8. 5) Similarly, the book is filled with images of relationship (God and people, husband and wife, father and son) connected to accusations of sin. This is explicitly present in such passages as 1:2, 6; 2:2ff., 16; 3:1ff.; 4:6; 9:1; 11:1ff., but it is also implicitly present in much of the rest of the book. These five lines of evidence should make it clear that Hosea was deeply steeped in a formulation of the Mosaic Covenant tradition current in the eighth century.[34] This tradition then would subsequently have been inherited by Jeremiah and Ezekiel.

4. A Suggestion for the Origin of the Oracle of Judgment

A simple and fairly obvious model for the structure of the prophetic Oracle of Judgment which, to the present writer's knowledge, has not been previously suggested, is the if/then, protasis/apodosis set of conditions by which the people are called to enter the covenant, to renew it, and by which they are threatened with the curses if they break it. In Exod. 19:5ff. we never learn what lies behind the "*if* you will obey my voice and keep my covenant." The laws in Exodus 20 help to show what the terms of covenant obedience are, but these chapters never stipulate what will happen *if* the people do not obey. That, however, does become quite clear in the covenant renewal text of Joshua 24. In verse 20 we read: "*If* you forsake the Lord and serve foreign gods, *then* he will turn and do you harm and consume you. . . ." The *protasis,* "*If* you forsake . . ." is a hypothetical Accusation of sin which has a meaning and function quite parallel to the first major element in the structure of the Oracle of Judgment. The *apodosis,* "*then* he will turn and do you harm . . ." is a hypothetical Proclamation of God's judgment; it declares God's readiness for punitive intervention, so that the two parts stand together in a cause and effect relationship. These negative or threatening pairs of protasis/apodosis conditions often occur immediately after a positive or promissory pair of if/then formulations. In 1 Sam. 12:14 and 1 Kgs. 9:4–5 we have the "if you obey, I will reward" type of construction; then in 1 Sam. 12:15 and 1 Kgs. 9:6–7 there follows the "if you disobey, then I will punish" warning. That same sequence occurs in the great covenantal blessing and curse liturgy of Deuteronomy 28. There, in classical form, we have this wording:

> 28:1–2 And if you obey the voice of the Lord . . . being careful to do all his commandments . . . then all these blessings shall come upon you. . . .
>
> 28:15 *But if* you will not obey the voice of the Lord . . . or be careful to do all his commandments . . ., *then* all these curses shall come upon you.

Clearly, the protasis in 28:15 anticipates violation of the Mosaic Covenant by having its commands broken. All that a prophet would have to do to turn this into the first half of an Oracle of Judgment would be to shift from a hypothetical to a factual Accusation. And the apodosis of 28:15 turned into a Proclamation of God's decision to intervene with judgment shows that these punishments are to be understood as an actualization of the covenant curses.[35]

C. Prophecy as a Setting[36]

1. The Rationale of Punishment

With this background, it ought to be a simple matter to show that the imagery and ideology of punishment within the prophetic Oracles of Judgment was covenantal. But the actual content of Jeremiah's and Ezekiel's oracles is surprisingly independent, in most cases, of any obvious ties with the covenant institution. The rigid dichotomy of Deuteronomy 28, in which the alternatives are obedience → life/disobedience → death, is not carried over into the judgment preaching of the sixth century prophets. As can be seen with the development of repentance summonses, much of the prophetic role was carved out *between* the Deuteronomic admonition to obedience and the announcement that God's annihilatory judgment was descending upon the people, that is to say, *between* the blessing and the curse. The older strata of Deuteronomy present the alternatives for the people as a black and white issue. As we will show below under the prophetic "Intentions" for the Oracle of Judgment, Jeremiah and Ezekiel assess and deal with the possibilities in nearly every shade of gray imaginable.

Even less do the sixth century prophets anticipate the contrived moderation of the chastisement → repentance → forgiveness pattern in Leviticus 26. The failure of chastisement to bring the expected repentance is a theme which runs through Hosea (6:1ff.; 7:11–14; 11:5), Jeremiah (5:3; 7:28; 13:22–23; 15:7), and Ezekiel (16:27–29; 23:8–11). Their development of this theme moves their threat of punishment beyond the framework of chastisement to a level not merely ignored but specifically denied by Leviticus 26. Both Jeremiah (9:16; 14:12) and Ezekiel (5:13; 13:13; 20:13; 22:31) use the image *kālāh,* "consume, bring to an end, annihilate," to express the eventual unqualified character of judgment, while Lev. 26:44 uses the same verbal root to deny that God will "destroy them utterly." And, as we will see below, Lev. 26:44 denies the rejection which Jeremiah and Ezekiel teach. From this evidence we conclude that Leviticus 26 intentionally repudiates or corrects a prophetic teaching on the intensity and purpose of God's punitive activity.[37]

While there are almost inevitably some conceptual or verbal parallels between the misfortunes which Jeremiah and Ezekiel promise in the Proclamations and the ills depicted in these two curse liturgies (Deut. 28 and Lev. 26), the Proclamations of judgment are never literally offered as curses. Moreover, each of these curse liturgies sets God's punishment at a level of alternatives which is alien to these prophets. In Deuteronomy 28 there are no degrees of punishment, and thus no just proportionality. In Leviticus 26 punishment is emasculated to the point at which it is not even just retribution, but merely chastisement at whatever level of intensity is needed to incite repentance. The prophets had to work out a plan of punishment related in a realistic way to an assessment of Israel's condition and actual historical events so that it would find its place between these two extreme poles.

For the most part, Jeremiah depicts both the people's sin and God's judgment on it in quite specific, concrete, and varied terms. But in three passages of unquestioned authenticity, exactly this same question is repeated: "Shall I not punish (*pāqad*) them for these things? and shall I not avenge (*nāqam*) myself on a nation such as this?" (Jer. 5:9, 29; 9:9). The root translated "punish," *pāqad,* and the root translated "avenge," *nāqam,* appear together in the Old Testament only in these three passages. Before Jeremiah used *nāqam* ("avenge") in this sense, it had associations primarily with old tribalistic ideas of retaliation and vengeance. In Gen. 4:23–24 Lamech boasted: "I have slain a man for wounding me, a young man for striking me. If Cain is avenged (*nāqam*) sevenfold, truly Lamech seventy-seven fold. . . ." Sometimes God himself acted to avenge a wrong done a person (Judg. 11:36; 2 Sam. 4:8), or he took vengeance on nations which had become his enemy by abusing his people (Deut. 32:41, 43; Isa. 34:8; 35:4). *Nāqam* ("avenge") was then a very powerful image when Jeremiah first creatively used it with God as the subject and Judah as the object of this action. It meant that God and his people were now at enmity with one another. The "avenging" (*nāqam*) action was a retaliation for the wrongdoing they did against him in sinning.

The verb *pāqad* ("visit-punish") was not used in a religious sense outside of a certain limited number of sources. Most of its uses meant "muster," "number," or "appoint." But sometimes it denoted a "visit" from one person to another with a positive purpose (Judg. 15:1), or God "visiting" a person for a beneficent reason (Gen. 21:1; 50:24). In perhaps the earliest "visitation" of its type, 1 Sam. 15:2 quotes God saying, "I will punish what Amalek did to Israel. . . ." *Pāqad* ("visit-punish") was used fairly often in the eighth century prophets to depict God's act of punishment: Amos 3:2, 14; Hos. 1:4; 2:13; 4:9; 8:13; 9:7, 9; 12:3.

The important points to note about the use of these images are: a) these are the verbs which come closest to the technical meaning of "punish" in the Old Testament; b) they were given that coinage primarily because of the way the prophets adopted and employed them to suit their own purposes; c) they express a highly personal dimension in punishment, with emphasis on God's prerogative to decide or act; d) they show a level of action which holds to some proportionality, between a curse and a chastisement.

It is interesting to note that in a series of bi-polar formulas combining an expression of God's readiness to judge as well as to show mercy, the verb used to express the punitive pole is *pāqad* ("visit-punish") in Exod. 34:6–7; Num. 14:18; Deut. 5:9; Exod. 20:5; *šālēm* ("requite") in Deut. 7:10; Jer. 32:18; and *nāqam* ("avenge") in Ps. 99:8. I think it is probable that these formulas have their setting in covenant renewal ceremonies.[38] Would that we knew their relation to the curse rationale within the covenant structure and the dates in which these passages came into their present form! Then it would be possible to make a reasonable estimate as to whether these formulas influenced the uses of the images for punishment in the prophets, or whether the influence moved from the prophets to these covenant-renewal formulations. Direct verbal influence on the prophets seems to be ruled out by the absence in their books of the participial construction of these verbs as we typically find them in the formulas and by the lack of direct combination of the two poles into one statement. However, as I understand the prophetic message, it *always* held together in tension the judgment and the mercy of God. So conceptual interaction between the prophetic understanding of punishment and this level of expression of covenant alternatives is an open possibility if not also a probability. *With these observations, what we have eliminated is a one-way influence of the covenant on the prophets; and the influence centering around the covenant curse formulations.*

Taken in perspective, the independence and creativity of the way Hosea and Jeremiah use the key terms for "punishment," *pāqad* and *nāqam,* remains very striking. This tradition was then carried on by the very effective use Ezekiel made of the common verb *nātan* ("give, put") to depict God's punishment in 7:3, 4, 8, 9; 9:10; 11:21; 16:43; 17:19; 22:31; and 23:49. If a common thread runs through all of these images, it is that *God returns the sin to the sinner* as a perfectly proportionate and just punishment. Here, of course, we are close to Koch's suggestion about an automatic act-consequence bond, which God supports like a mechanic or expedites like a midwife.[39] But if evil automatically returns to the evildoer, why is there any need to employ old vengeance metaphors and strongly anthropomorphic images to say that *God* accomplishes this? My suggestion is that in the prophetic understanding of punishment, *God expropriated and returned as his own prerogative the power of the cause and effect relationship between sin and punishment.* In the prophetic Oracles of Judgment, God's will and decision are far more prominent than in the covenant-renewal bi-polar formulas, and in them the pattern of divine response to sin is much less schematized than in Deuteronomy 28 or Leviticus 26.

What we have seen is that the rationale of punishment within the prophetic Oracles of Judgment is best appreciated if one does not come to the individual texts with preconceptions about covenant influence or an archaic act-consequence nexus. *To a striking degree the prophetic statement of punishment is original and unique with the prophets themselves, and independent of institutional determinism.*

In his 1970 paper R. Knierim said repeatedly that "settings change."[40] I take it that if the claim of a form-content congruence has any validity, then it holds most nearly true when the form is used closest to its original setting. By the time of Jeremiah and Ezekiel, the setting of the Oracle of Judgment had changed from whatever it was originally. Its setting has become prophetic. The sixth century prophets obtained their pattern for the use of this form primarily from the eighth century prophets, but added significantly to what was the unfolding prophetic institution or tradition. With this, we must bear in mind that for the sixth century prophets, the setting of this genre included not only the precedent of earlier prophetic tradition, but also those historical events which this genre purported to interpret.

2. The Historical Factor

The prophetic Oracle of Judgment rests on an implicit history of Israel's developing belief-structure, the assumptions and convictions which lie as the background for this speech-form. They are:

a. Israel's national, corporate accountability to Yahweh

b. Yahweh's immanent Lordship over Israel's history

c. The retributional model of providence, what God creates for Israel to experience: whether good times for obedience, or bad times for disobedience

d. The expansion of Yahweh's Lordship over events to include universal Lordship, so that international forces can serve God's retributional purposes

e. The notion that Yahweh's adherence to his principle of justice is a more irrevocable bond than his election of Israel, his mission for it to be his corporate servant in the redemption of history, his revelatory investment in and through the people of Israel, his contractual covenant relationship with them.

As one progresses from *a* to *e* there is a movement from relatively close dependence on the Mosaic Covenant matrix to an orientation which is increasingly unique, and distinct to prophecy. It would be hard to make a case that convictions *a–e* were present, at this level of clarity and application, on the slopes of Mt. Sinai or at the covenant renewal ceremony recorded in Joshua 24. But they are all present with the breakthrough of "classical," "reform" prophecy in Amos and Hosea.

We seem to see in the eighth and seventh centuries prophetic developments and innovations upon a fundamentally Mosaic Covenantal ideological base. That occurred in an interplay with the gradual internalization of those developments and innovations in normalized and institutional cultic expressions of covenant. Those expressions of covenant, in turn, became articulated in the various layers of tradition which made up the core of the Book of Deuteronomy and the "D" edition of Joshua—2 Kings. Seen this way, Jeremiah and Ezekiel may appear to have a dimension of dependence on Deuteronomy, but Deuteronomy in turn is dependent on how the eighth century prophets interpreted, developed, and applied the Mosaic Covenant ideology into a comprehensive retributional theology of history.

Thus the setting of the Oracle of Judgment in Jeremiah and Ezekiel is both prophetic and covenantal—in a limited sense perhaps also drawing upon law court and cultic matrices, through the lawsuit manner of stating the covenant grievance and the normative expression of these matters in the cult. It may be that the reason it has been difficult for scholars to reach agreement on the setting of the Oracle of Judgment is that it draws on a number of separate, but not mutually exclusive, matrices, while pulling together their influences and applying them to current history in a way which is a new contribution within the prophetic tradition.

Another aspect of the setting has to do with the fall of the Northern State in 722 and what significance that calamity retroactively gave to the words of Amos and Hosea. When covenant theology is correlated to a historical event such as this, as it is, then increasingly what is at stake is not just the covenant, but God's justice, God's Lordship over history, and Israel's election, identity, mission, survival. *Strictly covenantal concerns are largely superseded and prophetic theology is stretched to a breaking point.* This is a general statement of one of my principal discoveries derived from the study of the Oracle of Judgment in Jeremiah and Ezekiel. The consequences with which they have to deal are more grave and concrete than those ever envisioned in the institutional formulation of the covenant. Jeremiah and Ezekiel take on this task with individual creativity and freedom beyond expectation, but never contradict the basic logic of the Mosaic Covenant as it was understood and restated by their prophetic predecessors.

STANDPOINT

A. Context

It is difficult for us fully to penetrate the alternate patterns of light and darkness, hope and despair which ran through the community centered around Jerusalem in the last decade of the seventh century and the first decade of the sixth. Given the situation it is not surprising that juxtaposed to the harshest kind of judgment prophecy was a strong outbreak of what came to be recognized as false prophecy—persons promising peace as have the facile optimists of every era. We can summarize a few of the major factors in the context.

1. The Josianic covenant reform had largely failed;[41] there was a breakdown in the covenant community and in covenant observance.[42]

2. There was a deterioration of Judah's internal political situation; the kingship took on a very unstable character; visible evidences that Judah is God's theo-political state were discredited.[43]

3. Babylon replaced Assyria as the major imperialist power in the Middle East. Judah pursued policies which were offensive to Babylon, and Babylon made a series of aggressive acts which revealed that its movement against Judah was not far off.[44]

4. By the midpoint of Jeremiah's ministry and the beginning of Ezekiel's the main line of Israelite prophecy had had 150 years to establish itself if we date the starting point with Amos, and 250 years if we date the beginning with Elijah. Therefore by this time the prophetic role was so securely defined, and its predominant speech-form so widely understood (if not always accepted), that Jeremiah and Ezekiel could be quite innovative in the enactment of their role and in the language and purposes employed in the Oracle of Judgment.

5. As the initial destruction of Judah in 597 grew closer, and particularly between 597 and the final ruin in 587 it was impossible to avoid this equation:

$$\frac{\text{the eighth century Oracle of Judgment}}{\text{ruin of ``Israel'' in 722}} = \frac{\text{the Sixth century Oracle of Judgment}}{\text{ruin of ``Judah'' in 597-587}}$$

The inescapable analogy involved in this equation brought several consequences.

a. The prophetic word in the Oracle of Judgment was feared and hated like a magical incantation of malevolence, bringing the evil reality by speaking it. Jeremiah bore the brunt of the frustrated and terror-filled response to this word.

b. The theology of the "remnant" associated with the eighth century Isaiah collapsed.[45]

c. The Oracle of Judgment and Jeremiah's and Ezekiel's ministries ever more had to deal with the significance of an absolute end to God's initiative with Judah-Israel, and with the nullification of its identity as that had involved both a vocation in history for Yahweh and receiving his special favor and support.

d. The Proclamation portion of the Oracle of Judgment moved from threat to death sentence and from expression of God's righteous indignation within relationship to bill of divorce.

B. Intentions

The whole history of the patterns of employment of the Oracle of Judgment is recapitulated within the Book of Jeremiah.

1. It is probably correct to say that it began its career in the time of the ninth century prophets as a word of condemnation against individuals.[46] This we can see in Jer. 28:13, 15–16.[47]

2. It could be a negative Summons to Repentance (Jer. 26: 2–6).

3. Often it served as a promise of just and proportionate retribution on sin (as in Jer. 2:4–19).

4. Sometimes it condemned the people as beyond regeneration (Jer. 13:20–27).

5. It served to announce an unqualified and annihilatory level of judgment (Jer. 9:2–9).

6. In Jeremiah and Ezekiel we find it moving to state God's rejection of Judah and his cancellation of the covenant protections (Jer. 12:7–13).

7. Sometimes it served as a theodicy for the fairness and Lordship of God in face of the Babylonian catastrophe (Jer. 5:7–17).

8. An end point in the development of the functions for which the Oracle of Judgment was intended was in its adaptation to express God's judgment against foreign nations (Jer. 46–51).

In its emphasis on "typical" features, "generic" features, the exegetical discipline known as "form criticism" has had its attention turned away from the most exciting aspect of the thought expressed in units of prophetic speech: that they are addressed to very specific historical situations, and therefore to situations which are always being superseded by new developments. Thus what really speaks to these developments in an incisive and pertinent way is always subject to a reassessment of the exact nature of history's movement. The message needed changes, and the words called forth change. What we find in the prophetic books, is, as it were, an interpretive ideology of the passing scene articulated on horseback. Because of this it is nearly anti-philosophy. It is not even "truth" about history regarded as an abstraction. It is God's interpretation of particular developments in the concrete and dynamic reality of unfolding events. Any kind of theology of judgment is a theology worked out in the middle of a battlefield. Both the judgment and the deliverance which the prophets preach have this quality. We do not have to deal here with a shift from an entrenched, static deliverance, or from an abstract judgment to an equally theoretical deliverance. Just the opposite. The judgment moves. Through historical pressures it intensifies and radicalizes itself. It is because of this that the shift from doom to salvation is even more dramatic in Jeremiah and Ezekiel than what we find in the eighth century prophets. It is fascinating and challenging to try to understand this movement within the Oracle of Judgment. This is our concern in the next few chapters. Attention to this concern is not poorly invested, as though we are dealing with a quirk within the history of Israelite religion. As I see it *it is at the very essence of Israelite faith that radical innovation is combined with radical fidelity to inherited tradition.* That the same speech-form could be adapted to serve eight different intentions within one prophet is in itself proof of this.

Chapter II

RADICALIZATION OF THE JUDGMENT MESSAGE

THE FAILURE OF REPENTANCE

A. A Thematic Developmental Sequence in Jeremiah's and Ezekiel's Messages

One of the dimensions of a prophet's message which we are hard put to understand is whether it was characterized by repetition of the same themes, or whether there was a progression from an episode dominated by one theme, to a subsequent stage in which other emphases took prominence.

In the case of Amos, and to a lesser extent Hosea, their ministries were so short that any attempt at reconstructing a development is difficult. Added to this is the problem which exists, to one degree or another, with all of the prophetic writings, that we cannot date individual speech units and put them into chronological sequence with any degree of certainty. Hosea, for example, presents the impression of pronouncing severe Oracles of Judgment throughout his ministry, and his book is a kind of random alternation between admonitory words and suggestions of God's mercy.

Although the relative confusion and blurred picture which this leaves is not wholly escaped in Jeremiah and Ezekiel, there are differences. Jeremiah had a long ministry, perhaps extending over forty years; Ezekiel's ministry seems to have extended at least fifteen to twenty years. More importantly, the time during which Jeremiah acted out a prophetic vocation spanned many wrenching events for the life of his Judahite countrymen: most notably the disasters of 597 and 587. Ezekiel's proclamations fall on both sides of the watershed of 587. More than in Amos and Hosea, the possibility is raised with Jeremiah and Ezekiel that one can reconstruct at least the broad outlines of stages in the development of their understanding of God's will as that was related to changing circumstances.

The suggestion of a developmental sequence in Jeremiah's and Ezekiel's messages is one of the most basic hypotheses offered in this book.

The stages which can be most nearly substantiated are these: 1) a beginning phase which combines strong words of judgment with words of hope or calls to repentance; 2) a crucial transitional phase, the subject of this and the next several chapters, marked off when the failure of the people to repent is given as one of the grounds for punishment in the Accusation section of the Oracle of Judgment. When reference to the failure of repentance is present one knows that there had been a period in which repentance was urged, and when conversion, if enacted, was thought to have been able to avert the impending disaster. The frequent generalization that the prophets *always* qualified their judgment preaching by holding open the possibility of repentance and subsequent forgiveness is shown to be false when the people's failure to repent is given as one of the grounds for doom, and when the prophet says that they are incapable of repenting.[1] Often mention of the failure of repentance occurs together with statements that punishments on a chastising level have gone unheeded, that purgations have been of no effect. I will suggest that this leads to a level of "radicalization of the judgment message" in Jeremiah and Ezekiel not paralleled in any other prophets. 3) After a caesura in which profound revolutions take place in Judah's status and God's representation of his will for Judah, there bursts forth a radical and unqualified message of salvation from both Jeremiah and Ezekiel.

At this point in our study what we want to investigate is the movement from stage *1* to stage *2*. This is a crucial and underappreciated development, but it is still not so category-smashing as the movement from stage 2 to stage 3, which will occupy the latter chapters of this book.

The reader is forewarned that we do not see this as an interpretative scheme imposed on the prophets; even less do we see it as a rationalistic or evolutionistic progression within the thinking of Jeremiah and Ezekiel. Rather, we think that we perceive a hardheaded attempt on the part of these prophets to read the signs of their times in terms of how God's will was being addressed to a changing pattern of interrelated factors. Those factors included such things as: the international political situation, Judah's internal politics, and the state of covenant observance in Judah. The "episodes" in the movement toward judgment are at once interpretative configurations—phases in the prophet's understanding—and also episodes in God's will and self-disclosure, all occurring in a time span in which public events apply great pressure on the relationship between God and his people. The failure of chastisement, the collapse of the hope for repentance, and the rejection even of the idea of punishment as a purgational cleansing can be understood only if each prophet is studied in the light of his own situation. How Jeremiah and Ezekiel took up these negations, and what they mean for the radicalization of their judgment message will be the main concern of this section.

B. The Prophetic Summons to Repentance

The people could have been judged for a failure to repent only if they were clearly called to repentance earlier.[2] The suggestion of such a direct challenge from the prophet to the people is significantly attested by several narrative passages which place calls to repentance in their historical settings (see in 2 Kgs. 17:13–14; Neh. 1:8–9; Jer. 18:7–11; 25:4–7; 26:3–6; 35:15, Jon. 3:7–9; Zech. 1:4–6). An example of the speech-form together with an introductory word about its failure to win a response appears in Jer. 25:4–6:

> You have neither listened nor inclined your ears to hear, although the Lord persistently sent to you all his servants the prophets, saying, "Turn now, every one of you, from his evil way and wrong doings, and dwell upon the land which the Lord has given to you and your fathers from of old and for ever; do not go after other gods to serve and worship them, or provoke me

> to anger with the work of your hands. Then I will do you no harm."

The elements of exhortation ("Turn now") and promise ("Then I will do you no harm") combined here with an accusation ("from his evil ways and wrong doings") and threat ("or provoke me to anger") make it impossible to pass this off as an Oracle of Judgment. We miss seeing one of the most characteristic elements in the role of the pre-exilic prophet if we fail to recognize that crucial period in his ministry when doom and salvation both hung in the balance, and the fulcrum of the prophet's tension vis-à-vis the people was precisely whether or not they would respond to his calls to repentance. Like Moses, Joshua, and Elijah before them, the prophets presented the people with a clear set of alternatives and a demand for decision.

As in Jer. 25:4–6, so also in Amos 5:4–5 we find the basic elements of the structure of this speech-form. The *Admonition,* "Seek me," is followed by the *Promise* for those that respond: "and live"; this leads to the *Accusation* (anticipating a misdirected response) "but do not seek Bethel, and do not enter Gilgal" and its accompanying *Threat* "for Gilgal shall surely go into exile, and Bethel shall come to nought." In the group of six Summonses to Repentance in chapters 3 and 4 of Jeremiah, we find a good example of this structure in Jer. 3:12–13: *Admonition* "Return" (faithless Israel, says the Lord), *Threat* "I will not look on you in anger," *Promise* "for I am merciful" ("says the Lord"), *Admonition* repeated "only acknowledge your guilt," *Accusation* "that you rebelled against the Lord your God." Already here we see the flexible use of the structure. Elements can appear in various sequences. Sometimes the Admonitions accuse and the Promises threaten. Oracle of Judgment and Oracle of Deliverance do not ordinarily place an alternative before the people and do not confront the people with a demand for response. Where there is this demand it is not surprising that the alternative should be stated by counterbalancing promise and threat under the predominating motif of an urgent admonition.

Examples of the speech-form Summons to Repentance can be seen in the following passages: 2 Kgs. 17:13; 2 Chr. 30:6–9; Neh. 1:8–9; Isa. 1:19–20; 55:6–7; Jer. 3:12–13, 14, 22; 4:1–2, 3–4, 14; 7:3–7; 15:19; 18:11; 22:3–5; 25:5–6; 26:13; 31:21–22; 35:15; Ezek. 14:6–11; 18:30–32; Joel 2:12–13; Amos 5:4–5, 6–7, 14–15; Jon. 3:7–9; Zeph. 2:1–3; Zech. 1:2–6, Mal. 3:7. It is entirely basic to our description of the speech-form Summons to Repentance that this be in the form of a direct address from the prophet to the people. The presence of an Admonition is of course fundamental. Twenty-four out of twenty-nine times Admonition is combined with *both* positive grounds for compliance (the Promise) and negative grounds (the Accusation or Threat). It must be stressed that it is this combination of elements which makes it impossible to incorporate the Summons to Repentance under either an Oracle of Judgment or an Oracle of Deliverance. It is precisely this combination and juxtaposition of unusual elements which characterizes the Summons to Repentance and gives it its motivational power. Where tension over the response is most felt within a Summons to Repentance, we are closest to its original formulation. This double-edged structure of the repentance summons shows that the prophets saw a sharp tension between God's readiness to forgive and his readiness to punish. In this sense the repentance summonses testify equally to the love and mercy of God, and to his wrath and strict justice. The calling to repentance was probably the most humanistic and anthropocentric stage of the prophets' ministries. On man's response to God's call hung the outcome of history. In this sense the call to repentance rests upon a very optimistic view of man.

We believe the repentance summons to have been derived from covenantal challenges which used the protasis/apodosis (if/then) linguistic structure to sharpen the alternatives. When Moses first called the people to decision about entering the covenant at the foot of Mt. Sinai, he employed a positive set of protasis/apodosis conditions: "*If* you will obey my voice and keep my covenant" (*protasis*), " (*then*) you shall be my own possession among all peoples" (*apodosis*) (Exod. 19:5–6). The protasis here functions in the same way as the *Admonition* section of a Summons to Repentance, and the apodosis functions like the *Promise.* When Joshua called the tribes to renew their covenant relationship with God he formulated part of his challenge in a negative set of protasis/apodosis conditions: "*If* you forsake the Lord and serve foreign gods" (*protasis*), "*then* he will turn and do you harm and consume you . . ." (*apodosis,* Josh. 24:20–21). Here the protasis functions like the *Accusation* portion of a Summons to Repentance, while the apodosis functions like the *Threat.* All four elements are combined in the covenant curse liturgy of Deut. 28:1–15: "*If* you obey . . . (*then*) all these blessings shall come upon you . . . / *But if* you will not obey, *then* all these curses shall come upon you." This covenant renewal situation (in Josh. 24 and Deut. 28) is the setting in life out of which we think the prophetic Summons to Repentance originated, and the structural pattern of Admonition → Promise/ Accusation → Threat appears to have been derived from a double set of protasis/apodosis conditions.[3] We see Samuel, like Joshua, standing in the role of covenant mediator and using this language to call the people to decision in 1 Sam. 7:3. After him Elijah continues the tradition of that role and that pattern of challenge in 1 Kgs. 18:21. It naturally follows from what we have said that the prophet stands in the traditional role of covenant mediator as he brings to the people a moral challenge in a time-honored and widely recognizable form. Both the role in which the people understood him as appearing and the form in which he couched his exhortation supplied the prophet an engagement which the supportive rationale (Mosaic Covenant and traditions surrounding its renewal) needed to show the people the full implications of the decision placed before them.[4]

C. Failure of Repentance in Jeremiah

The evidence that Jeremiah did call the people to repentance with urgent exhortations and anxiously waited for their response is counterbalanced, but not contradicted, by evidence that Jeremiah felt that the repentance phase of his ministry was a failure.

The significant thing is that Jeremiah did not look back upon the repentance episode as an escape route to deliverance which unfortunately did not work out—a kind of blank or zero in Judah's record; no, Jeremiah was embittered and disillusioned by this failure. He made recalling it a very important part of the accusations upon which Judah's judgment was based. In this part of his teaching, no significant difference can be discerned between these related themes: the failure of repentance, chastisement, purgative punishment, or his pessimism that the people's behavior had shown them to be incapable of regeneration. For Jeremiah these sober assessments were supportive convictions, often intertwined in their expression, component parts of one basic thrust in his doom message.

Among the passages which are clearly original to the prophet himself, 5:1–6 provides a good initial illustration.[5] The announcement of judgment comes at the end, in verse 6a, introduced by "Therefore." What precedes the announcement functions as the accusation upon which the judgment is based. The first offense cited is their unpardonableness (v. 1). Seemingly God is angered by a nation which gives him no opportunity to show his mercy. This sets the tone for the main accusation which comes in verse 3: "Thou hast smitten them, but they felt no anguish; thou hast consumed them, but they refused to take correction. They have made their faces harder than rock; they have refused to repent."[6] Has Jeremiah forgotten what to put into an Oracle of Judgment? Amos and Isaiah never do this. They accuse the people of real sins, specific wrongdoings. But Jeremiah is ready to have the people torn to pieces by wild animals (v. 6), because they did not respond to an awakening and educating level of punishment or to the offer of conditional deliverance. "Feeling no anguish," "refusing to take correction," "becoming hard as a rock," "refusing to repent"—these are worse than sins! What can be done with people who not only violate the requirements of God, but seemingly cannot be made aware of what they have done? What is God to do with people who lack conscience and moral sensitivity? Clearly the prophet is becoming discouraged. Somehow time is running out. Caught between God, the people, and the course of external events, Jeremiah finds his level of frustration reaching a danger point. God's pathos speaks through his emotion, and we begin to sense that Judah has inexorably been brought a step closer to its doom.

In 9:5–9 God's feeling emerges through the prophet's words in a sequence of images which build up from the accusations "they commit iniquity and are too weary to repent"[7] (v. 5), and "they refuse to know me" (v. 6), to two judgment announcements put in the form of questions. In verse 7 it is a purgational punishment, "I will refine them and test them, for what else can I do, because of my people?" But this quickly leads to another kind of punishment in verse 9, "Shall I not punish them . . . shall I not avenge myself . . .?" There is a sense of movement toward a crisis here, the sources of which are not immediately apparent. It is not simply a matter of specific events of national wrongdoing and their appropriate recompense. Jeremiah simultaneously sees a buildup of sin, a decline in the people's capacity for moral relationship with Yahweh, and the entrapment of God in these circumstances. What is God to do? Punishment increasingly becomes a problem for him as it fails to bring the desired results first on the chastising and then on the purgative levels.

Was anything so new about God's people sinning? Had that never happened before? Who introduced a time limit on repentance? What necessitated this rapid escalation of punishment levels? Can it be believed that the people were actually further from maintaining their side of the covenant *after* Josiah's reform than they were before, under the reign of Manasseh, the prototype of wicked kings? Had any prophet before expressed such pessimism about the moral capabilities of the people: "foolish and senseless people, who have eyes, but see not, who have ears, but hear not" (5:21); "this people has a stubborn and rebellious heart" (5:23); "your sins have kept good from you" (5:25); "they have loved to wander thus, they have not restrained their feet" (14:10); "Can the Ethiopian change his skin or the leopard his spots? Then also you can do good who are accustomed to do evil" (13:23). After having started out with some hope, Jeremiah changes before our eyes into a prophet who has completely given up on his own people. One can suggest an explanation in the prophet's own personality, or in the uncompromising way that he applied God's covenant requirements to his contemporaries, or in his disillusionment that the Josianic reform was not more successful, or in an actual alleged moral deteroriation within the kingdom of Judah. But it is blind to ignore that the greatest turn toward radicalization of a prophet's judgment message coincided with the timing of Judah's fall into the hands of the Babylonians. I suggest *that* is why the time for repentance ran out then, when it had not suffered the judgment of a stop watch previously. That is why Jeremiah said that the people were no more capable of doing good than a leopard would be able to change its spots, when such clear-eyed and sensitive critics of corporate morality as Amos and Hosea never came down with a generalization as pessimistic as that. And that is why punishment escalated from a chastisement which did not immediately work, to a purgation which brought no direct results, to an annihilation. Jeremiah never says, "I will chastise more severely," or "I will more urgently call them to repent." What purpose then does it serve for the prophet to tell the people that they have failed to respond to chastisement, failed to respond to calls to repentance, that they have not listened or shown moral capacity, that purging punishment has not worked? I think that this development primarily explains that one era of God's action is over and another about to begin. And this crisis serves as an apology or justification for the next level of punishment.

We have raised the suggestion that the hidden factor in the radicalization of Jeremiah's judgment preaching was the pressure of external political events. The prophet apparently hoped that if the people would only repent, then God would turn back the Babylonians and not use them as the instrument of his punishment. And as the political threat became more ominous, Jeremiah at once became both more aware of the intensity of God's anger, and also the shortcomings of his countrymen were highlighted for him as never before. Compassion and outrage toward them grew in him side by side, until the recourse which they had, but failed to follow, seemed to justify God's severest judgment even more than specific wrongdoings. That connection is not difficult to demonstrate. After warning calls to the people were ignored (v. 17), in 6:19 God declares, "I am bringing evil upon this people . . . because they have not given heed to my words. . . ." Even more succinct is the word in 19:15: "Behold, I am bringing upon this city and upon all its towns all the evil that I have pronounced against it, because they have stiffened their neck, refusing to hear my words." The progression of thought in 15:6–9 is quite instructive. This will be seen if we pull out some key phrases in their sequence: "you have rejected me"; "so I have stretched out my hand against you"; "I am weary of relenting"; "I have winnowed them with a winnowing fork . . . I have bereaved them"; "they did not turn from their ways"; "the rest of them I will give to the sword before their enemies." The word for "relent" here (*niham*) also means "repent," but is often an image of God changing his intention from wrath toward forgiveness. So, sin leads to chastisement, the failure of chastisement undercuts God's motivation toward forgiveness, yet he chastises some more and still the people do not repent; then we hear of a judgment which moves from chastisement toward annihilation. In 6:27–30 the movement toward doom is more direct, as the failure of a purgational punishment (v. 29) leads God to reject his people (v. 30). In 7:23–29 God seems to exhaust every possibility—admonitions to obey, calls to repent, chastisements—every one of them failing to win a response, until the prophet announces God's fateful sentence: "the Lord has rejected and forsaken the generation of his wrath." When the failure of repentance is made the basis for God's refusal to forgive or for the rejection of his own people, we have reached the ultimate radicalization of Jeremiah's judgment preaching and pointed to themes to be taken up in sections which follow.[8]

When we speak of the failure of repentance as a sign and source of the radicalization of Jeremiah's judgment message, the question naturally arises "radicalized in relation to what?" Of course, we mean radicalized in relation to the first episode of his ministry when he directly exhorted repentance or pronounced God's judgment in the hope that it would promote conversion. But also we mean that Jeremiah's message is radicalized in relation to what Amos and Isaiah, and to a lesser extent Hosea, proclaimed.

D. Comparison with Earlier Prophets

Amos is often thought of as a very severe prophet of doom. The apparent basis for this characterization is that some of the sentences of God's judgment on sin which he pronounces are harsh and annihilatory in their thrust (8:2–3; 9:1, 7–10). The impression is amplified by the relative scarcity of notes of compassion within the book, and by the almost sadistic glee with which Amos reverses what the people are expecting in his promises of what they are going to receive from God (3:2; 5:18–20). But his litany on the failure of chastisement, 4:6–11, does *not* lead to a promise of doom or function as the basis for another level of punishment (unless something of that nature has been cut out of 4:12).[9] His calls to repentance in 5:4–5, 6–7, and 14–15 are all hopeful and unclouded. There is no direct indication that these calls failed. Unlike Jeremiah's attempted intercession for the people in chapter 14, when Amos asks God to forgive in 7:2 and 7:5, God repents of his intended judgment (7:3, 6). In Amos there are no words about the failure of repentance or purgational punishment, no direct tie of chastisement failure to doom, no generalized statements about the hopelessly unregenerate condition of human nature, no passages where God denies the possibility of mercy, no words of rejection. The surprising conclusion, then, is that in at least some ways Amos is less radical in his judgment preaching than Jeremiah. The repentance episode had not failed and ended during Amos' ministry, and God had not exhausted his options for responding to the people's sin; in the book there is less sense of being caught in the pressure of a historical vise.

Much of this climate disappears in the writings of Hosea who stood about fifteen years closer to the fall of Samaria than Amos did. He satirizes the people's insincere attempt at repentance in 6:1–4, comments on an instance of the failure of repentance in 7:10, and makes such a failure the basis of a severe judgment in 11:5ff. (although God repents of this judgment in 11:8–9). Yet, mixed throughout the book are more optimistic words about repentance (3:4–5; 10:12; 12:6; 14:1–2). The pessimism about Gomer's capacity for lasting rehabilitation at the beginning of the book sets the tone for much of what follows. There are generalized statements about the people's immorality (4:1–2), criticisms that they do not know God (4:6; 5:4), and such vivid indictments as these: "a spirit of harlotry has led them astray" (4:12); "like a stubborn heifer, Israel is stubborn" (4:16); and "their deeds do not permit them to return to their God" (5:4). A few times Hosea did say that God's mercy was cut off from Israel (1:6; 13:14), and as we will see below, in Chapter III, p. 75, Hosea may have originated the teaching that God rejected his own people (1:9; 2:2; 4:6; 9:17). By these criteria Hosea's judgment message is radicalized beyond any point reached in Amos (Hosea, like Amos, has his words of annihilatory doom—2:3; 5:14; 9:3; 13:16). Yet there are more outbursts of unrestrained compassion in the midst of Hosea's judgment message than in any other prophet. Hosea's is a very mixed message, bristling with polarities and tensions. The only times that he mentions chastisement seem to be with an optimism that it will work (5:2; 7:12; 10:10). In Hosea's book there is repeated emphasis on God's love overcoming Israel's sin. Because of these considerations, and the impossibility of dividing Hosea's ministry into distinct episodes (perhaps simply because of a haphazard arrangement of the separate speeches), Hosea's message appears to be less radical than Jeremiah's, although more radical in judgment than Amos'.

Isaiah's ministry in Jerusalem spanned the time from Hosea's work in the Northern capital through its fall to the Assyrians in 722 to the end of the century, around 700. Isaiah has quite a number of stern Oracles of Judgment, but they generally do not contain annihilatory imagery. While not to be confused with the false prophets, Isaiah was more optimistic in his outlook than either Amos or Hosea. There are calls to repent (1:16–17, 18–20; 30:15; 31:6), but no indictments against the people on the basis of their failure to repent. Isaiah clearly believes in the effectiveness and success of purgational punishment (1:25; 4:4). He is famous for his teaching that a remnant of the people will survive (1:8–9; 7:3; 10:20–23). And he even proclaims the inviolability of Jerusalem under the image of Zion (28:16; 31:5). One looks in vain here for any sense that the time for repentance or chastisement has passed, and there is no teaching that forgiveness is cut off or that God will reject his own people. All this is quite in contrast to the judgment message of the next great prophet to Jerusalem, Jeremiah.

In Amos, Hosea, and Isaiah we have found that the era of repentance admonitions, chastisements, and purgations was still operative. We assume that this era extended into the beginning years of Jeremiah's ministry on the basis of that prophet's authentic Summonses to Repentance, and his sharp personal disappointment that these failed. Much of the Book of Jeremiah reflects the agonizing transition from the era of repentance to the era of denied mercy, rejection, and annihilation. It is precisely this shift which justifies our speaking of a radicalization of the judgment message in Jeremiah.

E. Failure of Repentance in Ezekiel

By being among those taken captive to Babylon in 597, Ezekiel is physically and theologically a whole stage further into the judgment of the Exile than Jeremiah. It almost seems as though Ezekiel took up Jeremiah's judgment message where the earlier left it.[10] The tone of urgency in Jeremiah's doom preaching is largely missing in Ezekiel. Instead, his announcement of judgment is cool and matter of fact; it has an eerie visionary quality, but little compassion. Ezekiel apparently never went through a repent-chastise phase; thus, he has almost nothing to say of its failure. He begins with the assumption that there is no hope for Judah, and thus he preaches denied mercy, rejection, and annihilation from the outset. His public ministry begins in chapter 4 with punishment already inevitable, beyond a chastising or purgative level.

Along with this difference there are some threads of continuity with Jeremiah. In 3:7 God predicts that the people will not listen to his prophet; in 20:7–8, 18–21 we hear of repentance-type appeals and their failure. Ezekiel does not make the failure of repentance the basis for more severe judgment. In 16:27 and 20:26 God's chastisement brings no results, but an issue is not made of that. A progression of thought closer to what we found in Jeremiah appears in chapter 24 under the theme of a purgational punishment. The failure of the purgation further jeopardizes Judah's survival:

> Because I would have cleansed you and you were not cleansed from your filthiness, you shall not be cleansed any more till I have satisfied my fury upon you. I the Lord have spoken; it shall come to pass, I will do it; I will not go back, I will not spare, I will not repent. . . . (24:13–14)

Then a few verses later we learn that God has rejected them (24:21). In 22:15–22 what began as an image of purgation finally communicates a message of annihilation. Ezekiel is especially close to Jeremiah in his pessimism about the unregenerate nature of Judah considered as a corporate entity. The language is even similar at points. Ezekiel is called to preach to "a rebellious house" (2:7); they are people of "a hard forehead and of a stubborn heart" (3:7); they are those "who have eyes to see, but see not, who have ears to hear, but hear not" (12:2). In his allegorical review of Israelite history Jerusalem is shown as a whore beyond the reach of any rehabilitation (16:15–34); Jerusalem is seen by Ezekiel as worse than Sodom, worse than Samaria—two cities long since annihilated (16:46–51). The theme of Jerusalem as a whore, worse than Samaria, reappears in 23:11–21. Here, as in Jeremiah, the usual Old Testament optimism about man is reversed. The salvation preaching of both prophets assumed this perception of the problem as it is declared that God must improve human nature so that man can keep covenant requirements and have the hope of an unbroken relationship with God (Jer. 31:33–34; Ezek. 36:26–27).

Because those who had gone with him into Exile based their hopes not upon God but upon Jerusalem's escaping destruction and quickly returning from captivity, Ezekiel had to proclaim the destruction of Judah in the most uncompromising terms.

The only suggestion of the possibility of a national repentance which the book preserves is in 14:6. But in certain isolated sections of the book, especially chapter 18 and less so portions of chapters 33 and 3 which may well be dependent upon chapter 18, Ezekiel opens up the possibility of repentance for the individual.[11] There is no pessimism in these passages; failure to repent is never mentioned. To the present writer, this is an interesting and authentic interlude between the end point of Ezekiel's radicalized judgment preaching, and the development later of his salvation preaching. Having totally given up on national repentance, having promised the annihilation of Jerusalem and the departure of God's glory from the temple, and stung by questions of God's justice in letting the innocent suffer equally with the guilty, Ezekiel opens up this substantially new teaching of repentance for the individual to show that there is hope for those who accepted the Exile with faith in God's abiding Lordship and justice.[12]

In my view Ezekiel essentially accepts and underlines Jeremiah's already radicalized message of judgment. In his book we do not see so much the movement toward radicalization as its results: there is no hope for the nation; through the symbolism of the temple God has rejected it; without any evident compassion the refrain is repeatedly sounded that any possibility of mercy or forgiveness has been cut off.[13] The greatest authority on Ezekiel living today sees the message of judgment in Ezekiel as even more extreme than what we found in Jeremiah: "Ezekiel radicalizes to the last degree the announcement of disaster which had already been heard from the mouths of the earlier literary prophets."[14] The dimensions of this radicalization will be further clarified as we turn now to the teaching that God not only refuses to repent of his judgment but also refuses to forgive the sins which prompt it.

GOD'S REFUSAL TO FORGIVE OR SHOW MERCY

A. Scope of the Theme and Authenticity of Passages Expressing It

In what we found concerning the failure of the repentance-chastisement episode the spotlight was on man, on the arena of human initiative in maintaining or restoring the relationship between God and his people. Like a noose, the encirclement of Judah in doom is tightened by its failure to offer God's mercy a chance for expression without compromising the integrity of his justice. But radicalization of the doom message moves forward not only upon Judah's shortcomings. This thrust toward annihilation is signaled and propelled by two striking and unexpected expressions of God's own decision. We consider in what follows God's refusal to forgive or show mercy, and in the next chapter we take up the study of the suspension of the covenant relationship through God's rejection of Judah.

For reasons not apparent to the present writer, the substantial development of the theme of denied mercy and forgiveness in Jeremiah and Ezekiel seems not to have caught the attention of scholarly interest.[15] Yet what the prophets from Amos to Ezekiel have to say about the forgiveness of sins appears more often in the Oracle of Judgment than in any other speech-form.[16] We will study denials of mercy here along with explicit promises that God will not forgive, since either formulation appears to have the same function within prophetic judgment preaching. Allied with these motifs also is the gloomy depiction of the remnant hope in Jer. 6:9; 8:3; 15:9; Ezek. 5:10; 9:8; 11:13; 23:25.[17] Although the significance of the remnant belief in Isaiah, as in all prophets, has been greatly exaggerated,[18] it certainly underlines the shift we have already seen between Isaiah and Jeremiah-Ezekiel, that the latter two either explicitly deny a remnant hope or put it in a context which effectively does the same thing.

Our interest in the pages that follow centers upon the fifteen passages in Jeremiah and seven in Ezekiel where God's decision not to forgive and/or his refusal to show mercy appear as an important, perhaps even pivotal, component of the judgment preaching. The Ezekiel passages, apparently all original words of the prophet, repeat or closely follow a striking word pattern found in 7:9: "my eye will not spare (*ḥûs*), nor will I have pity (*ḥāmal*)." We have the pattern exactly in this form also in

8:18 and 9:10. Only minor variations occur in its expression in 5:11; 7:4; and 9:5. In 24:14 "spare" is used without "eye," "pity" is dropped, and "not repent" (*niḥam*) substituted in its place. The unusual but key verbal images which we focus on here in Ezekiel and will compare with analogous uses elsewhere are "spare" (*ḥûs*) and "pity" (*ḥāmal*), especially as they are used together.[19]

Jeremiah, on the other hand, brings the denial of mercy and forgiveness to expression under a greater diversity of imagery. In three contexts it is said that God or his anger will not "turn back" (*šûb*): 4:8, 28; 23:20. An equal number of times a closely related verbal picture communicates that God will not "repent" or "relent" (*niḥam*): 4:28; 15:6; 18:10. Twice the question of "pardon" (*sālaḥ*) is raised to show its unlikelihood (5:1; 5:7). In 6:20 God does not "accept" (*rāṣāh*) sacrifices; in 14:10 he does not "accept" (*rāṣāh*) his people. Only twice does Jeremiah employ anything anticipatory of Ezekiel's formula. In both 13:14 and 21:7 we have his verbs "spare" (*ḥûs*) and "pity" (*ḥāmal*), but a third verbal figure, "not have compassion," is added. In several additional passages the theme of denied forgiveness is expressed through imagery not found elsewhere in the book: 16:5, 13; 25:29. Most of these passages are considered genuine with Jeremiah (this applies to 4:8, 28; 5:1, 7; 6:20; 13:14; 14:10; 15:6; 23:20), but on some there is divided opinion (15:1; 16:5, 13; 18:10; 21:7; 25:29).[20] Before going into the function and meaning of the denial of mercy and forgiveness within Jeremiah and Ezekiel, we will see their employment of this motif in better perspective if we seek the antecedents for their formulations.

B. Sources of Jeremiah's and Ezekiel's Teaching

1. The Distinctive Imagery in Ezekiel

We need to inquire whether Ezekiel's "formula" was his own creation or borrowed from another source. The use in Jer. 13:14 alone stands earlier than Ezekiel since Jer. 21:7 is considered a late addition by source analysts.[21] In material which might be earlier than Jeremiah "spare" (*ḥûs*) and "pity" (*ḥāmal*) are put together only in Deut. 13:8. The construction of "nor shall your eye pity (*ḥûs*) him," and "nor shall you spare (*ḥāmal*) him" here is quite close to the pattern in Ezekiel,[22] but it is preceded by two verbal elements ("not yield," "not listen"), and followed by another ("nor . . . conceal") which are foreign to the Ezekiel passage. Another important distinction is that the subject of these verbs is the community of Israel, rather than Yahweh, and the object of the action is a wayward individual, rather than the whole people; thus, it does not communicate a denial of divine forgiveness at all.

The verb "spare" (*ḥûs*) appears three other times in a legal context within Deuteronomy (19:13, 21; 25:12), and once in the same pattern, "your eye shall not pity" in a holy war setting (Deut. 7:16). Beyond this, there are only eight additional uses of "spare" (*ḥûs*) outside of Ezekiel, Jeremiah, and Deuteronomy in the Old Testament—none of them in the sense of God's denial of mercy, and none of them in parallelism with "pity" (*ḥāmal*).[23]

Of "pity" (*ḥāmal*), by contrast, no uses are made within Deuteronomy beyond 13:8. It is employed a number of times in what could be earlier material, in 1 and 2 Samuel, with regard to sparing the lives of persons or animals (1 Sam. 15:3, 9, 15; 2 Sam. 12:4, 6; 21:7). Again, none of these depicts God's denial of mercy to his own people, none of them is in parallelism with "spare" (*ḥûs*), and none of them is in a context which suggests any direct influence on Deut. 13:8, or more notably, on Jer. 13:14 or the seven Ezekiel passages.

From this survey we can draw several conclusions: a) In the Deuteronomy passages which use "spare" (*ḥûs*), and the Samuel passages employing "pity" (*ḥāmal*), if the course of action depicted by these verbs was denied, it meant death; if it was pursued, it meant that life was spared. This then certainly underlines the gravity of the saying in Ezekiel. b) There is not enough evidence to warrant the claim that Ezekiel adopted an existing and well-known formula. The single combination of "pity" (*ḥāmal*) and "spare" (*ḥûs*) in Deut. 13:8 seems largely coincidental. Nor does its isolated appearance in Jer. 13:14 seem to have the fixity of a formula. And while either of those could have been a source for Ezekiel's structure, each includes elements which do not appear in Ezekiel. c) Our growing impression of Ezekiel's creativity in the use of this litany of denied mercy is further strengthened by a passage in which he uses the two verbs together, but in quite a different sense than in 5:11; 7:4; etc. Early in his allegory on God's election of Israel and Israel's subsequent apostasy, God says: "No eye pitied you (*ḥûs*) to do any of these things to you out of compassion for you (ḥāmal)" (16:5). We see, therefore, that Ezekiel knew more shades of meaning for these verbs than it might first appear (see also his use of *ḥāmal* in 36:21). Through use of this imagery Ezekiel allows us to see that Israel's predicament of being unloved and helpless before God adopted her has gone full circle after she had grown into adulthood and whoredom, standing helpless before the Babylonians, but then no longer pitied by God.

2. The Distinctive Imagery in Jeremiah

For Jeremiah's teaching that God will not turn from his punitive purpose, nor forgive, we also find very little earlier precedent. Isaiah never takes up this theme. Amos employs the image "never again pass by them" (*'ābar*) in 7:8 and 8:2, probably with a meaning equivalent to denying forgiveness;[24] but this expression is not found in Jeremiah. Hosea uses "have mercy" (*rāḥam*) in verb form in 1:6 and 2:4, declaring that God will not pity his people any longer. This usage could have influenced Jeremiah's addition of that verb to "spare" (*ḥûs*) and "pity" (*ḥāmal*) in 13:14 and 21:7. The key terms for expressing the denial of forgiveness in Hos. 8:13, "not accept," "remember their iniquity," reappear in Jer. 14:10. Yet, even with these threads of possible influence from Hosea, the truly characteristic and distinctive imagery Jeremiah uses for expressing the denial of forgiveness motif is not anticipated.

It is generally recognized that Jeremiah is "the great prophet of repentance," unexcelled in the variety of effective word plays he achieves with *šûb* and *niḥam*, the two words for "turn back, repent."[25] A promise appears in 26:3 stating that if the people "turn" (*šûb*) from their "evil" (*rā'āh*) way, then God opens the possibility: "I may repent (*niḥam*) of the evil (*rā'āh*) which I intend to do to them because of their evil doings.") In another development, Jeremiah said that when the people failed to repent (*šûb*), God's response was "I am weary of relenting" (*niḥam,* 15:6). Instead of the people turning (*šûb*) from immorality, in 4:8 and 23:20, we find that it is God who refuses to turn (*šûb*) his wrath from the course of judgment. In 18:8–10 God declares that if a nation "turns (*šûb*) from its evil, I will repent (*niḥam*) of the evil that I intend to do to it"; but if the nation refuses to repent "then I will repent (*niḥam*) of the good which I had intended to do to it."[26] Whatever earlier uses "turn back" (*šûb*) and "repent" (*niḥam*) may have had, Jeremiah obviously gave them an expression unequaled in brilliance and effectiveness. It seems fitting that the prophet who agonized so much over the failure of repentance should not only make that failure a basis for severe judgment, but also convert images of turning (toward God) into expressions denying God's forgiveness. This establishes the strongest possible bond between the failure of repentance episode and the denial of forgiveness as a further radicalization of doom. The two themes are thus virtually brought into a cause and effect relationship.

As far as we can determine, "turn" (*šûb*) has no earlier usage in the sense of denied mercy or forgiveness. And while "repent" (*niḥam*) has earlier employments as a metaphor for forgiveness, it is never previously used to express the denial of forgiveness. Probably the earliest comparable uses of it come in Gen. 6:6 where God "repents" of having created man and in 1 Sam. 15: 11, 29, 35 where God "repents" of having made Saul king. The verb *niḥam* in the sense of granting the equivalent of forgiveness appears in Exod. 32:14; Amos 7:3, 6; Hos. 11:8; Joel 2:13, 14; and Jon. 3:9, 10; 4:2 (see also in Jer. 26:13, 19; 42:10). Therefore, while Jeremiah has some sources to draw upon, his own use of *niḥam* remains quite distinctive, especially when used in juxtaposition with *šûb*.

Beyond the forgiveness denials which we have already considered in Amos and Hosea, the only other sources of possible conceptual influence on this teaching in Jeremiah and Ezekiel come in early narrative literature. In the covenant renewal ceremony of Joshua 24, the people are warned that if they forsake Yahweh to serve other gods "he will not forgive (*nāsā'*) your transgressions or your sins" (24:19). This is to be compared with Exod. 34:6–7 and Num. 14:18 where the same root, *nāsā',* is used in covenant renewal settings to promise that God *will* forgive the people's sins. But Josh. 24:19 is supported by Exod. 23:21, toward the end of the Sinai Covenant ceremony, where the people are warned that God's angel who is to lead them in the wilderness "will not pardon (*nāsā'*) your transgressions." In yet one other covenantal context, Deut. 29:20, the individual who turns to serve other gods is promised, "The Lord would not pardon (*sālaḥ*) him." The possibility of influence on Jeremiah and Ezekiel from these divergent statements of the relation of forgiveness to the covenant tradition can be considered as we turn now to look at the function and meaning of this theme in its context in the two prophets.

C. Function and Meaning of Theme of Denied Forgiveness in Context

One of the striking aspects of Ezekiel's use of the "my eye will not spare, nor will I have pity" formulation is that it is always accompanied in the same verse with a phrase depicting the act of judgment. Sometimes it precedes, but equally often it follows, the event of judgment. This raises for us the question what is the function of this formula in Ezekiel, or the function of the various ways Jeremiah brings God's refusal to forgive into expression? Is it to interpret the judgment, or to justify it, or to reinforce it? The outline below shows the range of uses.

1. The saying (about no forgiveness, no mercy) appears in the Accusation: Jer. 5:1, 7; 6:20.

2. The saying introduces the Proclamation: Jer. 15:1; 16:5.

3. The saying accompanies the Proclamation: Jer. 15:6; 23:20; 25:29; Ezek. 7:4, 9; 9:5.

4. The saying is the Proclamation: Jer. 14:10; 18:10.

5. The saying leads up to the most severe part of the Proclamation: Ezek. 5:11.

6. The saying is the final element in the Proclamation: Jer. 4:8, 28; 13:14; 16:13; 21:7; Ezek. 8:18; 9:10; 24:14.

The Oracles of Judgment in Jeremiah 5:1 and 5:7 have as their beginning note (as in point *1* in this outline) the doubtful possibility of forgiveness: "Can you find anyone that deserves forgiveness?" in 5:1, and "How can I pardon you?" in 5:7. At once this very effectively stresses that God wants to forgive and that Judah has made it impossible for him to forgive. Its unforgivableness is not merely part of Judah's sin, it also serves as the justification for God's punishment.

When it comes at the end of a Proclamation (point *6* in outline), the denial of mercy or forgiveness carries a chilling sense of finality. It is almost like a judge telling a defendant: "You are sentenced to death and denied the possibility of appealing your case." Certainly this reinforces the word of doom by putting a kind of unbreakable seal upon it.

Cutting off the flow of forgiveness, or access to God's mercy, may come earlier, perhaps reflecting the turning point or decision toward an annihilatory judgment. This is the sense in Jer. 15:1; 16:5; and Ezek. 5:11 (points *2* and *5* in outline). Standing by itself, it implies the judgment to follow in Jer. 14:10 and 18:10 (*4* in outline). In the instances in which it accompanies the Proclamation of judgment (cited under *3* in the outline), it is well integrated into the whole doom pronouncement and does not especially call attention to itself. Our overall impression is inescapable that *in any judgment passage in which a denial of mercy or forgiveness is present the tone of severity is strengthened, the images of judgment seem less rhetorical and more literal, and the thrust toward annihilation appears accelerated.*

Is the "no forgiveness, no mercy" motif a good criterion for the radicalization of judgment? Not if it requires the assumption that the prophets at an earlier stage taught that God's mercy and forgiveness were readily accessible. Although we know of occasions when both Amos and Jeremiah interceded with God for the people's forgiveness (Amos 7:2, 5; Jer. 14:7ff., 19ff.; compare Ezek. 9:8 and 11:13), the prophets avoided promising forgiveness as the reward for repentance. It would have ill suited their purpose, either in repentance preaching or in the judgment preaching before it developed an annihilatory thrust, to have emphasized God's readiness to forgive. If anything, the evidence seems to indicate that the people were already overconfident of God's mercy, perhaps basing this on hopeful passages in any of a number of Psalms or upon the version of the Exod. 36:6–7 liturgy then current (which may well *not* have included a judgment pole from the outset, since so significant a majority of its echoes know nothing of such a pole).[27] Yet, a call to repentance necessarily included some promise of mercy from God if the people heeded it. And it is difficult to imagine what happened in a covenant renewal ceremony unless there were included calls to repentance and promises of forgiveness.[28] Exod. 34:6–7 and Num. 14:18 support this; but Josh. 24:19; Exod. 23:21; and Deut. 29:20 warn that the people cannot count on God's forgiveness in the event of substantial covenant-breaking sins. In the Old Testament as a whole there is nothing approaching a normative understanding of how accessible God's mercy or forgiveness is, nor how far forgiveness when granted goes in removing the stain of guilt and the burden of punishment.[29] This warns us against generalizations, and forces us to deal with specific situations on an individual basis.

Nevertheless, we can summarize our impressions. 1) At the beginnings of their ministries Amos, Hosea, and Jeremiah held open the possibility of averting a tragic judgment by the workings of God's mercy if the people wholeheartedly repented. 2) When Hosea, Jeremiah, and Ezekiel promise that God will not forgive, there is probably present some element of polemical corrective of the Exod. 34:6–7 expectation on the basis of the Josh. 24:19 type of tradition.[30] 3) That polemical corrective is not enough to explain the function or meaning of the "no-forgiveness"–"no-mercy" passages as they now stand in Jeremiah and Ezekiel. 4) We have already seen that, in light of their terminological background found in Deuteronomy and 1-2 Samuel, when

Ezekiel says that God is not going to "spare" (*ḥûs*) or "pity" (*ḥāmal*) he is saying that life will *not* be spared. And with Jeremiah we found that God's refusal to repent of his plan of judgment was a response to the people's failure to repent of their sins. After repentance-chastisement failed, the only remaining recourse was within the sphere of God's initiative. The "no-forgiveness"–"no-mercy" passages make clear that this final alternative to doom is now also excluded. They demonstrate radicalization of the judgment message in that they take us one step farther along the line of movement indicated in the repentance failure passages. Doom is justified and inevitable when the people are unforgivable; the denial of mercy or forgiveness reinforces and seals doom. Without this restraint the movement toward annihilation is accelerated.

Even in these passages the bi-polar formulas (see Chapter I, pp. 27–29), rooted in Yahweh's mode of action, find a reaffirmation. This is so because the dynamics of God's inclination toward mercy and forgiveness are present and affirmed, even as the possibility of their coming to expression in this circumstance is denied. It is as though these passages say: Even though my inclination is toward mercy and forgiveness, yet in this circumstance I am denying you and myself the expression of that. What comes forth now in this radicalized judgment and doom is the pole expressive of God's readiness to punish. But it must be clearly seen that while everyone can now count upon *that* plan of action, this is the denial of the *operation,* but not the *existence* of the possibility, of God's forgiveness. Indeed, only a God who is very ready to forgive has to emphasize that at this point in history he will not forgive. It is that which gives the negation of the affirmation its double-edged effectiveness. Even as they learn of this further radicalization of their judgment, the people of Judah are reminded that it is a God of mercy who is about to destroy them. Without this tension present in the doom preaching, the later salvation preaching either contradicts the judgment or is itself inexplicable.

Chapter III

THE REJECTION MOTIF

A. An Introduction to the Rejection Motif

A cursory examination of any pre-exilic prophetic book shows that the most prominent theme in the doom preaching is the accusation of transgressions committed. The endless repetitions of this motif, lacking any sense of redundancy, indicate that the prophets were primarily concerned to convince the people that they had sinned grievously against God. Although the next most evident element in doom preaching, the threat or promise of judgment, announces what punishment will impinge upon Israel from the outside, this only indirectly reflects what continuity Israel will have into the future. In the final analysis the two most important things to know in order to grasp the meaning of the doom preaching at its point of greatest severity are God's own plan and intention, and the status of Israel's internal, personal relationship with God. Some key questions then become: Is the covenant "broken" in the sense that it can be said that a covenant relationship no longer exists between God and his people? Is the election of Israel by God reversed so that they become his rejected people, or suspended so that they are, at least for a time, abandoned or forsaken?

We deal with this question under the terminology of the "rejection" of Israel, not because that is the best word—indeed, in many ways it is too severe a word—but because there is some precedent for using that term to designate this issue in scholarly work, and because there is a solid basis for it in the Hebrew vocabulary used to depict a caesura in Israel's relationship with God. Although there is substantial textual evidence for the presence of a rejection teaching, especially in the prophets, nothing like a comprehensive study of it has yet appeared. Within the Old Testament itself the question of rejection was sometimes a controversial issue. Most passages affirm it, but a few emphatically deny it.

Since it would be meaningless to negate the validity of a belief unless it earlier had been promulgated, we are immediately alerted to the possibilities that the idea of God's rejecting Israel was not held by all faith circles in Israel. If it was fairly widely accepted at one period in Israel's history, perhaps it was later denied or nullified by an affirmation taking its place. So, in examining this motif within the doom preaching of Jeremiah and Ezekiel, we need to be sensitive to restrictions on its applicability, whether temporal or otherwise.

There can be no doubt that Israelite faith ever raised the possibility of God's rejecting the people he has chosen. The suggestion of this rejection becomes unmistakably clear when the verb "choose" (*bāḥar*) is set in direct juxtaposition to the verb "reject" (*mā'as*). We find some good illustrations of this juxtaposition. 2 Kgs. 23:27: "And the Lord said: 'I will remove Judah also out of my sight, as I have removed Israel, and I will cast off (*mā'as*) this city which I have chosen (*bāḥar*), Jerusalem and the house of which I said, My name shall be there.' " Ps. 78:67–68: "He rejected (*mā'as*) the tent of Joseph, he did not choose (*bāḥar*) the tribe of Ephraim; but he chose (*bāḥar*) the tribe of Judah, Mount Zion, which he loves." Jer. 33:24: "Have you not observed what these people are saying, 'The Lord has rejected (*mā'as*) the two families which he chose (*bāḥar*)?' " Isa. 41:9: " 'You are my servant, I have chosen you (*bāḥar*) and not cast you off (*mā'as*).' " This demonstrates that Israel not only has the notion of rejection as a conceptual equivalent, in reversal, to the idea of election, but also that the verb *mā'as* ("reject") specifically negates what *bāḥar* ("choose") affirms.

B. The Rejection Motif in Jeremiah

While the cumulative evidence that Jeremiah preached God's rejection of Judah is conclusive, it would go beyond the evidence to suggest that this was a dominant theme in his message. What we maintain is that the employment of this theme in Jeremiah is authentic, and that it played a significant role in his understanding of Judah's status in relation to God within the context of his whole doom preaching.

A fruitful passage for our introduction to the employment of this motif in Jeremiah, not without some critical problems,[1] is found in 14:19–15:4. In the first part of this passage (14:19–22) the words of grievance, confession, and petition are put on the lips of the people, perhaps envisioned as a congregation standing in the temple and giving voice to their concern in a style known to us from the corporate laments of the Psalter.[2] It is probably correct to see the lament as an accurate historical remembrance of the people's concern, but to understand the wording and the thought pattern as stemming from Jeremiah who in this situation speaks for the people.[3]

The main points are: 1) It begins with "reject" (*mā'as*) doubled for emphasis[4] in an agonized question-accusation: "Hast thou utterly rejected Judah?" 2) God is immediately pressed with a second question: "Does thy soul loathe (*gā'al*) Zion?" In a slight shift of mood the latter part of verse 19 laments their misfortune, while verse 20 contains a confession of sin. Verse 21 returns to the rejection motif with three new images. 3) "Do not spurn (*nā'aṣ*) us, for thy name's sake." 4) "Do not dishonor (*nābal*) thy glorious throne." 5) "Remember us and do not break (*pārar*) thy covenant with us." 6) God's answer, beginning in 15:1, denies their request and commands, "Send them out of my sight." 7) Verses 2–4 of chapter 15 promise a judgment of unlimited severity.

Our two main observations on this passage are that the most specialized word for rejection (*mā'as*) introduces the passage in a way which obtains the maximum emphasis from that word. Then, rather than simply repeat this verb, Jeremiah enriches the vocabulary and understanding of rejection with three new images. The verb *mā'as* thus further establishes itself as a normative point of reference for the rejection motif, while at the same time we see that other verbs used in parallel expressions to phrases containing "reject" (*mā'as*) derive something from that association while at the same time providing a rather free development on the language by which the rejection motif can be expressed. Secondly, more than the specific vocabulary of rejection, we want to emphasize the pattern of ideas associated with this theme. The first element would normally be a description of the people's flagrant transgressions. This element is presupposed in the confession in verse 20 of chapter 14 and found earlier in the chapter, but is not explicitly given in the segment immediately under observation. Otherwise the components of rejection are well demonstrated here, and we can summarize them with a numbering which correlates to our numbering in the survey of the passage just above: 1) the end of the election status has come; 2) God's hostility toward Zion implies that his blessings and mercies no longer flow out through the temple there; 3) God's personal relationship with Judah is canceled; 4) the throne and the election and covenant promises attached to the figure of David are negated; 5) the covenant itself is specifically abolished; 6) God is alienated from the people, wants physical separation from them, and turns away his face so that any protective power or possibility of appeal to his mercy is withdrawn; 7) the judgment resumes at a level of even greater intensity than before, a level which is unqualified and which moves toward annihilation.

With the addition of the missing accusation of transgression at the beginning, these points make sense and fit together as a coherent sequence. We can hypothesize that God's rejection of his people is a kind of preliminary step to the final stage of judgment. This rejection deals with the temple, with David, and with the Mosaic Covenant—it embraces all three traditions on which any hope of security was founded. It also articulates the rejection of the more personal dimension of the relationship between Yahweh and his people. While it will gradually become clear that these words have only a limited historical application, it must be admitted that the theme of rejection in a passage like Jer. 14:19–15:4 is made to be quite comprehensive and, for the generation to which it was addressed, ultimate in its meaning.

We can round out our understanding of Jeremiah's use of the rejection motif by placing what he says in 14:19–15:4 alongside of a survey of the other relevant passages. We are strongly reminded of Hosea when in 3:1–11 Jeremiah depicts the people as the harlotous wife and God as the offended husband threatening divorce. At the outset, the question is raised in this form:

> If a man divorces his wife, and she goes from him and becomes another man's wife, will he return to her? Would not that land be greatly polluted? You have played the harlot with many lovers; and would you return to me? says the Lord. (3:1)

Hosea, generally acknowledged as a source of direct influence on Jeremiah,[5] makes the basic theme of his preaching the extended metaphor that Israel has broken the marriage bond with Yahweh by adulterous relations with Ba'al. That Hosea preached doom as God's divorcing his people becomes evident in two passages at the beginning of the book: (1:9) ". . . you are not my people and I am not your God"; (2:2) "Plead with your mother . . . for she is not my wife, and I am not her husband. . . ." The first quotation is the reversal of the "Covenant Formula";[6] it is therefore clear that in Hosea's imagery divorce equals nullification of the covenant. In the development of Jeremiah's adoption of this metaphor, the latter prophet argues that Judah failed to learn a lesson from the historical tragedy of her sister: "She saw that for all the adulteries of that faithless one, Israel, I had sent her away with a decree of divorce; yet her false sister Judah did not fear, but she too went and played the harlot" (Jer. 3:8). Here, in an application consistent with Hosea's warnings, the destruction of Israel in 722 is looked back upon as substantiating that God *had* divorced the Northern Kingdom. The interpretation of 722 as God's rejection of Israel is explicit and clear in Ps. 78:60–67. What we actually have in Jer. 3:1–11, accordingly, is God warning Judah that he will divorce her as he divorced Israel, annihilate her as he annihilated Israel.

Another rejection passage of some significance comes within Jeremiah's famous "Temple Sermon." In the midst of persuading the people not to put mechanical trust in the temple as a source of security, Jeremiah invokes the remembrance of what happened in Shiloh, the first sanctuary for the Ark during the time of the Judges. Its destruction—probably at the hands of the Philistines around 1050—is interpreted as God's judgment on it for the wickedness of the people (7:12). Then this equation is made: "I will do to the house which is called by my name . . . as I did to Shiloh. And I will cast you (*šālak*) out of my sight, as I cast out all your kinsmen, all the offspring of Ephraim" (7:14–15). An interesting sequence here, bearing some comparison with Ezekiel's thought, shows that the people's immorality and idolatry (7:9, 11, 13) lead to the destruction of the temple (7:14), and then the temple's destruction becomes a prelude to God's forsaking Judah as he forsook Israel (7:15). There is no unambiguous statement in 7:8–15 that God rejects the election, or cancels the covenant, but that seems assumed by the passage as a whole.

Into the same context there has been brought a second and more explicit expression of rejection. Verse 29 begins the last section within chapter 7 and seems to set the tone for what follows: "Cut off your hair and cast it away; raise a lamentation on the bare heights, for the Lord has rejected (*mā'as*) and forsaken (*nāṭaš*) the generation of his wrath." What follows is an indictment: they have defiled God's temple by their abominations (7:30–31). This leads to the threat of relentless judgment (7:32–34). Just as the marriage relationship could be corrupted through adultery and lead to divorce, so also Israel's access to God's mercies through the temple could be defiled. And in a coordinated response, God removes that channel of approach to his blessings, rejects the people, and brings judgment down upon them. Although it is visible and tangible, the temple functions not unlike covenant, or election, in that it represents yet another way in which God has related to the people, and shown them his grace. If the covenant has been broken by the people's sin, it would be inconsistent to let them exploit God's dispensation of mercy through the temple, as though it had no relation whatever to the Exodus traditions. So we see in this passage that what began as a violation of the law led to elimination of the temple (i.e., as a threat), and then the theological meaning of the loss of the temple is expressed as the reversal of election.

One other point in this passage deserves our attention before we leave it: what God rejects and forsakes is "the generation of his wrath." One is reminded of the generation at the time of Moses which incurred God's wrath and was not allowed to cross into the promised land. We have here a suggestion of the limitation of applicability of this rejection. *It is not Judah, nor even less the Jewish people, being rejected in principle.* But *this generation which evoked God's wrath is being rejected, denied the temple, and threatened with annihilation. Thus, what is said about rejection here is entirely within the framework of a judgment preaching which is comparatively specific and practical in intent.*

Another good example of Jeremiah's rejection preaching appears in 12:7 where he says: "I have forsaken (*'āzab*) my house, I have abandoned (*nāṭaš*) my heritage; I have given the beloved of my soul into the hands of her enemies." It is notable in this unit, 12:7–13, how frequently God speaks of his people in an image which shows great affection for them. Weiser's comment seems particularly apt: ". . . the prophet opens a unique glimpse into the heart of God, in which love and hate, justice and mercy struggle with one another, so that the thoughts of election and judgment appear in tension with one another."[7] It is precisely because God's election so uniquely expressed his own loving initiative toward Israel that the word of rejection is always an agonized word, a word which seems to carry with it elements of extremism and despair.

A more comprehensive analysis of the imagery of rejection would make this point even clearer. For example, in the present passage, 12:7, the image "forsake" (*'āzab*) is introduced in parallelism with "abandon" (*nāṭaš*), which we found associated with "reject" (*mā'as*) in Jer. 7:29. In the great majority of the times that *'āzab* is used in the Old Testament in any theologically significant context it depicts the people's forsaking God (Judg. 10:6ff.; 1 Sam. 8:8; 1 Kgs. 11:33; Deut. 28:20; Jer. 2:17–18;

5:7ff.; 16:11; 22:9 to give just a few examples). Because of the frequent use of this verb in covenant contexts it is fair to say that "forsaking Yahweh and serving other gods" seems to be the language which epitomizes covenant breaking (see Josh. 24:16ff.; Deut. 31:16; 2 Kgs. 17:13–14; Hos. 4:10). Precisely this predominant association for "forsake" (*'āzab*), giving it an unforgettable coloring, makes it a harsh, ironic, and bitter word when put on God's lips. In itself it is not a technical word for the reversal of election, but in Jer. 12:7 it takes an object, "my house," which is a frequent metaphor for what God has elected. This is strengthened in the parallel passage—"I have abandoned my heritage"—so that a rejection motif here is unmistakable. The end of this verse "I have given the beloved of my soul into the hands of her enemies" rounds out the meaning of "forsake" (*'āzab*), and helps us better to understand the consequences of rejection. At the onset of the full destructive power of the Exile's punishments, God was understood to have ended his relationship with his people and to have left them. This means that his protective presence with them temporarily ended so that they would be entirely abandoned to the ravages of the Babylonians. Obviously there is an unreconciled ambivalence here. God used the Babylonians to punish his people. But his presence was always understood to be a source of blessing and protection. So that even though the Babylonians were interpreted as being the agents for the enactment of his will, God had to abandon, forsake, reject, leave, turn his back upon his people, in order that the judgment he had decreed could pursue its course. Thus there is a quasi-spatial sense in which rejecting or forsaking his people was necessary in order that judgment not be thwarted; but, at the same time, that rejection described the status of the people's relationship to God when judgment came in full force.

There is a use of "reject" (*mā'as*) in Jer. 6:30, and of "abandon" (*nāṭaš*) in 23:33 and 39. These probably mean reject in a sense similar to what we have found above, but in neither case does the context of the passage contribute significantly enough to what we have already learned to warrant a closer examination. There are, however, some direct and indirect contributions to the rejection motif in Jeremiah's salvation preaching. We shall return to that portrayal of the theme—examining all such passages in Jeremiah, Ezekiel, and the rest of the Old Testament together—after we have first studied the rejection motif in Ezekiel's doom preaching.

C. The Rejection Motif in Ezekiel

From a superficial examination of Ezekiel, one might move quickly to the judgment that this prophet does not teach God's rejection of Judah. The helpful "control word"*mā'as* is totally lacking, as also is most of the vocabulary of rejection that we have come to know up to this point. However, if we understand this prophet on his own terms, we will see that his interpretation of the Exile contains a dramatic sense of the rift in God's relationship with Judah—what we have been calling "rejection."

Ezekiel was a priest who took up the task of being prophet to the exiles in Babylon after the deportation in 597. His doom preaching was concentrated into a short period between the beginning of his ministry in 594 or 593 and the final destruction of Jerusalem in 587. It would be difficult to exaggerate the importance which Ezekiel's audience, the deportees in Babylon, attached to the survival of Jerusalem and especially the temple on Mt. Zion as the basis for all their trust in God's power and purpose and their hope for quick deliverance out of Exile. Ezekiel had the almost impossible dual task of surgically detaching their faith from these doomed physical tokens of God's presence and graciousness and also creating a basis for hope that there was a new dispensation being formed by which God could deliver them out of Exile. The difficulty of this, for Ezekiel, was increased manifold by his own emotional attachment to the temple and by his saturation in the priestly outlook. It is readily demonstrable that Ezekiel differs from all his prophetic predecessors who primarily spoke of sin as "rebellion" (*pęša'*), by converting a word for cultic uncleanness (*ṭāmē'*) into a metaphor which was his predominant way of depicting sins of all types. As for Ezekiel's preoccupation with the temple, D. N. Freedman makes the point well. "The theme of the Temple runs through the entire book, and is the key to its unity. In a sentence, it is the story of the departure of the glory of God from the Temple, and its return."[8]

Although Ezekiel is well versed in the Exodus and Davidic election traditions, it is understandable that anyone who was trained as a priest and who never lost his priestly instincts might have a uniquely visceral attachment to the tradition of the election of Zion, and to the embodiment of that tradition in God's holy presence radiating blessing out through the Jerusalem temple. If Ezekiel was to take up the theme of rejection, it would be hardest and yet most important for him to think through God's rejection of Zion. Accordingly then, W. Zimmerli interpets that the ". . . process of judgment reaches its climax . . . when the prophet sees Yahweh's glory withdrawn from the sanctuary and desert the land." "Yahweh has disposed himself to forsake Jerusalem, the holy center of the 'house of Israel.' " "In all this, Ezekiel radicalizes to the last degree the announcement of disaster which has already been heard from the mouths of the earlier literary prophets."[9] Hosea or Jeremiah seemingly would have had no more than mixed feelings if the temple had been desecrated and abandoned, but we only do justice to Ezekiel and understand his frame of thought if we understand with Zimmerli that such an announcement, on his lips, "radicalizes to the last degree" the doom preaching of his prophetic predecessors.

Our interpretation is that Ezekiel basically gives expression to the rejection theme through the verb "pollute, defile, profane" (*ḥālal*), and once by its virtual synonym "make unclean, defile, pollute" (*ṭāmē'*), in passages where God directly or indirectly defiles his own temple. Some background on his usage of *ḥālal* ("pollute, defile, profane") will help us grasp the sense of his use of it. It quickly becomes clear that, as Ezekiel understands God, the last thing God can endure, and the first thing God wants to rectify in the salvation preaching, "is having his holy name profaned in the sight of the nations." "Profaning God's name" is a recurrent image Ezekiel employs to epitomize

Judah's sin. One of the important parts of Ezekiel's judgment preaching is the historical recital in chapter 20. There the people are condemned four times because they "profaned (*ḥālal*) my sabbaths" (20:13, 16, 21, 24). Over against this, three times it is said ". . . but I acted for the sake of my name, that it should not be profaned (*ḥālal*) in the sight of the nations" (20: 9, 14, 22). Since it is violating sabbath and committing idolatry (20:7, 8, 16, 18, 30, 31) which profane God's name, there is a mixed perspective here, in which ethical transgressions cause a cultic type of defilement. In the portion of the book dealing with rebuilding and reconsecrating the temple, God retrospectively condemns Judah, putting in near parallelism the charge of their "profaning" (*ḥālal*) "my sanctuary," and the accusation, "You have broken (*pārar*) my covenant with all your abominations" (44:7). Perhaps it is fair to say that in Ezekiel what begins as an act of cultic defilement finally breaks the (Exodus tradition) covenant. Then the kind of transgressions which Jeremiah would see as covenant violations Ezekiel interprets as being also an infringement upon God's cultic presence. This comes out in 5:11 ". . . as I live, says the Lord God, because you have defiled (*ṭāmē'*) my sanctuary with all your detestable things and with all your abominations, therefore I will cut you down; my eye will not spare, and I will have no pity." Covenant-breaking sins defile the temple and bring down an intensity of judgment which Ezekiel's prophetic predecessors could hardly have expressed more emphatically. The integration of cultic requirements flowing out of the temple ideology and covenantal terms, with Exodus and Sinai as their background, is further seen in a passage out of Ezekiel's salvation preaching, where light is also shed on the meaning of *ḥālal* and *ṭāmē'*. "I will vindicate the holiness of my great name, which has been profaned (*ḥālal*) among the nations, and which you have profaned (*ḥālal*) among them." "I will sprinkle clean water upon you, and you shall be clean from all your uncleanness (*ṭāmē'*) and from all your idols I will cleanse you." "You shall dwell in the land which I gave to your fathers; and you shall be my people and I will be your God" (36:23, 25, 28). Profaning God's name apparently breaks the harmony between the people and the land, so that they cannot live there; it breaks the relationship between God and his people. Before they can return and the temple can be rebuilt God has to cleanse them. Toward that end the cultic act of sprinkling cleanses them from idols, which are the source of their uncleanness. That is in actuality a metaphor for God's forgiving them for the most flagrant kind of covenant violations. The problem created by Judah's polluting and defiling actions is rectified when God re-covenants with them by repeating the "Covenant Formula" to them.

With this background we have some preparation for understanding what Ezekiel meant in chapter 24 when he used the tragic news of the death of his wife (in Jerusalem) as a sign to interpret to the exiles God's will for the temple: "Thus says the Lord God: 'Behold, I will profane (*ḥālal*) my sanctuary, the pride of your power, the delight of your eyes, and the desire of your soul . . ." (24:21). G. Fohrer takes special note of the context—Ezekiel's receiving the news of the death of his wife (24:16, 18) and being told not to mourn for her (26:16, 17) and the parallel terms of endearment ("the delight of your eyes" in 24:16 meaning Ezekiel's wife and in 24:21 meaning the Jerusalem temple). He perceptively observes: "What the bereavement of his beloved wife signifies for the husband, the profanation of the temple signifies for the Israelites."[10] Ezekiel tells the exiles not to mourn for the temple, following his example of forgoing mourning for his own wife. In this, Ezekiel assumes that the exiles will take the profanation of the temple in a way similar to his response to the news of the death of his wife. A relationship was ended, abruptly, because the other component in the relationship had ceased to exist. In a sense, by having the temple desecrated, God killed the temple; he killed that dispensation, that manifestation, that means of access to himself. But at the same time the people were not to grieve about that. No future for the exiles would come out of Jerusalem. Every personal and theological hope tied to the inviolability of Zion was smashed, because *God desecrated his own temple.* With it, God's protective presence was withdrawn from Jerusalem, and the immediate and horrible consequence is described in the last half of verse 21: "... and your sons and your daughters whom you left behind [i.e., in Jerusalem] shall fall by the sword." The content of this passage is God's rejection of Zion from election status; the relationship with God through the temple is broken. And as we have seen so often before, the immediate consequence of rejection is judgment on a new level of severity.

In chapter 7 Ezekiel takes up a theme from Amos 8:2 to declare that "the end has come." A succession of pictures of God's annihilatory fury (7:4, 7, 8, 9, 10, 13) leads up to the verses which interest us (7:20–24):

> Their beautiful ornament [the temple] they used for vainglory, and they made their abominable images and their detestable things of it; therefore I will make it an unclean thing (*nidāh*) to them, (21) and I will give it into the hands of foreigners for a prey, and to the wicked of the earth for a spoil; and they shall profane it (*ḥālal*). (22) I will turn my face from them, that they may profane (*ḥālal*) my precious place; robbers shall enter and profane (*ḥālal*) it, and make a desolation. . . . (24) I will put an end to their proud might, and their holy places shall be profane (*ḥālal*).

Although it is not immediately certain what is being desecrated in verses 20 and 21, verses 22 and 24 help to make clear that Ezekiel has the temple in mind. Eichrodt, Fohrer, and Zimmerli all support the view that this deals with defiling the temple.[11] Eichrodt's point is helpful: "'Seeing' Yahweh's face is a regular synonym for a visit to the temple. Yahweh must now turn away from Israel that face which hitherto he had graciously turned towards her" (v. 22); "as a result, the temple loses its dignity and, as Jeremiah says, becomes a robbers' den (Jer. 7:11) and ceases to be under God's protection" (v. 22).[12] Thus there are associations here which are already quite familiar to us. With Fohrer, we see "desecration and annihilation" of the temple interconnected.[13] And that of course is a component of the annihilation of the city and its inhabitants, although here the "rejection" is the climax of the judgment rather than its prelude.[14] Once again here God's turning his face away is a component of the rejection which allows the attackers to destroy without restraint. In this passage God profanes the temple through the Babylonians, but they are so clearly the agents of his will that the changed status of the temple is a direct enactment of his purpose.

That we are not forcing an unnatural meaning on *ḥālal* becomes even clearer when we recognize that shortly after the time of Ezekiel there erupted five similar uses of this verb outside of his book, the only time in Israelite history that the verb was employed in anything approaching this sense. For example, Lam. 2:2:

> The Lord has destroyed without mercy all the habitations of Jacob; in his wrath he has broken down the strongholds of the daughter of Judah; he has brought down to the ground in dishonor (*ḥālal*) the kingdom and its rulers.

This passage deals with the Davidic Covenant and the discrediting of its visible symbols. The same tradition is invoked in Psalm 89 in which there is a dramatic shift from firm promise (vv. 33–34) to bitter lament (vv. 38–39):

> but I will not remove from him my steadfast love, or be false to my faithfulness. I will not violate (*ḥālal*) my covenant. . . . But now thou has cast off and rejected, thou art full of wrath against thy anointed. Thou has renounced the covenant with thy servant; than has defiled (*ḥālal*) his crown in the dust.

The verb *ḥālal* has been removed even farther from its literal meaning here than in the passages we have examined in Ezekiel; and in Psalm 89 its being equated with reversal of election and nullification of covenant is self-evident. Second Isaiah picks up the image in two passages: "Therefore I profaned (*ḥālal*) the princes of the sanctuary, I delivered Jacob to utter destruction . . ." (43:28); "I was angry with my people, I profaned (*ḥālal*) my heritage; I gave them into your hand, you showed them no mercy . . ." (Isa. 47:6). From these passages it is hard to escape the conclusion that other sources found an apt image in Ezekiel's use of *ḥālal* for God's defiling his temple.

Even more than with *'azab* ("forsake") it is wholly unexpected and even shocking to make God the subject of *ḥālal* ("defile"); precisely this gives the image its power. Commenting on Ezek. 7:22–23 Eichrodt has a good insight when he says, ". . . it is Yahweh himself who wills its [the temple's] destruction and . . . it is he himself who strips Israel's pride of its strongest protective coating."[15] The Davidic and Zion traditions never contained the conditional element found in the Sinai tradition, and thus they were more intrinsically tied to visible manifestations of the theo-political state. As the people understood these physical manifestations they had the "protective coating" about which Eichrodt spoke. *Ḥālal* as God's action was an excellent image for negating the glib confidence that a blanket of holiness eternally protected David's throne and Zion's temple. And after 587 it was no prophetic theory but an empirical fact that Zion and David had suffered rejection. No doubt these are some of the reasons why other sources picked up on Ezekiel's use of *ḥālal,* and building on that, unfolded even further the implications of this metaphor.

What we have already said about Ezek. 24:21; 7:20ff.; and the five uses of *ḥālal* outside of Ezekiel just discussed gains further support from Ezek. 9:7, even though there *ṭāmē'* replaces *ḥālal* in the key phrase. The overall setting here is significant, and it is worth a quick survey: 1) God's glory leaves its resting place on the cherubim and rises up—and presumably out of the temple (9:3). 2) His avenging angels come and are given instructions on destroying Jerusalem (9:4). 3) There is to be no pity, none spared, and the slaughter is to begin with those in the temple (9:5–6). 4) Then comes the metaphor epitomizing rejection of the temple: "Defile (*ṭāmē'*) the house, and fill the courts with the slain. . . ." 5) Ezekiel is overpowered by his vision, and in a rare outburst of emotion and intercessory zeal, reminiscent of Jeremiah in 14:19–20 and paralleled in Ezekiel only in 11:13, he asks, "Ah Lord God! wilt thou destroy all that remains of Israel in the outpouring of thy wrath upon Jerusalem?" (9:8). 6) God's answer is fatefully negative (9:9–10). Several parts of this passage have parallels to elements in the latter half of Jeremiah 14. And the overall association of motifs is one which correlates readily with what we have repeatedly learned about the context of the rejection motif, so long as we acknowledge the originality of Ezekiel's thinking. *God separates himself from his people, rejects the dispensation of the temple which formerly made him accessible, and initiates an annihilatory judgment which is understood as an outpouring of his wrath.* The timing of Ezekiel's outcry is instructive: what hope is left when the slaughter begins in the temple and defiles it? We are thereby reminded once more that for the generation to which it was addressed this kind of doom preaching contained an ultimacy.

We have now examined the most explicit and significant rejection passages in Ezekiel's doom preaching. One might also compare 22:16 (*ḥālal*), 8:12 and 9:9 (*'azab*), 5:8 ("Behold I, even I, am against you"), and 15:7 ("I will set my face against them"). While we began this study of rejection in Ezekiel by stressing his dissimilarity from his prophetic predecessors, one very strong strand of continuity between Hosea, Jeremiah, and Ezekiel is the theme of the people as the adulterous wife and God as the estranged husband. Ezekiel develops this theme even more than Jeremiah, and makes it the basis of the complex, almost allegorical, sermons of chapters 16 and 23. He never explicitly says that God divorces either of his wives, Israel or her sister Judah. But it is clear that the fate of Israel will become the fate of Judah (16:52; 23:11, 18). And more to the point, God's contempt, his wrath, and his punishment are to be poured out on the adulterous wife, utterly without restraint (16:35–43, 48–52; 23:9–10, 13, 18, 23–31, 35, 46–49). Certainly this language justifies our saying that Ezekiel's understanding of rejection is not restricted to the Zion and David traditions, even though it comes to its most explicit expression in those connections. Through the husband-wife imagery and the dimension of judgment on the unfaithful wife, Ezekiel stands in substantial continuity with Hosea and Jeremiah in preaching a suspension in the election status of Judah within the framework of the Exodus-Sinai tradition.

D. A Survey of the Use of This Theme outside of Jeremiah and Ezekiel

In order to present a complete and balanced picture we need to show where the rejection motif occurs outside of Jeremiah and Ezekiel. This listing is limited to the passages in which God threatens rejection, or it is lamented or stated that he has already rejected, or God is petitioned not to reject. In the section which follows we will deal with the passages within and outside of Jeremiah and Ezekiel in which it is either explicitly said or implied that God rejects no longer, or restores the people to election status. Since we have had occasion to refer to many of these passages before, this survey needs to provide only a brief comparative listing.

The rejection theme is found five times in the Deuteronomistic literature: 2 Kgs. 17:20; 21:14; 23:27; Deut. 31:17; 32:19–20; five times in Lamentations: 2:2, 6, 7; 5:20, 22; seven times in Psalms: 53:5; 77:7–8; 78:59, 60, 67; 89:38, 39; five times in Hosea: 1:9; 2:2; 4:6; 9:15, 17; five times in Second Isaiah: 43:28; 47:6; 54:6, 7, 8; once in Isaiah of Jerusalem: 2:6; and once in Zechariah: 11:10–11. There were approximately ten uses each (depending on how one counts multiple expressions in one passage and circumlocutions) in Jeremiah and Ezekiel.

Taking an overview of this usage, we are struck that the theme does not occur in the core of Deuteronomy, nor in Amos (although Amos makes up for the lack with an abundance of annihilatory images), nor in Micah. We would have to conclude that the rejection motif began in Hosea, was given its classical expression by Jeremiah and Ezekiel, and then was picked up from them by Lamentations, the Deuteronomistic historian, Second Isaiah, psalmists, and others. Hosea, Jeremiah, and Ezekiel are each very creative, independent, and original in the imagery they use for the rejection motif.

E. The Rejection Motif in the Context of Salvation Preaching

An important part of the evidence for prophetic teaching on

rejection occurs in the salvation preaching of Hosea, Jeremiah, Ezekiel, and Second Isaiah. It naturally follows that if the events of judgment were interpreted as signifying a break in the relationship between God and his people, a suspension of the election traditions which served as the dispensation through which God's mercy flowed, then there could be no salvation preaching unless God reinitiated a relationship and opened some channels through which his love could flow. One is equally susceptible to overstating or understating the discontinuity. Salvation preaching does not negate the validity of doom preaching, or ignore the threat and promise a return to "business as usual" before the theological and political crisis ever arose. There is more discontinuity than that. On the other hand, salvation preaching is neither addressed to an audience different from that of doom preaching, nor does it promise totally new dispensations with no relation at all to Israel's great Exodus, David, and Zion traditions. There is more continuity than that.

Everyone acknowledges that salvation preaching finds its richest development in Second Isaiah, whose message is at once amazingly innovative and disarmingly traditional. As well as anyone, he shows us the status of the rejection theme, when by God's chronology the time of salvation has displaced the time of judgment:

> Fear not, for you will not be ashamed . . . you will forget the shame of your youth, and the reproach of your widowhood. . . . For your Maker is your husband, the Lord of hosts is his name. . . . the Lord has called you like a wife forsaken (*'āzab*) and grieved in spirit, like a wife of youth when she is cast off (*mā'as*). . . . For a brief moment I forsook (*'āzab*) you, but with great compassion I will gather you. In overflowing wrath for a moment I hid my face from you, but with everlasting love I will have compassion on you. . . . (54:4–8)

This passage clearly presupposes that there was rejection preaching, that such preaching was fully valid in its time, that salvation preaching must pick up where judgment preaching left off, but that the time of rejection is past. Rejection's negations are counterbalanced and historically superseded by the affirmations of God's love and his will to reinitiate a relationship.

A similar development already occurred earlier within the ministries of Jeremiah and Ezekiel. Jeremiah begins his most famous Oracle of Deliverance with these words:

> Behold, the days are coming, says the Lord, when I will make a new covenant with the house of Israel and the house of Judah, not like the covenant which I made with their fathers when I took them by the hand to bring them out of the land of Egypt, my covenant which they broke (*pārar*), though I was their husband, says the Lord. But this is the covenant which I will make with the house of Israel after those days, says the Lord; I will put my law within them, and I will write it upon their hearts; and I will be their God, and they shall be my people. . . . (31:31–33)

It becomes clear here that God is not dealing with simple continuation of the covenant from the Exodus tradition. That did not work because the people broke the covenant. The passage assumes that the relationship between God and his people has lapsed. God thus initiates a "new covenant" which is "not like" the earlier one. Rejection, and all that led up to it, is taken seriously. And there is clearly an attempt to resolve the problem of the broken covenant, the lapsed relationship, by the initiation of a new state in God's redemptive plan for history through Israel.

Ezekiel envisions that the people are not only rejected, they are dead (Ezek. 37). His salvation preaching involves a vision of their resurrection. Later in the same chapter, he pulls together many lines of tradition and promises the reinitiation of dispensations that were nullified by the rejection-judgment.

> My servant David shall be king over them; and they shall all have one shepherd. They shall follow my ordinances and be careful to observe my statutes. They shall dwell in the land where your fathers dwelt that I gave to my servant Jacob; . . . I will make a covenant of peace with them; it shall be an everlasting covenant with them; and I will bless them and multiply them, and will set my sanctuary in the midst of them for evermore. My dwelling place shall be with them; and I will be their God, and they shall be my people. Then the nations will know that I the Lord sanctify Israel, when my sanctuary is in the midst of them for evermore. (37:24–28)

Read forward, the doom preaching discloses what all God's salvation must accomplish. Read backward, such a brilliant salvation sermon as this serves as an index of what the prophet understood to be destroyed, or at least suspended during the judgment. David, the land of their heritage, the covenant, and then the temple: Ezekiel fits it all together. An especially beautiful part of this oracle is the way Ezekiel interweaves the promises of the temple and the promise "I will be their God, and they shall be my people." This seems to confirm what we suspected earlier: that when the temple was desecrated the personal relationship, the election and covenant relationship, between God and his people was broken. Rejection, and the judgment of which it was a part, has an almost creative function, because to reconstruct what fell apart required from both God and his people a deeper effort, a movement closer to actualizing in history a full expression of God's divinity and man's humanity. A chapter earlier, Ezekiel made clear that salvation entailed God's cleansing his people, giving them a new heart, pouring his spirit into them (36:25–27). The last nine chapters of the book are devoted to a fond description of a new temple—a fit place for God's glory to return (43:4) and dwell forever (43:7).

There is a sense in which every Oracle of Deliverance inevitably moves on the conviction that the time of rejection is over, or at least gives that appearance by reaffirming what the explicit rejection passages nullified. If the people go back to Jerusalem, that tends to reaffirm the Zion traditions. See Jer. 3:17; 31:6; and 33:9; the affirmation of Zion comes in the last nine chapters of Ezekiel, but is movingly anticipated in 37:26–28. The restoration of David is clearly promised in Jer. 23:5–6; 30:18–22; 33:14–16; and in Ezek. 34:23–24; 37:24–25. Reinitiation of the Exodus Covenant came to expression in our three quoted passages: Isa. 54:4–8; Jer. 31:31–34; Ezek. 37:24–28, under imagery of restored personal relationship, reference to the covenant, and recital of the "Covenant Formula."

An interesting challenge to the line of thought that we have followed comes from one passage in Leviticus and two in late Jeremiah which appear to be polemical denials, *in principle,* that God ever could have rejected his people. Leviticus 26 in its present form seems to represent a post-exilic rethinking of the prophetic and Deuteronomistic interpretation of the Exile. At the end of the Exile and even in the salvation preaching that began during the Exile, there was a very strong tendency to stress that God's (new) election of Judah and his (new) covenant would endure forever. Leviticus 26 tries to take account of the implications of the exilic judgments under the dogmatically dominating motif of the *continuity* of God's relationship with his people. The unconditional and annihilation-threatening dimension of judgment which we have found in Jeremiah and Ezekiel is replaced by a judgment which never goes beyond a stern chastising punishment. It fits into the context of such a liturgy that God would promise: "I will not spurn (*mā'as*) them, neither will I abhor (*gā'al*) them so as to destroy them utterly (*kālāh*) and break (*pārar*) my covenant with them; for I am the Lord their God" (26:44). Obviously the author of this passage does not agree with what Hosea, Jeremiah, Ezekiel, and Second Isaiah taught about the relation of doom and salvation to Israel's election and covenant traditions.

With less development of the setting, the same thing appears in Jer. 31:35–37 and 33:24–26. The argument in both passages is put in the form of a riddle. Essentially, God says, "If I have not established the sun for the day and the moon for the night, if this fixed order is about to disappear, then I will surely reject (*mā'as*) my people." This gives election a *natural* basis, and that would be antithetical to everything which Amos, Hosea, Jeremiah, and Ezekiel ever taught. Unlike Second Isaiah and Job and later sources, Jeremiah never argues from nature to history. Thus, I can only agree with those scholars who insist that the words of these two passages come from a source outside the Jeremianic circle.[16]

Before dropping this topic it is worth pointing out that both Lev. 26:44 and Jer. 31:35–37; 33:24–26 affirm a rejection teaching in their very negation of it. Such carefully constructed polemical correctives of a rejection teaching would be redundant, would not have been called forth, had there not been a rejection preaching which disturbed the authors of these passages. So even here our argument becomes stronger, although we must admit that rejection was not only limited to fairly short periods of time, it also won acceptance only in certain "theological" circles.

F. An Evaluation of Scholarly Discussion on Rejection

Having made our own examination of the textual evidence, we have an independent basis now to evaluate what has been written on the topic of rejection in the literature of Old Testament scholarship. Aside from studies that give it passing attention,[17] the only time that it is afforded anything like a systematic analysis is in a chapter of a book by T. C. Vriezen.[18] Vriezen wrestles with the idea that the Old Testament has a dogma of rejection which has equal status with its opposite, the dogma of election.[19] Within the limited scope of the number of images and passages which he considers, Vriezen offers some good observations. However, we disagree with him on several basic points: 1) He traces the origin of the harsh or unconditional aspect of rejection teaching to the earlier strata of Deuteronomistic literature, the more qualified dimension of this teaching to the later Deuteronomistic sources, and in either case the prophets are seen as standing in a dependent position on these sources.[20] By contrast our study enabled us to see only a thread of influence from Hosea toward Jeremiah and Ezekiel. More significantly, we found the rejection teaching undergoing its basic development and growth within each of these prophets. Then it passed from them to Second Isaiah, the Deuteronomistic historians, and other sources. 2) Vriezen puts passages containing the rejection motif alongside of rather randomly selected passages urging repentance, promising the end of rejection, or otherwise emphasizing God's love and forgiveness. He then tries to decide if rejection actually did have the status of a dogma. His conclusion is that what is said about rejection is qualified by the possibility of repentance and by the unfailing presence of God's grace. Thus rejection is subordinated to election, to repentance, and to God's grace. Vriezen does not deny that for a time it was an issue or a question, but he does deny that it had independent, theologically significant, doctrinal status.[21] Such a view ignores the interrelationship between this message and the immediate historical situation which was one of the main factors we carefully considered in the formulation of the message. As part of the radicalization of the judgment message in Jeremiah and Ezekiel, what is said about rejection anticipates the theological meaning of the Exile.

If one attempts to see the situation through Jeremiah's and Ezekiel's eyes—around 590 B.C.—when chastising levels of punishment had brought no response, when calls to repentance had gone unheard, when Babylon had already decimated Judah but not yet done its worst, *then* judgment preaching incorporating the terrible message that God had rejected his own people looms very large, and smacks of an authenticity which had an ultimacy for the generation to which it was addressed. That fact is no more qualified by what Isaiah of Jerusalem said about the remnant, or what Second Isaiah said about the new Exodus, than those messages were qualified by Jeremiah's and Ezekiel's teachings on rejection and annihilation. If Second Isaiah had said the same thing two hundred years earlier he would have been a false prophet, and if Amos had given his same message two hundred years later he would have been an irrelevant fanatic. Distortions quickly arise if Jeremiah's and Ezekiel's words about rejection are taken out of their temporal context. Given the way that the prophets worked, their proclamations must be understood in the matrix of the events which gave rise to them. Sometimes that is a limitation, always a clarification, and usually a pivotal guideline if we seek to apply their words to our own time.

G. Summary

1. God's rejection of his people is not an isolated theme but takes its place in a recognizable pattern: a) the people are accused of covenant-breaking sins; b) these sins fill God with wrath; c) he rejects the people from their election or covenant-partner status; d) God is alienated from the people and removes his presence or hides his face; e) the judgment returns at a new, annihilatory level. Elements may be dropped or added, and the sequence can be altered, but these are the most basic and frequently expressed ones. One might observe that a rejection sermon is an expanded Oracle of Doom, with elements *b, c,* and *d*

added between the Accusation and the Proclamation. These elements help to explain the movement from Accusation of sin to Proclamation of judgment, especially in terms of changes in God's attitude and in the people's status.

2. One conclusion which we draw from this fact is that God's rejection of his people is a kind of preliminary step to the final, annihilatory, stage of judgment. This point has two facets. God removes from the people anything which would be so closely associated with blessings, protection, and graciousness that it would seem to restrain the full exercise of judgment: the temple, the wilderness covenant, David's throne, God's own presence. And secondly, God removes the people from any status in which it would be self-contradictory for them to be subjected to unqualified judgment: God's elect or covenant partner in either the Exodus, David, or Zion traditions.

3. There is never any suggestion that the people are being rejected in principle. Nor is there a basis for the possibility that the temple, or David's line, or the wilderness covenant is being rejected in principle. The teaching on rejection fits into the framework of prophetic judgment preaching, and that always has a specific historical meaning and never a meta-historical intention. Thus rejection has its full validity within a very limited period of time. Jeremiah and Ezekiel intended their message for the generation living at the time of the destruction of Jerusalem in 597 and 587.

4. Given the suggestion that the task of salvation preaching was largely defined by the content of judgment preaching, one of its most urgent requirements was to respond to the negations contained in the rejection teaching. As much as any one factor, this response pushed salvation preaching forward toward an eschatological level of thought and expression. When the rejection motif appears in Oracles of Deliverance, it is included not to be negated, but to be answered by a new and forceful affirmation taking its place. In the very thoroughness of its questions and negations the prophetic preaching of judgment laid the basis for a period of great creativity and theological growth as soon as it became possible to proclaim God's word of salvation.

Chapter IV

THEODICY

A. The Clash between History and Theology at the Onset of the Babylonian Exile

It is not simply the case that prophetic theology *developed in* the Exile. Prophetic theology *explained* the Exile, and the Exile *explains* prophetic theology. It is a fact of verifiable public history that by 587 Judah was demolished and exiled, just as by 722 Israel was demolished and exiled. Both events would have no less factuality had there been no prophets to interpret the meaning of these events in theological terms. The prophets were not merely dealing with sin, covenant breaking, defilement of the temple, or acts to demonstrate God's Lordship in judgment as well as in salvation. The Exile was not a prophetic theory; it was a historical fact. I think that the concrete actuality of the Babylonian Exile and the eclipse of Israel in 722 pushed prophetic theology to positions it otherwise would not have taken. To ignore this possibility is a little like reading over the transcript of a discussion between doctors attempting to diagnose a patient's illness while overlooking that in addition to this transcript we have the data that during their conversation the patient was in a coma. Knowing about the coma helps us to interpret the doctors' conversation. It has something to do with why their dialogue did not have much to say about poison ivy, chicken pox, or the common cold. This is not to suggest that the prophets only worked *backward* from public events and raised or lowered the theological tempo in direct proportion to the drama of political developments. They worked *forward* from Israel's faith traditions and the right of God's judgment on the people's sin which those traditions made understandable. Yet in all probability Babylon would have conquered Judah in the beginning decades of the sixth century whether Judah had been sinful or not. It is this factor which is the catalytic agent in the reaction of God's judgment on Judah's sin. Thus, three different ingredients are mixed together as causative factors leading to the Exile: Judah's weakness and irritation to Babylon, Babylon's strength and aggression, and God's judgment on Judah's sin as part of his plan for history. Who can say which proportions of which were present? It is even difficult to say whether Judah's weakness and Babylon's aggression were theologized, or whether God's judgment and Judah's sin were politicized.

The direct relevance of these observations to the issues which we have been considering is that the prophets had no control over the amount of time between when they summoned the people to repent and when Babylon's "punishment" of Judah took effect. And the prophets could not control the nature, extent, or duration of the Babylonian "punishment" so that it clearly stayed within a just and proportionate relationship to Judah's sin. In their doom preaching Jeremiah and Ezekiel are wholly captive to the framework of the so-called Deuteronomistic philosophy of history which rests upon the following assumptions: 1) Yahweh is Lord of history. 2) He is just. 3) Human life ends with the death of the body. 4) Therefore, justice is expressed through historical events: righteousness is promptly and visibly rewarded while wickedness is promptly and visibly punished.

Jeremiah and Ezekiel *never* entertain the possibility that Babylon's attacks on Jerusalem in 597 and 587 were reflections of the chance character of life, or demonstrations of the power of a divine agency in competition with Yahweh, or results of Judah's military weakness, or indications of Babylon's evil. They apparently envisioned no alternative but to interpret this catastrophe as God's direct and proportionate punishment on Judah's sin. We can diagram the simple and implicit equation which arises from these combined theological and historical circumstances:

Babylonian ravages		God's will to judge, punish, reject, annihilate
Deterioration of external evidence of Judah as Yahweh's theo-political state	=	Deterioration of Judah's interior relationship with Yahweh; blessing, repentance, forgiveness removed, and then loss of election status

The crux of the problem arising out of this equation is the degree to which the speed and intensity of the development on the right-hand side of the equation (the "theological" part) is determined by the speed and intensity of the development on the left-hand side of the equation (the "historical" part). A consequence of the interaction is that Judah is damned and Babylon made a neutral instrument in order to safeguard God's justice and his Lordship. The possibility is present in every Oracle of Judgment which Jeremiah and Ezekiel uttered that they are defending God's justice and his control over history. This I understand as theodicy.[1]

The basic issue in any theodicy is that a pattern of faith-assumptions used to interpret life's happenings may prove to be inadequate to this task when calamitous events occur. Resolutions put forward to solve the problem are a theodicy. What is at stake is fundamentally God's justice in the face of disproportionate suffering, calamity, evil. What we find in Jeremiah and Ezekiel is no full blown, systematic theodicy in the sense that present-day theologians would use that term. Rather we see *pieces* of evidence that the questions which prompt theodicy were being asked, together with answers offered which bear favorable comparison with the theodicies of any era.

The term "theodicy" is postbiblical, a theological designation first used by Leibniz in 1697. It is composed of the Greek *theos*="God" and *dike*="justice," and literally means the "justification or vindication of God."[2] The modern statement of theodicy in terms of the conflict between a good and all-powerful God vis-à-vis the presence of evil in the world has to be translated before it makes sense in terms of the Old Testament framework of understanding.[3] It would be anachronistic to understand "evil" in the Old Testament in an abstract or absolute sense. The prophets know of moral evil (Amos 5:14), natural and political evil (Jer. 5:12), and evil as God's judgment (Jer. 26:19). But they do not know of evil as a power opposed to God, or as an imperfection in God's creation, or as an inconsistency in a philosophically conceived system. We must understand "evil" in the Old Testament as misfortune assumed to be God's punishment. Jeremiah and Ezekiel faced the challenges of those who felt that the Exile was not just. It was an "evil" in the sense of a calamity moving beyond any reasonably deserved retribution. As such it threatened to destroy the people's faith. Even though it was partly a consequence of the severity of their own judgment preaching, the two prophets of the onset of the Exile had to deal with this threat.

B. The Issue of Theodicy as a Question on the People's Lips

Theodicy begins with a question. To the extent that the issue in a theodicy is a theological statement posing the dilemma of God's goodness and the force and presence of evil in the world, the Bible voices an anguished response to the dilemma posed. It is an answer which forms itself in the process of questioning God's seeming injustice. Instead of a sophisticated statement of an inconsistency, biblical theodicy begins by asking: Why? Why should we suffer? Why should our cherished places be destroyed? Why should such a nation as Babylon be allowed to devastate our inheritance?

It would indeed be difficult to understand the speeches of Job's friends, or God's speech out of the whirlwind, if we had not first heard Job's words. And his words were filled with questions—not theoretical questions, but deeply felt hurts turned into accusatory questions. In theodicy the question and the complaint always come first.

It is especially the common people who raise the question.[4] Therefore, we will need to move outside the prophetic books to Psalms and Lamentations to hear the voice of the people. But to a remarkable degree this questioning of God also is attested within the prophetic books, where we have little reason to expect to find it. It is not part of the prophet's role to cross-examine God or accuse him of wrong. Rather, his main function is to interpret the acts of God in history and to recommend their acceptance in faith. But even the prophets were disturbed by the things which troubled their countrymen.

To anticipate ourselves a bit, it may be helpful to state our thesis that theodicy exists in the prophetic literature on four levels: 1) the questioning of God which raises the issue: here either the people are quoted, or the prophet speaks with his own voice; 2) answers to those questions, offered by the prophets, in the form of the sin-punishment rationale within the Oracle of Judgment; 3) counter-questions from God which both defend his justice and demonstrate his compassion for the people; 4) a final resolution in terms of new alternatives created by God and announced in the Oracles of Deliverance. There is neither a structural nor a logical relationship among these four levels. They cut across various speech-forms. That there should be expression on level *3* and level *4* could not be predicted; those involve an element of surprise and shifted perceptive comparable to God's whirlwind speech at the end of the Book of Job. As the Exile neared, doubt and anguish over God's justice were like a spiritual wound which festered in the community of would-be believers until the problem was healed. The relationship among the various levels on which we encounter the expression of theodicy is episodic, and part of an ongoing dialogue between God and his people.

It is especially within community laments from the time of the Exile that we hear Judah's corporate voice asking the questions that called forth a prophetic theodicy. There are four Psalms, 44, 74, 79, and 89, designated by S. Mowinckel as "National Psalms of Lamentation,"[5] which can be dated with reasonable certainty to the time of the Exile.[6] There are many other Psalmic sources, but these raise most of the important concerns. With these must stand another very valuable source for the popular response to the Exile, the Book of Lamentations. There is very little scholarly question about the exilic date of these poems, and it is generally seen that community and individual laments are the predominant form of speech within both books.[7]

We want now to give an overview of the kind of concerns voiced in the four representative corporate lament Psalms from the Exile and in Lamentations, as these supplement and interlace with the questions and complaints expressed directly within the prophetic books: 1) *God has not shown mercy, or compassion, or restrained his anger*: "How long, O Lord? Wilt thou be angry for ever? Will thy jealous wrath burn like fire?" (Ps. 79:5). In question form also are Ps. 89:46b and Lam. 5:22; it comes as a complaint in Lam. 2:2, 17, 21, and in this forceful expression: "Thou hast wrapped thyself with anger and pursued us, slaying without pity" (Lam. 3:43). 2) *God has allowed the domination and ridicule of Judah by its enemies*: all the nonprophetic sources under consideration include one or more instances of this predominant concern. The only question comes in Ps. 74:10 "How long, O God, is the foe to scoff? Is the enemy to revile thy name for ever?" As complaint we find it in Pss. 44:13–16; 74:4–8; 79:1–4; 89:41–42, 50–51; and Lam. 2:17b; 3:45–46. 3) *God has rejected or forsaken his own people*: The question that begins Ps. 74:1 is "O God, why dost thou cast us off for ever?" A similar question ends the Book of Lamentations (5:22a). It appears as a complaint in Pss. 44:9, 23; 89:38–39; Lam. 2:6–7. Acting as intercessor for his countrymen, Jeremiah asks, "Hast thou utterly rejected Judah? Does thy soul loathe Zion?" (14:19a). A people's complaint of being forsaken and forgotten is quoted in Isa. 49:14. 4) *God has become neglectful, indifferent, or inaccessible to his people*: "Rouse thyself! Why sleepest thou, O Lord? Awake! . . . Why dost thou hide thy face? Why dost thou forget our affliction and oppression?" (Ps. 44:23–24). With the exception of Lam. 3:44, all the other reflections of this concern are also in question form (Pss. 74:11; 89:46a; Lam. 5:20). This issue is touched on briefly in Isa. 49:14b. 5) *God's punishment is excessive*: "Look, O Lord and see! With whom hast thou dealt thus? Should women eat their offspring . . . should priest and prophet be slain in the sanctuary of the Lord?" (Lam. 2:20). It is in the form of a complaint in Ps. 44:11–12. This theme occurs a number of times in Jeremiah and Ezekiel, always as an accusatory question: Jer. 9:12; 14:19b; Ezek. 9:8; 11:13. Each time it is from the prophet's lips, most obviously in the two extraordinary Ezekiel passages as the prophet's own question: "Ah Lord God! Wilt thou make a full end of the remnant of Israel?" (Ezek. 11:13). 6) *God has not been faithful to the terms of his relationship with Judah*: "Lord, where is thy steadfast love of old, which by thy faithfulness thou didst swear to David?" (Ps. 89:49); this deserves comparison with the complaint in Lam. 2:1. 7) *The mocking questions of Judah's enemies are quoted back at God*: "Why should the nations say, 'Where is their God?' " This quotation is from Ps. 79:10, but the specific and devastating question from the "nations" is raised in identical terms in Joel 2:17b, "Where is their God?" In Jer. 22:8 the nations are quoted as asking over Jerusalem: "Why has the Lord dealt thus with this great city?" The enemy's taunts and questions are bitterly recalled also in Lam. 2:15–16. 8) *The people have to bear the sins of their fathers*: This is expressed, critically, in the form of a statement in Lam. 5:7 and in Ezek. 18:2. The problem underlying it is expressed in question form back in Gen. 18:23. 9) *God's justice is directly questioned:* This is rather widely attested in the prophetic literature, but it does not appear explicitly in Psalms or Lamentations. We see it in Jer. 12:1; 16:10; Ezek. 18:25; 33:17, 20; Isa. 45:9–11; Hab. 1:4, 13; Zeph. 1:12; Mal. 2:17. The last of these cited puts the issue most succinctly: "Where is the God of justice?" We should not overlook the despair behind this doubting; it calls to our attention "those who say in their hearts, 'The Lord will not do good, nor will he do ill' " (Zeph. 1:12).

It is important to recognize through this survey the sensitive spots which led the people to dismay and disillusionment, and to even more basic questions about God's ways. We do not find examples of these nine themes in eighth century prophecy. There was less sense of weariness, betrayal, and crushed hope then. Theodicy is primarily a phenomenon of the sixth century, of the Babylonian Exile. Our survey has made it clear that the prophets were deeply identified with the popular questioning of God at that time.[8] It was a problem to them, to the people, and above all an external challenge to the prophetic mediation of the truth of God's word and the rightness of his acts. Although the common people pushed harder on some questions than the prophets did (themes *1, 2, 4, 6*), it finally remained for the prophets to raise the hard question, the theological question, about God's justice. As we move on to various levels of responses to these stated problems, it will be important to remember that the prophets are not speaking in either a theoretical or a patronizing way. They themselves are listening to the answers which they are led to give and to transmit.

C. The Oracle of Judgment as a Sin-Punishment Theodicy

How does a prophet explain to the people the consequences of their sin? He employs the Oracle of Judgment. How does a prophet explain to the people the basis for a punishment descending upon them? He employs the Oracle of Judgment. As we have already seen, Israel's basic theodicy designates the misfortune as God's punishment, and insists that it is proportionate to a sin of equal seriousness. If we had no other clues to help us, we would strongly suspect that some Oracles of Judgment delivered at the time of national calamity embodied as one of their functions the work of theodicy. But we do have direct evidence that this was the case. In Jer. 16:10–13 we read:

(10) And when you tell this people all these words, and they say to you, "Why has the Lord pronounced all this great evil against us? What is in our iniquity? What is the sin that we have committed against the Lord our God?"

(11) Then you shall say to them: "Because your fathers have forsaken me, says the Lord, and have gone after other gods and have served and worshiped them, and have forsaken me and have not kept my law,

(12) and because you have done worse than your fathers, for behold, every one of you follows his stubborn evil will, refusing to listen to me;

(13) therefore I will hurl you out of this land into a land which neither you nor your fathers have known, and there you shall serve other gods day and night, for I will show you no favor."

There are three parts to this speech. Verses 11–12 provide the Accusation and verse 13 the Proclamation of an entirely typical Oracle of Judgment.[9] But the phrase "then you shall say to them" directly ties it to the first element, the series of the people's disturbed, accusatory questions quoted in verse 10. The promised judgment is quite obviously exile. Therefore we have here a typical Oracle of Judgment which functions as an answer to a series of accusatory questions quoted from the lips of the people. The Oracle of Judgment functions as a theodicy both because it stresses the extreme gravity of the people's sin, and also because it directly ties the Exile ("this great evil") to the sin as God's irrevocable punishment.[10]

This passage may be compared with a similar formulation in Ezek. 9:8–10. Here in a rare outburst the prophet himself complains in question form about what seems to be excessive punishment: "Ah Lord God! Wilt thou destroy all that remains of Israel in the outpouring of thy wrath upon Jerusalm?" (9:8). Because the temple has been defiled (9:7) this priest-prophet has momentarily had his faith shaken. God is not fair; the destruction he brings goes too far. The only answer given to this outcry is a typical two-part Oracle of Judgment with the Accusation coming in 9:9 and the Proclamation in 9:10. Since this oracle is explicitly directed to Ezekiel (9:9a), as an answer to his question, it functions as a justification for God's action, and hence as a theodicy.

Another interesting text in Ezekiel runs from 14:12 to 23. The general theme of this passage is a justification of judgment and its terms. One major commentator says that in these verses the issue is "the justice of the divine retribution."[11] He cites a series of precedents "to refute the idea that God must give preferential treatment to guilty individuals out of regard for the merits of their devout fathers."[12] Others have noticed the similarity of the concerns in the argument here and the line of reasoning in the early classic exposition of the theodicy theme in Gen. 18:22–33.[13] Toward the end of the section there is a form of an Oracle of Judgment (14:21–22). This is followed with the words: "You shall know that I have not done without cause all that I have done" (14:23). With those words it is clear that the issue of theodicy is being addressed.[14] But again even here in this extended discourse, there is but a two-part explanation for the devastation visited on Jerusalem: the people's sin, and God's fitting punishment of that sin.

There are other examples of Oracles of Judgment in settings

which make clear that they answer the people's accusatory questions. In Jer. 9:12 the outraged criticism is: "Why is the land ruined and laid waste like a wilderness, so that no one passes through?" An Oracle of Judgment follows in classical form with the Accusation in verses 13–14 and the Proclamation in verses 15–16. In Jer. 22:8–9 this pattern is abbreviated with foreign peoples raising the question in verse 8, followed by an Accusation without any Proclamation in verse 9. In Ezek. 33:20 there is an abbreviated version of the question from 18:25, now put into a complaint ("The way of the Lord is not just"), followed by a brief Proclamation of judgment ("O house of Israel, I will judge each of you according to his ways"). An interesting remembrance of this usage occurs in Second Isa. 42:24–25.

We suggest that an Oracle of Judgment can serve either as an expression of covenant theology or theodicy depending on the point at which the prophet's thought originated and the direction in which it moved. This can be diagrammed:

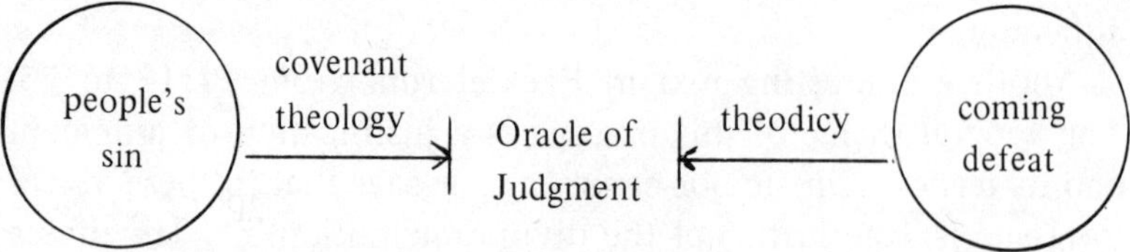

Covenant theology begins by focusing on the people's sin and asking, "What punishment should be forthcoming for this?" The Accusation-Proclamation structure of the Oracle of Judgment is the simple but perfect expression of this movement of thought. Prophetic theodicy begins by focusing on a great evil that is about to occur in history, a political catastrophe. Theodicy asks: "How can this evil be explained in terms of God's justice? What can the people have done to deserve such a fate?" The Proclamation will refer to the catastrophe under some harsh image, and then fill the Accusation with the most extreme charges of sin imaginable.

These two movements of thought, covenant theology and

theodicy, often meet in Oracles of Judgment and become indistinguishable. It is entirely possible that the prophet's attention was drawn to *both* the people's sin and the coming defeat. The prophet's concern then moved both theologically and empirically-apologetically to a convergence on the Oracle of Judgment. I see no reason why both themes could not be present in the same oracle, and both functions intended for it. These two lines of movement were also forces or *pressures which put the Oracle of Judgment into a kind of vise.* It was covenant theology pressing from one way, intensified by the failure of repentance (and the frightful precedent of the eclipse of Samaria in 722), together with the impending defeat by Babylon pressing from the other way, which radicalized the judgment preaching of Jeremiah and Ezekiel into the form of expression in which we find it. So, we are suggesting that many Oracles of Judgment contained as one of their purposes a sin-punishment theodicy, while admitting that in most cases we lack direct proof for that claim.

A supplementary criterion for the presence of theodicy is the exaggerated depiction of sin which some scholars see in certain Oracles of Judgment. Y. Kaufmann, for example, insists: "It is the inner necessity of religious faith, of theodicy, that has produced the biblical doctrine of Judah's sin—a doctrine that was shared alike by Jeremiah and Ezekiel."[15] Perhaps we have a better check on the presence of theodicy if an excessive statement of sin in the Accusation is combined with a military image used to depict the punishment. By these criteria, a tone of theodicy would seem to run through the Oracle of Judgment in Ezek. 5:5–12. The Accusation contains these extreme generalizations: "She has wickedly rebelled against my ordinances more than the nations, and against my statutes more than the countries round about her. . . ." (v. 6). The Proclamation of that oracle includes these words: ". . . a third part shall fall by the sword; and a third part I will scatter to the winds. . . ." (v. 12). Within the Oracle of Judgment in Ezek. 22:1–16 we call attention to the sweeping moral indictment in verses 7–12, and the allusion to exile in verse 15. Comparable elements can be found in the Oracle of Judgment in Jer. 15:5–9. Probably the most extreme estimates of Judah's sin appear in contexts in which Jerusalem is declared equal or greater in evil than Sodom and Samaria, cities that had already suffered annihilation. This is seen in Jer. 7:8–15; 23:13–15; Ezek. 16:48–52; and 23:11–35 in which the basic Accusation/Proclamation pattern of the Oracle of Judgment is still visible, even though each is set in a broader context.

When the various lines of evidence are combined, *whether* Jeremiah and Ezekiel used Oracles of Judgment to express a theodicy hardly remains in question. What remains an open issue is *how often* they intended this usage, and how this intent interacted with what the diagram above calls the "covenant theology" thrust. Our assumption, of course, is that in the passages quoted or cited *it is the prophet who is creating a theodicy for God* by the new application which he gives to a quite conventional speech-form. Here there is more analogy with the speeches of Job's friends than with God's words from the whirlwind. We will return to the implications of that comparison in the latter portions of this chapter.

D. A Pathos Theodicy in God's Counter-Question

As long as the theodicy issue is raised with accusatory questions or answered with a sin-punishment explanation for events, we have not left the frame of reference supplied by the Sinai Covenant. It is important to recognize that the exilic prophets got into the theodicy problem because of their fundamental acceptance of assumptions about the relationship between moral cause and effect which prevailed from the time of Moses through the discovery of the Book of Deuteronomy. Yet these same early exilic prophets got out of the theodicy issue and came nearest to resolving it by first stretching the limits of that traditional framework of interpretation, and then by leaving it behind. *Yahweh is both the God of the covenant and the God above the covenant.* The turning point toward such a perspective is seen when Jeremiah and Ezekiel hear God chafing under the strictures of the quid-pro-quo logic of the Sinai Covenant. And it is known when they hear God trying to achieve a very personal and compassionate level of communication with the condemned community of Judah apart from the roles of "Judge," "King," and "Lord" imposed on him. If the lamenters challenge the logic of orthodoxy by accusatory questions, God challenges assumptions made about his aloofness, concern, and responsibility for evil with a series of very striking counter-questions.

In our ordinary patterns of conversation, what prompts us to answer a question by questioning the questioner? Is it not when the question states the issue in a way which is unacceptable to us, or when the question so pointedly incriminates us that to accept it as put would be to admit guilt? If a Christian visiting Israel were to ask a native of that old-new country, "Why is Israel so aggressive and militaristic?", the Israeli would probably not answer this question as put. Rather, one might expect in answer a counter-question which challenged what were seen as offensive and unfair assumptions contained in the perspective of the questioner.

Most of the time there is a separation between the people's accusatory questions and God's counter-questions. This is not always the case. In Ezek. 18:25 we hear: "Yet you say, 'The way of the Lord is not just.' Hear now, O house of Israel: Is my way not just? Is it not your ways that are not just?" The persons who raise the issue of theodicy say that guilt for history's tragedy rests on God, while protesting their own innocence. God's twofold question suggests that he neither instigated the present dilemma nor pushed it toward irresolvability. Because Israel had alternatives which it did not use, and because it acted against its own integrity, then *God is just* in acting out the only alternatives left to him.[16]

The climax of the Book of Job bears close comparison with this passage in Ezekiel. After all of Job's anguished and near-blasphemous questions, God's answer out of the whirlwind is: "I will question you, and you declare to me. Will you even put me in the wrong? Will you condemn me that you may be justified?" (40:7–8). From a twentieth century perspective it seems unfortunate that the Old Testament usually saw the alternatives as *either* God *or* his people bearing the guilt for an evil turn of events. That God bears responsibility as first cause of evil is made emphatically clear by Amos ("Does evil befall a city, unless the Lord has done it?" 3:6) and Second Isaiah (45:7). But Judah, of course, is morally responsible for any evil it has elicited as a punishment. Almost all of the answer that Job receives out of the whirlwind comes as a series of questions. Their purpose is to humble him, to show that God is Lord of nature (which he never doubted), and at best, to demonstrate that God's ways are mysterious and beyond human comprehension. I do not find compassion in the formally structured kind of "disputation speeches" found in Job 40:7–8 or Ezek. 18:25. While these are important points of reference, prophetic theodicy in the form of counter-question does not appear to come in a special "disputation" speech-genre, and, as we will demonstrate, its keynote is compassion.[17]

We can highlight what distinguishes the prophetic perspective by singling out five thematic emphases:

Is God a sadist? Does he not prefer repentance to punishment?

> Have I any pleasure in the death of the wicked, says the Lord God, and not rather that he should turn from his way and live? (Ezek. 18:23)

In this verse God's mercy breaks free from any possible (contemporary) caricature of his tendency toward judgment. God loves conversion so that he can forgive, and hates annihilatory punishment.

Why have they acted in a way that offers God no alternative to harsh punishment?

> Why have they provoked me to anger with their graven images, and with their foreign idols? (Jer. 8:19)

Like a father, God nostalgically wishes for the simplicity and purity Israel manifested in an earlier stage in their relationship.

God suffers under a poverty of limited alternatives.

> Behold, I will refine them and test them, for what else can I do, because of my people? (Jer. 9:7)

God is chafing under his entrapment within the terms of the Sinai Covenant. He has no zeal to execute full punishment, yet Israel's sins are such that they require just that.

The circumstances do not permit God to grant forgiveness.

> How can I pardon you? Your children have forsaken me, and have sworn by those who are not gods. (Jer. 5:7; cf. 5:1)

God loves his people and would like to forgive them, but their actions preclude that and frustrate God's merciful intentions.

Although God does not want to punish, he cannot contradict his nature and his integrity. Can the people show cause why he should not punish?

> Shall I not punish them for these things? says the Lord; and shall I not avenge myself on a nation such as this? (Jer. 5:9, 29; and 9:9, the same wording in three refrains)

The issue here hangs on God's responding in the form of a question. If it were a declaratory statement, "I shall punish, I shall avenge," the suggestion of theodicy would not arise. To whom is the question directed since Israel is cast in the third person? Is God talking to himself, the heavenly council, the nations? It seems clear that God is not comfortable with the punishment. And yet the question makes clear that punishment is inescapably the next step unless someone can put forward a persuasive objection or offer a viable alternative. It is the willingness of God to raise this question in a brief interlude before the act of judgment which shows that he is struggling with the problem of impending evil in history no less than is Israel.[18]

To a series of questions which express human doubt that God cares about Judah in its time of distress, God responds with a series of his own questions which show that he is more disappointed than vengeful in his attitude toward Israel; frustrated and even angry at the situation in which he finds himself and Israel. This kind of theodicy goes beyond the sin-punishment logic contained in the Oracle of Judgment in that God makes himself open, speaks directly to the needs of human understanding, and strains at the limits of inherited religious institutions. Some of the main points in this kind of theodicy can be profitably summarized.

1. Judgment is a problem to God as well as to Judah.

2. Judgment is externalized from God, and through his compassion he empathizes with his people, even though it remains clear that full punishment will be exacted.

3. This is certainly a God who takes the questioner, if not the question, seriously, who reaffirms his love and sensitivity in the midst of judgment.

4. Job never got an answer to his questions like those given in Jeremiah and Ezekiel. It may be that theodicy in the prophets has not only been largely ignored, but that it is deeper and more subtle than anything in the Book of Job. These same questions, which serve to show that God is as disinclined toward punishing as the most loving parent, at the same time very delicately shift the burden of responsibility for history's impending evil back onto Judah. This is at once more compassionate and more pertinent than if God has asked Judah if it had ever seen the warehouses where the snow and rain are kept (Job 38:22).

5. There is here a theodicy in the form of God expressing pathos toward the people. He stands close to them in their predicament, is willing to share their anguish, clarifies that his inclination is toward being loving, forgiving, merciful even as the punishment begins.

6. There also is here a theodicy in the form of God's asking the people to feel pathos with his situation. Judah is asked to feel into what it means for God to act in integrity with his own righteousness and justice. The people are asked to understand God's own alternatives from God's point of view.

7. In the pathos theodicy God is not aloof and inscrutable; he sacrificially communicates his own inner struggle.

8. These divine counter-questions which we have found are, almost without exception, within Oracles of Judgment. But words like these do not belong in Oracles of Judgment. Therefore, all the more do they call attention to themselves. They

communicate that God's compassion and sensitivity to his people do not disappear, even in the most severe judgment. God cares. He is more than a judge. We see here a tension between God as he acts out a role *in* the covenant and yet stands *above* it looking for fresh alternatives.

There is no level of theodicy in Job comparable to the pathos–counter-question of Jeremiah and Ezekiel.[19] Through the whirlwind God does not identify with Job; rather he changes the framework of concern from problems of providence in history to the glories of God's creator role in nature. A similar thing happens in the apocalyptic literature of Daniel. There theodicy arises within history when evil empires, pictured as beasts, persecute God's people for their religious faithfulness. It is resolved by God's terminating history and creating a kingdom beyond history. From the perspective of the Christian tradition, I see Jeremiah's and Ezekiel's pathos theodicy feeding into a broadly based biblical incarnational thrust: God identifies with the human situation and participates in it.

What we have set into relief is that the pathos theodicy of Jeremiah and Ezekiel is a distinctive, important, and uncommon model for faith dealing with God's presence in calamity. It need not be urged that this is any final answer. Evil has no final answer. But within the context of a rather anthropomorphic conception of God, it breaks out of the tit-for-tat logic of the Sinai Covenant and the Deuteronomistic view of history. Yet it does not move so far, as with apocalyptic, to give up on the redemption of history. Nor do we find a resolution, as in the Book of Job, through affirming God's inscrutable transcendence at the expense of his immanence. Above all we find here that God has seized the initiative; he has done a theodicy for himself!

E. Deliverance to a New Era as the Final Resolution of Prophetic Theodicy

We will detail in the chapters that follow an abrupt, unexpected, surprising shift from an oppressively heavy judgment message to a hope-filled, joyous deliverance message. There we will see that God's act of deliverance creates both its preconditions and its goals. Within the deliverance oracles God no longer lives with the old alternative of waiting to see whether or not his people will obey. The law does remain as the central norm to give structure to the God-people relationship, but in the deliverance preaching there is no longer any question about the fulfillment of the law, and thus no conditionality about total forgiveness and the eternal duration of a newly instituted covenant. Israel's defeats are no longer going to be God's defeats. Israel's misuse of its freedom is no longer going to deny God freedom for an open-ended future.

I see theodicy as a component of the judgment preaching, and as an indication of how radical that proclamation became in Jeremiah and Ezekiel. If the people had *known* that salvation was just around the corner, or that a remnant of Judah was going to be saved, then the theodicy would not have been evoked.[20] What could possibly follow an annihilatory judgment, in which God rejects his own people? To get beyond this point we have to deal with a radical break between the judgment preaching and the deliverance preaching in Jeremiah and Ezekiel. But by stripping everything bare, their rigorously faithful interpretation of covenantal judgment opened the way for a deliverance proclamation which had as its main quality repeated indications that God had ushered in a new era within history.

This "new era deliverance," proclaimed toward the end of Jeremiah's ministry and in the middle of Ezekiel's, does not merely *answer* the questions which earlier prompted a theodicy, but more it is the *final resolution* of that type of concern, in that it promises the elimination of the conditions in which questions of that type could arise. New alternatives are created. They do not include either the possibility that some new Babylon will be allowed to prevail, or that God's people will sin in a way that will cause a breach in the relationship and a new historical catastrophe interpreted as God's judgment.

If theodicy is visualized as an act of rationalization within the constraints of a very small box, within a poverty of alternatives, the ultimate resolution is to get out of that box. Through what is announced in the Oracles of Deliverance, God creates new freedom for himself and his people by getting out of the box. It is not a redemption inside the terms of the old Mosaic Covenant structure; this is what sets apart the prophetic deliverance oracles of Jeremiah and Ezekiel from passages like Deuteronomy 30 and Leviticus 26. In *this* act of deliverance God *creates* new terms, *creates* a new structure, *creates* new rules, *creates* new possibilities. *Second Isaiah's tremendous emphasis on the synthesis between God as Creator and God as Redeemer is here significantly anticipated.*

It can be observed that whenever the Old Testament gets into deep trouble over God's governance of history so that a theodicy is elicited, the problem of God's providence is resolved by shifting to God's power or new activity in nature. This is how the theodicy issue in the Book of Job ends. And, I would suggest that the ultimate answers to the theodicy articulated in the depths of Jeremiah's and Ezekiel's judgment message are the new alternatives which God achieves in his eschatological intervention acting as the Creator of new possibilities in human nature and new possibilities in history.

We must emphasize, however, that with the teaching of a radicalized judgment and a theodicy, prophetic thought exhausted its options and threatened to put itself out of work. Thus it called forth a specially fashioned new era, a historical turning point, an eschatology in the sense that eschatology was the only way out of this blind alley, the only real answer *to* theodicy. From the framework in which Jeremiah and Ezekiel worked, salvation eschatology was an extremely creative answer to the problem of theodicy—far better than Job's resort to natural theology.[21] It was the real beginning of a "theology of hope," which obviously is still quite viable today. If Jeremiah and Ezekiel had not plumbed the depths of judgment—dealing with elements like failure of repentance, rejection, annihilation, theodicy—as deeply as they did, their salvation preaching would have been no better than the words of the false prophets. And in this we are more prepared for what follows than we realize.

It will become increasingly apparent that the more one understands judgment preaching, the more the pattern and content of salvation preaching seems sensible, even necessary.

I want to leave the reader with my impression that, in the context of the writings of Jeremiah and Ezekiel, theodicy and eschatology are very different phenomena. Instead of introducing the concept of an eschatological level of judgment to account for its extremity and severity, we need only recognize and understand the presence of theodicy in *response* to the radicalized judgment preaching of Jeremiah and Ezekiel. Theodicy is basically an attempt to make an apology for beliefs in an existing structure, or existing dispensation, so that these will fit, or speak to new actualities, and not be negated by them. Theodicy, in that sense, is man's effort to rationalize or accommodate elements in the existing faith structure to fit events which are out of size for that structure and which thereby threaten to invalidate it. Thus, while eschatology is the first chapter in a new era, theodicy is the difficult last chapter of an old era.

F. Theodicy in Theological Perspective

1. Jeremiah and Ezekiel Compared with Job's Friends

In the Introduction of this study we suggested that Jeremiah and Ezekiel played the role of Job's friends to Judah as it lay prostrate in grief and doubt with the onset of the Exile. In most of the modern treatments of the Book of Job there is little respect shown for Eliphaz, Bildad, and Zophar. A. Farrer's comments are a case in point.

> Job's comforters are liars; and their mendacity is a moral fault, not simply a speculative failure. It is the hardness of a heart which refuses to feel the sorrow it dares to explain. Eliphaz and Zophar close their eyes upon the fact which it is their boast to interpret; and in forcing the case for God's compassion, they destroy their own capacity for pity. In justifying Providence they come near to justifying evil; and evil can never be justified; it is theologically defined as what God himself detests.[22]

Are Jeremiah and Ezekiel subject to these same criticisms?

There are some differences. 1) Job was sick and his friends were healthy. Jeremiah and Ezekiel shared in the affliction of those to whom they ministered. They questioned. The fate of the people was their fate. Both went into exile. Like all those who represent and lead a people, they carried, in addition to their own doubts, the sufferings and mental torment of others. The answers which they offered the people were interpretations by which they tried to keep their own faith alive.

2) There is a sense in which answering theodicy consists in smug rationalizations and facile sophistries thrown at the base of the cross of life's greatest mystery and sorrow. In another sense, answering theodicy is a profound *yes* in face of the negations involved in all the alternative interpretations. What options were conceivable in their context: God is not Lord of history? God is Lord, but he is not just? Jeremiah and Ezekiel wholly rejected those alternatives, and would not compromise the faith that they had before the disaster struck. When evil times descended, the lamenters cried out, "Take this cup from me!" But Jeremiah and Ezekiel answered for themselves first and then for all of Judah with "Thy will be done." Certainly it took more faith for Jeremiah and Ezekiel to say that God was destroying Judah through the Babylonians than it did for Second Isaiah to say that God was redeeming Judah through the Persians. Jeremiah and Ezekiel trusted God unto death—the death of their state, the death of Judah's historical mission, the death of their countrymen. They trusted God's goodness, justice, and his effective plan for history as they faced the abyss. And they did not promise what, if anything, was to come afterward. Judah was asked by them to accept its end, on faith, without assurance of anything beyond.

2. Exile and Holocaust

The Babylonian Exile was the first in what has become a long series of calamities through which believing Jews have had to struggle. As I see it, Jeremiah and Ezekiel helped Judah face its hour of trial in the "garden of Gethsemane" and accept the bitter cup. In doing that, in the affirmations implicit in their Oracles of Judgment, these prophets provided the groundwork for a theology of crucifixion. Now after Auschwitz and the Holocaust, after centuries of medieval pogroms, after the cruel destruction of the Second Temple by the Romans in 70 A.D., after Antiochus Epiphanes' persecutions of Jews precisely for their religious faithfulness in 167 B.C., Christians have to admit that Jews have come to know the meaning of crucifixion in a way that Christians have not: through participation unwillingly in unjustified victimization. The whole people of Israel have suffered mocking, persecution, and death time and time again. There is no way that a decent person can say that this has been good for them, or that they have brought it upon themselves. It has tested faith beyond reason. What Christians hoped that Jews might learn about the human condition through seeing what their ancestors did to Jesus, Christians can better learn by seeing what we and our civilization have done again and again to the Jews. For many centuries now Christians have been in the role of the emperors, the warriors, the crucifiers.

Israel's times of calamity have strained the traditional faith structure and forced some changes. The anguish and injustice of 167 B.C. was so great that the kind of believers who produced the Book of Daniel in the midst of that struggle broke with the traditional optimism about history and professed that God would bring a kingdom of heaven beyond and after history.

Those Jewish thinkers who only recently have found it possible to reflect about the Holocaust see in it a horror, an obscenity that makes theologizing it difficult if not inappropriate.[23] Yet, one sees a reluctance here to allow a resolution in terms of otherwordly hopes. Arthur Lelyveld comes close to a "pathos theodicy" and also shows us the difference between the Holocaust and the Babylonian Exile when he says: "While I cannot say that God 'willed' Auschwitz, I can say that God 'wept' over Auschwitz."[24]

None of the Jewish tragedies after 587—the persecution under Antiochus in 167 B.C., the second destruction of Jerusalem under the Romans in 70 A.D., the systematic annihilation of six million

Jews with the acquiescence and support of Western Christendom between 1939 and 1945—none of these has been interpreted as authored by God, as his just punishment. The Babylonian calamity of 587 B.C. was as far as Israelite-Jewish thought ever went in interpreting a historical catastrophe almost entirely theologically. That is a beginning point for understanding the grim side of Jewish history. To the extent that we have found in it a penetration beyond smug answers and formulas, a heroic struggle of faith, a speechless silence confronting the mindless violence of events, an effort to find faith beyond despair, then it has been a good introduction. But in light of what the twentieth century holds over us and will not let us forget, it can only be the beginning of a lifetime effort to understand God's ways. The time will come when each of us, individually, needs that kind of faith. Sooner than we expect America corporately may need such a faith—to say "yes" in the face of darkness—as the flow of events turns toward favoring younger, more flexible nations.

Chapter V

THE SHIFT FROM DOOM TO SALVATION

A. After the Judgment

We have found a harshness in prophetic judgment preaching, and an interaction of thought with events. In actuality, Jeremiah's and Ezekiel's theology of doom somewhat exceeded the empirical dimensions of Judah's fate at the hands of the Babylonians. As a group, the exiles were not subject to anything approaching genocide. And there was no wholesale extermination of all Jews in the rural areas surrounding Jerusalem. Perhaps it would be fair to say that Jeremiah and Ezekiel provided a theological framework for accepting a total disaster with unbroken faith. If Judah was to fare better at the hands of the Babylonians than Israel had with the Assyrians, these prophets could not have anticipated that. But this is to speak about survival in inappropriate secular and modern terms. As the early sixth century prophets understood their task, it was to interpret the main outline of historical events in "theological" terms, or as those happenings reflected God's will and his relationship with his people. In this sense, the fall of Judah as the visible manifestation of God's theo-political state was complete enough by the time the Babylonians had finished with Judah in 587. And in light of this, the turn of their message toward salvation at this time is simply amazing. This was a different kind of faith than was required to accept Judah's death. They trusted God in the face of heavy punishment then. *Now, with no empirical suggestion that Judah would ever be enabled to return from Exile, with no real moral transformation among the chastened but dis-*

heartened survivors of the Exile, they began to promise God's deliverance. We have shown that God's will toward mercy was always latently present, if necessarily restrained from expression, during the circumstances of the doom preaching. Suddenly for those to whom the Exile had become a fact, this pent-up love from God burst forth out of the mouths of the two prophets who had so rigorously denied any hope of escape from judgment. This unexpected and undeserved good news came fifty years before Cyrus liberated the exiles from Babylon.

Because Jeremiah's and Ezekiel's theology of salvation was ahead of its time historically, we become all the more curious to understand the bases and implications of this shift theologically. Certainly one example which demonstrates the new mood is that in their salvation preaching God freely promises forgiveness. In the judgment preaching forgiveness was only mentioned as a problem, or impossibility; it was never even explicitly designated as God's response on condition of repentance. But after the Exile began, forgiveness is promised within the salvation preaching utterly without suggestion that it had the people's repentance as its precondition. How Jeremiah and Ezekiel dared announce such a shift in God's requirements and God's intention is a fascinating question.

There are some concerns which require our consideration before we move into the analysis of the content of their salvation message. These issues concern the authenticity of the salvation passages, the genre of speech containing this new word, and the traditio-historical sources of the genre. A review of these issues will reveal the inadequate examination given to salvation preaching within the ministries of Jeremiah and Ezekiel up until now.

To indicate where the next two chapters are moving, it may be helpful to the reader to offer an initial statement of some basic hypotheses for this part of our study. 1) The salvation preaching in Jeremiah and Ezekiel—concentrated in Jeremiah 24, 29–33 and in Ezekiel 11, 34–37—opened an authentic and dramatic new episode in their ministries. 2) They expressed this message through a speech-form not previously described. It was not developed by analogy with the Oracle of Judgment. And I hold it as illegitimate methodology to derive this form by working backward from Psalms to Second Isaiah and from Second Isaiah to Jeremiah and Ezekiel as has been the case in prior studies. 3) There was a striking absence of qualifications and preconditions within this salvation preaching. It did not depend upon the people's repentance. It did not assume that their moral capacity had improved since the time of the judgment preaching. It was not a backward reading of history, because as yet there was no sign of the end of the Exile. It is therefore entirely basic to recognize that this salvation preaching was *unconditional.* 4) In the Oracles of Deliverance which we will describe in the pages to follow there was a very prominent *eschatological* thrust. We find here a new election, new covenant, new theophany, and a new divine dispensation for history. 5) Two primary factors made possible and justified the shift from a radicalized judgment message to an unqualified salvation message. On the human side, the people's accountability for sin was transformed once the Exile, interpreted as God's punishment, was in full force. On the divine side, by his own will and prerogative, God initiated a new chapter in his relationship with his people. He liberated himself from the burden of the people's past failures and started anew on a different level through some familiar structures such as an elected people, a covenant relationship, a divinely ordained law.

B. Authenticity of Ezekiel's Deliverance Oracles

In the chapters of this study in which we examined aspects of Jeremiah's and Ezekiel's judgment preaching, the authenticity of the passages we considered seldom was a pressing issue. In both books the number of unquestioned judgment verses is many times longer than the number of salvation verses, questioned or not. Thus there were always enough examples of a motif we wished to consider within material which could be confidently ascribed to the original two prophets. We did not have to argue for the genuineness of a passage before we could examine its content. But a whole series of factors converges to prejudice the case against the authenticity of salvation passages in Jeremiah and Ezekiel. It is no exaggeration to say that there is hardly one oracle of weal in either prophet whose authenticity is unquestioned. This situation is partly a function of a circular line of reasoning in which Second Isaiah is taken as *the* prophet of salvation. All earlier prophetic words of deliverance either shrink under comparison with his words or have their authenticity doubted. Then since one supposedly cannot be really confident about vigorous deliverance oracles being pronounced earlier, Second Isaiah is made to stand apart as *the definitive prophet of salvation.*

The issue of authenticity in deliverance oracles has been less questioned in Ezekiel than in Jeremiah (no doubt in part because Ezekiel stands closer to Second Isaiah). We shall search for solid ground, therefore, with the later prophet first. There are only fifteen salvation oracles in Ezekiel; this makes a discussion of their authenticity at once manageable and urgent. Much potential importance rests on relatively few words. It is unfortunate that literary criticism went through a period of radical uncertainty regarding the source analysis of Ezekiel from which it has only recently emerged. In 1924 Hölscher trimmed down the 1,273 verses of the book to 170 genuine ones; by 1943 this radical skepticism still found a voice in Irwin who allowed Ezekiel himself only 250 verses; in 1930 Torrey argued that the entire book was an invention from the third century.[1] Fortunately, this extraordinary skeptical tendency has been reversed in recent decades. Today the great majority of chapters 1–37 is attributed to Ezekiel. This includes most of the salvation passages, which have traditionally been harder for scholars to accept than judgment passages. Today four leading source critics—W. Eichrodt, G. Fohrer, R. Pfeiffer, and W. Zimmerli—unanimously support in most cases, and by a three out of four majority in all other instances, the genuineness of eleven deliverance promises in Ezekiel: 11:16–21; 20:40–44; 34:11–16, 20–24, 25–31; 36:8–15, 22–32, 33–36; 37:11–14, 19–23, and 24–28.[2] This means that of the fifteen Oracles of Deliverance in Ezekiel, only 16:59–63; 17:22–24; and 28:25–26 are almost certainly late, while 39:25–29 remains a question mark. Our argument in this and the following chapters concerning aspects of the deliverance message will be based on the eleven most clearly genuine oracles in Ezekiel.

C. The Authenticity of the Deliverance Oracles in Jeremiah

There has never been much question that most of the poetic words of judgment in the first half of Jeremiah are from the mouth of the prophet himself. But the second half of the book is a critic's nightmare. The material runs the gamut from biographical narratives, through autobiographical pieces, salvation oracles, and historical chronicles, to oracles against foreign nations. There are at least four different sources for this material—material which obviously went through a long and complicated development before reaching its present form.

Worsening the problem, a series of judgments and prejudgments conspire to deny Jeremiah any authentic words of salvation amidst the admittedly perplexing latter half of the book: 1) Standards of expectation for Jeremiah are based on the pattern of authentic words of the eighth century prophets, rather than by approaching Jeremiah as the first of the sixth century prophets. 2) In the view of some scholars, none of the prose passages of the book is thought to be the original words of the prophet. With this conclusion there often is joined the assumption that Jeremianic prose is primarily shaped by a (vaguely defined) school of "Deuteronomists."[3] 3) Since the false prophets whom Jeremiah roundly and repeatedly condemned were prophets of salvation, the assumption often made with any words of unqualified promise is that they are inauthentic until proven otherwise. 4) Some scholars claim that oracles containing references to "Israel" were intended by Jeremiah for the survivors of the Northern State and come from a time in the earliest part of his ministry.[4] 5) A recurrent assumption is that any oracles of weal which presuppose exile, or catastrophe on Jerusalem, have to have originated after Jeremiah's death, even though he had the clear precedent of 722 made real for Judah by the events of 597 and the increasing inevitability of their recurrence as 587 drew closer.

Accepted and taken together, these considerations eliminate each of Jeremiah's thirty salvation oracles as evidence that the prophet turned toward deliverance preaching in the latter part of his ministry. But nearly everyone who has studied Jeremiah is ready to affirm that Jeremiah did make a transition from judgment to deliverance promises toward the end of his ministry. It is much easier to find affirmations of this generalization than it is to find firm support for texts which would corroborate it. Are we thus actually reduced to a situation in which it can only be affirmed *that* Jeremiah proclaimed deliverance to the survivors from Judah toward the end of his life, but are unable to say *what* he proclaimed? We seem to be left with the anomalous situation that the Book of Jeremiah attracted thirty salvation oracles, yet none of them can readily be taken as evidence for the content of the salvation phase of his ministry. This impossible, self-contradictory state of affairs is not the result of any scholar's conscious attempt to eliminate Jeremiah's salvation preaching. We have no choice but to challenge some of the basic assumptions which make it impossible to recover Jeremiah's preaching of deliverance to Judah.

It is a commonplace of biblical scholarship that, if any genuine Jeremianic words of salvation are to be found, they will be seen within the collection of poems in chapters 30 and 31. However, close examination of these chapters leads to disappointment. Even with certain verses excepted, they hardly present the unified poem which P. Volz and W. Rudolph thought to find there.[5] The following verses do not even contain a message of deliverance, but instead communicate judgment or admonition: 30:4–7c, 12–15, 23–24; 31:15, 18–19, 21–22, 29–30. Many verses are rightly rejected as being composed outside of the Jeremianic circle: 30:1–3, 8–9, 10–11, 31:7–9, 10–14, 23–25, 26–28, 35–37, 38–40.[6]

It seems gratuitous that these chapters have been so frequently entitled "The Little Book of Comfort." At best they are highly composite and fragmented. Aside from the great prose passage 31:31–34, which will be considered in the following section, the only two significant promises which remain are 30:18–22 and 31:2–6. Since the authenticity of these two promises is almost universally supported, we must at least consider them in relationship to Jeremiah's deliverance preaching. But we are left with the conclusion that if any solid basis for a deliverance message to Judah is to be found within Jeremianic material dating after 597, that foundation will be discovered outside these chapters.

D. Six Pivotal Prose Oracles of Deliverance

It is one of the central claims of this chapter that Jeremiah's message of deliverance to Judah has its textual foundation in a series of the following six prose passages: 24:4–7; 29:4–7, 10–14; 32:6–15, 42–44; 31:31–34; 32:36–41; and 33:6–9.[7] These are listed in a sequence approximating the degree of certainty which we can have that the words and ideas are authentically Jeremianic.[8] In a sense the sequence also gives priority to the passages which are most basic for understanding this phase of Jeremiah's ministry after 597 when he promised salvation to the survivors of Judah. I claim that: 1) these passages, taken together, represent the mind of Jeremiah as concerns Judah's future *after it has gone into exile;* 2) there is a strong probability that they are from a single source; 3) this source is Jeremiah together with his own first circle of faithful disciples. With three of the passages—24:4–7; 29:4–7, 10–14; 32:6–15, 42–44—we have the significant advantage of possessing Jeremiah's word of deliverance in the midst of the narration of undoubted episodes in his ministry which provide the context for understanding his promise. This circumstance affords us tools for analysis which are not available in the heterogeneous series of speeches in chapters 30–31.

I think that the earliest and paradigmatic passage of this group is 24:4–7. Nine of the most prominent scholars who have written on Jeremiah underline its authenticity.[9] J. P. Hyatt stands alone in denying this passage to Jeremiah.[10] His reasons are disproved by the exegetical observations which follow. Perhaps the most obvious feature of Jeremiah chapter 24 is the radical distinction made between the deliverance which God promises to bring to the exiles (vv. 5–7) and the severe judgment which he announces he will visit on their brethren who escaped the deportation of 597 (vv. 8–10). The basis for this distinction has not generally been well understood. The injustice which Hyatt thinks he sees in the contrasting treatment of the two groups is a major consideration in his denying the passage to Jeremiah.[11] But in fact the distinction found here is consistently carried out in the deliverance preaching of Jeremiah and Ezekiel and supplies one of the most fundamental reasons for their shift from a message of judgment to one of deliverance. In chapter 29 Jeremiah sends a letter to the people *in exile* expressing God's encouragement to them to live (vv. 5–7), and promising God's deliverance to them when the years of the Exile are completed (vv. 10–14). When Jeremiah buys a field as an act symbolic of hope, it is clear that the restoration of the people to their land will come only *after* an intervening period when they are separated from it (32:14–15). The one Oracle of Deliverance assuredly uttered by Ezekiel before 587 (11:16–21) is specifically designated for those *already in exile,* while the earlier part of the chapter expresses a harsh judgment for the part of Judah yet in Jerusalem (11:1–12).

If Rudolph is correct that the only words of salvation spoken by Jeremiah early in his ministry—otherwise marked by a proclamation of judgment on Judah—were directed to the survivors of the Northern State Israel,[12] then this further illustrates the consistency of the principle. *Jeremiah and Ezekiel never proclaim deliverance to Judah on its land as a continuation of the theocracy and the traditional understandings of their relationship to God.* An obvious sequence suggests itself to us here: first, prophetic threats of divine judgment; second, actual historical catastrophe interpreted as God's punishment; third, prophetic promises of God's merciful deliverance. *The people's accountability for their sin together with God's attitude and intention toward them are radically shifted when the Exile becomes a fact. The punishment itself creates an entirely new situation.* At least ten years of Jeremiah's ministry take place *after part* of his Judean countrymen had suffered the punishment of Exile. Many scholars hold that Jeremiah stayed on in Jerusalem for one or two years *after* the final calamity in 587.[13] The difference that those events might have made in at least part of his message has been largely overlooked. If a message of peace before the Exile-punishment was false, then continued predictions of annihilatory judgment to those already in exile would be rigid fanaticism. *The deliverance is never spoken at a time, or promised as taking effect at a time, before the threats of judgment would have become a historical fact.* I think that a large part of the prevailing misunderstanding of prophetic deliverance proclamations, and estimates of the authenticity of speeches containing this message, results from a failure to come to grips with the points just made.

Even W. Rudolph, whose commentary on chapter 24 I find the most insightful,[14] fails to see the distinction grounded in the punishment. Although he begins by saying that "this judgment, good/evil, is not conditional on their characteristics, but concerns itself with their fate,"[15] Rudolph fails to follow through with his own insight, and ends, like so many others, by a misplaced emphasis upon the interior differences between the two groups of people.[16] Actually Jeremiah 24 never says that God is going to treat the exiled community with favor because they are good, nor does the passage say that those left are bad. *The "good" finds its primary rootage in the intention of God's action:* "I will regard as good," "I will set my eyes upon them for good." One should compare this substantive use of "good" (*ṭôb*) with Jer. 8:15 ("We looked for peace, but no good came, for a time of healing, but behold, terror"), Mic. 1:12 ("The inhabitants of Maroth wait anxiously for good, because evil has come down from the Lord to the gate of Jerusalem") and Isa. 3:10. Amos 9:4 has a phrase identical with Jer. 24:6, "I will set my eyes upon them" (*śamtî 'ênî ^{a}lêhem*), the only difference being that the positions of "for good" (*l^{e}ṭôbāh*) and "for evil" (*l^{e}rā'āh*) are reversed. This employment of "good" (*ṭôb*) to designate the content of God's decision as regards an action of deliverance instead of an action of judgment needs to be carefully distinguished from the uses of "good" (*ṭôb*) indicating God's blessing.[17] This term is also used to describe God's plan for deliverance in Jer. 32:39, 42; 33:9 (cf. Jer. 15:11; 18:10; 21:10). In these Jeremianic deliverance passages "good" (*ṭôb*) refers to the quality within an episode of the divine plan and is a near synonym of "peace-well-being" (*šālôm*). The emphasis in its employment within chapter 24 is on the divine sovereignty: God's will, his prerogative. His decision only sounds arbitrary when one ignores what has happened to the exiles: the punishment has made them more fully aware of their sins, the punishment has helped to preserve the integrity of God's justice. Although it is not yet said, as in Isa. 40:2, that "her time of service is ended" or "her punishment accepted" so that the moment of deliverance is in the present, a time of salvation for the future *is assured.*[18] It is a future characterized by God's setting his eyes upon them for good and *making them good,* as 24:7 shows so clearly. *Thus judgment and its requirements are not glibly forgotten; deliverance is affirmed in tension with judgment.* This makes for an altogether realistic and convincing movement from judgment toward deliverance on the part of the prophet Jeremiah.

It will be useful for us to compare the basic components in Jeremiah's promise of weal in 24:4–7 with the other prose salvation passages which, as we have already suggested, are the primary texts for understanding Jeremiah's deliverance message to Judah (29:4–7, 10–14; 32:6–15, 42–44; 31:31–34; 32:36–41; 33:6–9). As counter-checks we can also compare the passage with the two poetic oracles thought to have come earlier in Jeremiah's ministry (30:18–22; 31:2–6), and with Ezekiel's only promise of salvation assuredly dated before the fall of Jerusalem (11:16–21). This comparison has been reduced to diagram form for the convenience of the reader (see Diagram A).

The meaning of the element in the left-hand column is as follows:[19]

1. The oracle addresses and has its application for those

Judeans who are experiencing exile in Babylon, or for whom it is assumed that such experience is inevitable.

DIAGRAM A

	Jer. 24:4–7	29:4–7, 10–14	32:6–15, 42–44	31:31–34	32:36–41	33:6–9	30:18–22	31:2–6	Ezek. 11:16–21
1. To Judeans in exile	X	X	X	X	X	X			X
2. Tension with judgment remembrance	X	X	X	X	X	X			X
3. God gives them a new heart	X	X		X	X				X
4. "Covenant Formula"	X	(X)		X	X		(X)		X
5. Know God, obey God	X			X	(X)				X
6. "Restored," "returned"	X	X	X		X	X	X		
7. Repentance is a consequence	X	X			X				
8. Priority of God's "I will"	X	X	X	X	X	X	X		X
9. God's act not "motivated"	X	X	X	X	X		X		X

2. There is a remembrance of a time of judgment, so that the promised deliverance exists in a residual tension with the judgment without that recognition's diminishing or qualifying the dimensions of salvation in the new era.

3. God gives to the people or creates in them a new capacity to respond to him, most often with the image of "heart."

4. There is recited a form of the Covenant Formula—"I will

be your God and you will be my people" (Smend's *Bundesformel*) as one of the goals of God's saving intervention.[20]

5. Knowing God, or obeying God, is specified as another goal of the divine intervention.

6. God restores their fortunes, or returns them to their land, by use of the imagery of *šûb,* often doubled.

7. The saving act involves repentance and turning toward God not as a prerequisite but as a consequence.

8. The proclamation of God's initiative, his "I will," comes prior to the mention of any human initiative.

9. This "I will" initiative may have a goal or intended result (changed conditions, changed relationship, changed people), but it does not have an explanation in a "ground," "basis," or "motivation" like the Accusation section of an Oracle of Judgment.

We can summarize some of the main implications of Diagram A as follows. The oracle in 32:36–41 agrees with 24:4–7 on at least eight out of the nine characteristics. In 29:4–7, 10–14 and 31:31–34 there is accord on at least seven out of nine. The oracle in 32:6–15, 42–44 (five out of nine) is focused on the external condition of the people and does not go into the theological implications of their inner relation to God. By comparison the allegedly genuine poetic oracle in 31:2–6 has none of these points in common with the "prose six," and 30:18–22 has only three or four. That is striking when we compare our six focal oracles with the earliest of Ezekiel's salvation promises. Ezek. 11:16–21 shares seven out of the nine characteristics. To take a comparison from further into the development of Ezekiel's message, his oracle in 36:22–32 shares eight out of nine of these elements (all but #5). What we see here is that the six prose oracles in Jeremiah have a great deal more in common with one another and with Ezekiel's deliverance oracles than they do with allegedly Jeremianic passages like 30:18–22 and 31:2–6. In the section to follow we will find that these six in Jeremiah are markedly different from clearly Deuteronomistic oracles of weal outside of Jeremiah and from those Jeremiah promises which are most commonly thought to be from the Deuteronomistic editors of the book. What does it communicate if these six are like one another and like Ezekiel's salvation oracles but unlike supposedly early poetic passages in Jeremiah on the one hand and unlike supposedly late Deuteronomistic passages on the other hand? At the same time their similarity with Ezekiel is one of content, not style or vocabulary. *It reveals that in the six oracles to the left side of Diagram A we have found the beginnings of authentic early sixth century prophetic salvation preaching in a pattern which then continues throughout Ezekiel.*

Out of all the elements in Diagram A, I take "Tension with judgment remembrance" as the most pivotal quality. It is singularly lacking in the (early) poetry of 30:18–22; 31:2–6. What gives 24:4–7 "tension" is that God's regarding them as "good" is never removed far enough from his regarding them as "evil" for the latter possibility to recede from being a frighteningly close alternative. 24:6b also puts the alternatives together in an explicit way. There is, then, no forgetting here of the reality of the judgment, or ignoring that *at this singular moment of history* there are two tracks in God's plan for his people: evil→judgment/good→deliverance running in parallelism. In 29:11c the good (*šālôm*) /evil juxtaposition is clearly stated, and it is implied in 29:11d (before this they had no future or hope). 32:6–7 follows hard on a prophecy of doom for Jerusalem (32:3) and its king (32:4). The whole action of 32:6–15 is courageously hopeful, probably intended to give heart to those who otherwise saw cause for nothing but despair. Again in 32:42 the evil/good tension is made explicit. One has the feeling here, as in 32:6–15, that the time of "evil" is not yet over, even though the time of "good" is warmly assured. 31:31–34 has some emphasis on the people's sin and covenant breaking, and it is implicit in stating the need for a whole new covenant and a time of unconditional forgiveness that the deliverance will follow a time of thoroughgoing judgment. 32:36–41 has stronger accents on divine judgment than 31:31–34, which it is often said to "echo." These accents appear in verses 36, 37ab, 40b.

It is on this point of "tension" between a freshly remembered, or residually present, if not actively concurrent, time of judgment and the promised time of deliverance that the poetic oracles of 30:18–22 and 31:2–6 most clearly reflect a different aura (and intention) than the prose deliverance passages. In 30:18–22 there is no direct mention of any judgment or previous time of "evil." Of course the "restore" and "rebuild" of verse 18 assume a destruction, but the impression here is that the judgment is a thing of the past. Since there is no reference to a restoration of relationship, the judgment does not seem to have been taken with such deep implications. Therefore, the deliverance is less dramatic. This is all the more true of 31:2–6 which has an altogether lyrical and optimistic tone. Verses 2 and 3 could refer to the period of wilderness wanderings after Egypt, or the survival of the Northern State. One should note the verb tenses in 31:2–6 and the stress on continuity. The series of "agains" are only mild remembrances of a time of distress—that is, we are further into a mentality of salvation here, and the future is assured in a far more relaxed way than in chapters 24, 29, 32.

As we see from Diagram A the continuities of 24:4–7; 29:4–7, 10–14; 32:6–15, 42–44; 31:31–34; 32:36–41 are too strong to permit serious doubt that they are all from the same source. I would say that these speeches were addressed to the same audience, belong in their first formulation to within less than a decade of one another, and speak to the same constellation of concerns from the same basic theological perspective.

E. Alternate Examples of Salvation Oracles

We can best see these six (authentic-early) Jeremianic prose salvation passages in perspective if we compare them with other deliverance type passages. A good beginning point would be to look at undoubted Deuteronomistic promises of hope outside of Jeremiah. If there is any objective basis for saying what a deliverance promise of Deuteronomistic authorship would look like (within the Book of Jeremiah or not) then surely such passages provide the foundation for it.

The Deuteronomistic promises of a good future which envision or presuppose a time of exile are very limited in number. They are: Deut. 4:26–31; 30:1–10; and 1 Kgs. 8:46–53. We can briefly compare them on key points with the six passages in Jeremiah just examined. 1) The turning point from the time of judgment to the time of deliverance hangs dramatically on whether or not the people repent (4:29, 30; 30:2, 10; 1 Kgs. 8:47, 48). Thus the turning point is not God's decision. What these passages promise is sharply conditional. By contrast, in none of the six key passages in Jeremiah (24:4–7; 29:4–14; 32:6–15, 42–44; 31:31–34; 32:36–41; 33:6–9) is there *any* reference to repentance as a precondition for God's gracious act; quite the reverse: God's gracious initiative is unconditional, is usually stated first, and dominates the tone of the entire promise. 2) In each of the three Deuteronomistic promises the restoration is performed with some consideration given to God's prior commitment to "the fathers" of the present, troubled generation (Deut. 4:31, 30:5, 9; 1 Kgs. 8:53). The assumption is that new conditions have not invalidated old promises, and that there are tradition-historical threads by which the people can lay claim on God. In our six (early-authentic) prose Oracles of Deliverance in Jeremiah there is never any reference to "the fathers" or to any promise made to them which might be a favorable consideration in God's action to deliver. The amazing thing about these Jeremianic oracles is that they are as unmotivated by institutional considerations as they are unconditional upon human initiatives. 3) The three Deuteronomistic passages all make explicit that God's response involves not only concrete restoration but an expression of unconditional and womblike love (using the distinctive image *rāham*: Deut. 4:31; 3:3; 1 Kgs. 8:50). This is not found in Jeremiah's oracles.

When we look at these comparisons, what really sets the six Jeremianic passages apart from the three Deuteronomistic promises is that the Deuteronomistic passages operate strictly within the sin→punish/repent→forgive logic of the (Mosaic) covenant. It becomes quite clear that Jeremiah can only proclaim deliverance because the terms of repentance, as also the terms of the conditional covenant, have been left behind and transcended in God's manifestation of a new unconditional readiness to deliver his people as the beginning act of a new era. The Deuteronomistic historians know nothing of this important shift. Their so-called promises of weal are nothing more than Summonses to Repentance projected into the future. Our conclusion is that the six Jeremianic passages are informed by a different set of theological priorities, a distinctly separate vision of the course of the prophetic vocation, and a different constellation of thematic preferences from the three Deuteronomistic passages.[21]

Beyond the six prose passages in Jeremiah which I have suggested are authentically Jeremianic, there are twelve additional prose passages in Jeremiah that are generally attributed to later stages in the development of the prophetic book: 3:15–18; 16:14–15; 23:3–4, 5–6; 30:2–3, 8–9; 31:38–40; 33:14–16, 17–18, 19–22, 23–26; and 50:18–20. Certain observations and comparisons can be made with regard to them. 1) There is a more relaxed tone in them than in the (earlier-authentic) six. The problem here is not the people's sin, or the tension in God's plan between judgment and mercy because of that sin, or in what has happened to the personal relationship between God and Judah as interior consequence of the judgment-exile. The problem is presented as being simply the *fact* of the Exile. These oracles seem to have been spoken at a time when the Exile as God's justified punishment was forgotten, or so thoroughly accepted as no longer to be an issue. 2) Given this perception of what the people need deliverance from, the solution is not regeneration of their humanity, cleansing, or reinitiating the relationship. The distress is resolved simply with the promised return of the people from Exile to Judea and the reestablishment there of the visible signs of the theo-political state (faithful rulers patterned after David; Levitical priests; restoration of Jerusalem; repossession of the land as the people's promised inheritance). 3) It is difficult to see how these oracles could escape the charge of being false prophecy unless they had been delivered well after the fall of Jerusalem was an accomplished fact.[22] Had they been delivered before 587 they would be promising a continuation of all the reassuring tokens of God's favor as manifest in the visible signs of the theo-political state without any regard to the people's sin and without realism concerning the impending invasion by Nebuchadnezzar (interpreted as God's judgment). The only realistic position, it seems to me, is to affirm that the twelve prose promises within the Book of Jeremiah, beyond the six discussed earlier, were addressed to an audience not in peril of an imminent historical cataclysm, but were spoken well after such a judgment had taken place.[23]

Compared with the twelve (late) prose promises in Jeremiah, the six (earlier-authentic) Jeremianic oracles promise deliverance in awareness of the Exile *as God's judgment,* and with a conviction that the people of deliverance *must be transformed* from the condition of the people who went into judgment. In these six the relationship between God and Judah is seen to be a fragile variable, yet it is negotiable. But, there is no sense that restoration will mean a return to the status quo before the judgment.

F. Comparisons with Ezekiel's Deliverance Promises

If we are to take seriously our suggestion in the opening pages of this chapter that Jeremiah is the first of the sixth century prophets, then it is now time to compare our suggested evidence for his actual deliverance message to Judah with the unquestioned oracles of deliverance in Ezekiel. As compared with the six Jeremiah promises of deliverance in prose which we think to be genuine, the eleven Ezekiel promises of deliverance differ in the following ways. Ezekiel's promises have certain trademarks. 1) Unlike Jeremiah he shows a repeated concern about the observer nations, and the shame and disgrace which Judah has brought upon God by what has happened to it (20:40–44; 36:8–15, 22–32, 33–36; 37:24–28). 2) In conjunction with this it may be stressed that God is taking the saving initiative "for his name's sake" and not out of consideration for Judah

(20:40–44; 36:22–32). 3) True to his priestly background, Ezekiel's description of the people's wrong gravitates toward imagery involving some idea of uncleanness, like "abominations" or "detestable things" (11:16–21; 20:40–44; 36:22–32; 37: 19–23). 4) Accordingly, Ezekiel carries the idea of God's forgiving through the imagery of a cleansing action (36:22–32, 33–36; 37:19–23). 5) Also in accord with Ezekiel's background, with regard to the election of Zion, the temple, and David, he stresses repossession of Jerusalem, resanctification of the temple, reinitiation of the Davidic kingship, and restoration of the people to the land (seen as originally as inheritance) much more than Jeremiah did (only in 32:36–41 and 33:6–9 in Jeremiah, but in all of the eleven except 11:16–21 and 34:11–16 in Ezekiel).

However, in many important ways Ezekiel's oracles are quite like the six in Jeremiah, in some cases showing a further development of Jeremiah's tendencies. 1) All are in prose. 2) There is recurrent use of the Covenant Formula (11:16–21; 34:20–24, 25–31; 36:22–32; 37:19–23, 24–28). 3) God endows the people with something to make them more able to live in relationship with him (11:16–21; 36:22–32; 37:11–14). 4) We have some mention of the covenant's being reinitiated (34:25–31; 37:24–28). 5) Most important of all, in every case except 37:24–28 there is some clear remembrance of the judgment and the implication that the deliverance is in tension with it.[24]

We hypothesize that only prophets who preached judgment included within their promises of (uncondtional) deliverance the otherwise anomalous and extraneous element of a vivid remembrance of some component of the judgment message. This element may have come in one of a variety of forms: 1) the explicit indication that God himself has been the source of the misfortune; 2) a reference to those being promised as sinful, disobedient, full of abominations, even though the promise does not set the precondition that the people be qualified to receive it; 3) the explicit or implicit suggestion that the deliverance constitutes a new beginning—more than just a restoration of what existed before 597—even though it is with the same people who received the judgment; seen in: a) Covenant Formula as re-election; b) forgive-cleanse; c) God giving new heart and spirit; d) obedience made internal; e) resurrection; f) new covenant. This can be compared on Diagram B.

DIAGRAM B
EVIDENCES OF JUDGMENT IN RESIDUAL TENSION WITH PROMISED DELIVERANCE

	JUDGMENT ELEMENT		DELIVERANCE ELEMENT				
	God is source of judgment	Deliverance recipients remembered as sinful	Bundesformel	Forgive cleanse	New heart & spirit	Obedience internalized	New covenant
Jer. 24:4–7	5		7		7	7	
29:4–7; 10–14	4, 7, 10		12			12, 13	
32:6–15, 42–44	42						
31:31–34		32	33	34		33	31,33
32:36–41	37		38		39	39	40
33:6–9		8′		8			
Ezek. 11:16–21	16	18	20		19	20	
20:40–44		43, 44		41			
34:11–16							
34:20–24			24				
34:25–31			30				25
36:8–15							
36:22–32		22, 23, 32	29	25, 29	26	27	
36:33–36		33		33			
37:11–14					14		
37:19–23		23	23	23			
37:24–28			27				26

It is clear that Ezekiel is further into the mentality of deliverance than Jeremiah and gives relatively more stress to deliverance, as over against remembrance of judgment themes, than does Jeremiah. But even on this point there is considerable overlap. As we have already seen, Ezek. 11:16–21 balances judgment with deliverance and keeps a very sharp, explicit tension between them. And of course Jer. 31:31–34; 32:36–41; and

33:6–9 all put quite a strong stress on the deliverance and elaborate its details.

When all the salvation promises in the prophetic books are added together, the seventeen in Jeremiah and Ezekiel shown in Diagram B emerge from about fifty prophetic Oracles of Deliverance as singularly preoccupied with how the word of salvation stands against a vividly remembered background of doom. Therefore, it is quite intentionally affirmed that the deliverance is juxtaposed to the judgment. What is very striking in the earliest authentic deliverance promises to Judah in Jeremiah and Ezekiel is that God is explicitly said to be the cause of the evil, or judgment, or catastrophe (column *1*, Diagram B), but this is also the earliest element to drop out. The first stage of transition from this view is when the judgment-exile is expressed by the verb in the passive (Ezek. 20:41 "where you have been scattered," also 34:12). Then, it is merely left implicit that the misfortune of Exile is a fait accompli; but that is not equated with God's punishment. As this happens there is a concern to show that those in Exile had sinned (Jer. 31:32; 33:8; Ezek. 20:43; 36:22; etc.).

I would suggest that *these are primary ways in which the early deliverance message was brought into a kind of organic connection with the judgment message,* and *it was made clear that the mercy of the deliverance did not ignore the integrity of the judgment.* In other words, this was perhaps the way that early deliverance preaching was shown to be distinct from false prophecy. As events progressed, and the survivors of Judah were in Exile, and the misfortune-punishment of Exile was a lived experience, this component dropped out, and (as in Second Isaiah's salvation oracles) the concern shifted toward making the deliverance really convincing. But besides this primary integration of the judgment and deliverance messages, Jeremiah and Ezekiel were unique in the emphasis given to a secondary or indirect recognition of the judgment and its consequences. We find a striking distinction between the weal oracles added to Jeremiah (the prose twelve)—where the promise is one of simple restoration to the same condition the people were in before the disruptions of the kingdoms ever began—and Jeremiah's and Ezekiel's very clear recognition (in their authentic oracles) that God's chosen have not merely met with a political and historical problem that can be described in physical terms. The Covenant Formula, forgiveness promises, words of new covenant presuppose that a relationship has been broken; the words about gifts of new heart and internalization of obedience suggest that God must creatively further perfect his people; and the image of resurrection suggests that the corporate entity had died.

If the six prose passages in Jeremiah (24:4–7; 29:4–7, 10–14; 32:6–15, 42–44; 31:31–34; 32:36–41; 33:6–9) were added after the time of Jeremiah by Deuteronomistic editors, it then becomes inexplicable why these passages have this very striking residual judgment component in common with the genuine deliverance promises in Ezekiel, while in twelve other prose oracles of weal in Jeremiah (3:15–18; 16:14–15; 23:3–4, 5–6; 30:2–3, 8–9; 31:38–40; 33:14–16, 17–18, 19–22, 23–26; 50:18–20), the judgment component is strikingly absent. Nothing outside of Jeremiah and Ezekiel can attest the remarkable combination of unconditional promises of deliverance together with a vivid awareness of the validity and profoundly serious implications of the judgment. The evidence from Second Isaiah shows clearly that it was important to hold these two elements together only in a limited period of Israel's history. And, interestingly enough, Second Isaiah documents a remembrance that they were held together.[25] *I suggest that only the major prophets had the authority, influence, and respect to proclaim an unconditional salvation to Judah, including not merely restoration of what was lost physically, but reinitiation of the whole inward, spiritual, covenantal relationship. And only in the primary strata of tradition stemming from Jeremiah and Ezekiel,* and in a quite modified way also in Second Isaiah, *do we find an acceptance of the burden of responsibility to make sense of the movement of God's initiative toward salvation without ignoring the reality and justice of the judgment God brought on Judah.* The second and third generation of Jeremiah's disciples and editors contented themselves merely with attaching promises of a restored theocracy. Thus Jer. 24:4–7 and the five passages which followed its pattern mark the beginning of a development of extraordinary significance and theological depth. Their promises, so clearly transitional from the proclamation of judgment to the proclamation of deliverance, are integrally related to the pattern also seen in eleven authentic Ezekiel prose promises. In the sum of them we find one of the most interesting and important developments in the history of Israel's faith.

Chapter VI

THE PROPHETIC ORACLE OF DELIVERANCE

STRUCTURE

For many years a strange situation has prevailed in the study of the prophetic Oracle of Deliverance. Most studies have begun with the last great prophet who gave this speech-form extended expression, and at least by implication have left the suggestion that further investigation of this genre should proceed backward from Second Isaiah. With negligible exceptions, scholarly analyses of the Oracle of Deliverance speech-genre have also begun by accepting the premises of Joachim Begrich's 1933 article that Second Isaiah got this speech-form by borrowing it from a hypothesized priestly "oracle of favorable hearing" offered in response to individual laments within the cult.[1] It is time for a fresh start in the investigation of this speech-form. We will work first of all with the textual evidence that we find in the prophets. Beginning with the eighth century prophets, we will move from them to Jeremiah and Ezekiel, and then compare what we find in the prophets of the beginning of the Exile with what we find in the text of Second Isaiah.

Since in the opinion of the present writer nothing approaching a satisfactory analysis of the structure, intention, and setting of this speech-form exists—especially as it is employed in Jeremiah and Ezekiel—we have some basic work to do before we will have before us the data needed to understand the genre of speech which carried Jeremiah's and Ezekiel's message of deliverance. The process of trying to understand this "form" cannot be separated from a growing sensitivity to the distinctive features and patterns of emphasis within its content. The form or genre is really just a generic description of the main aspects of the contents of the message in the pattern and packaging of their expression. Therefore, this chapter is not a technical digression from our concern to appreciate the content of the deliverance message as that compares with the judgment preaching. Rather, what we now undertake is a necessary preparation and a natural transition to a more theological analysis of the content of the deliverance message.

We have found thirty-nine oracles in Amos, Hosea, Micah, Jeremiah, and Ezekiel which have some claim to represent the *genre* "Oracle of Deliverance." The criteria for inclusion in this group will become clearer as we work to delineate the typical structural features. But as a starting point, the following minimal requirements were imposed: 1) the oracle must include some sentences which are presented as direct speech from God; 2) the divine word is addressed to the corporate entity Israel/Judah; 3) the message carries the assurance or promise of weal, better times or conditions, relief from distress.[2]

It is not a simple matter to determine the structure of a particular kind of biblical speech. One must not give in to dogmatism and determinism in form-critical study. It will not do to suggest that this genre in relation to its setting rigidly predetermines what will be found in a particular example of the speech. As often as not one will find a sentence or two in each pericope which is completely unique to that individual passage, and which therefore gives it creativity, novelty, and freshness. It is only after a prolonged process of comparison of these units of speech that one begins to discern the patterns, the common themes, the typical expressions, the generic structural components beneath the confusing diversity of language.

In some eight years of study on this genre I have slowly moved from a sense of complexity to a growing impression of the essential simplicity of the backbone of the Oracle of Deliverance. First of all, *it is all divine proclamation.* Taken as a whole this speech-genre is singularly lacking in explanations, justifications, motivational clauses, qualifications, conditions, and exhortations. I do not mean to make a special appeal for divine revelation here. My point is that the prophets understood the word of deliverance to come in the form of something originating solely in God—perhaps understandable, in its wellsprings, only to God—and couched, therefore, entirely in the language of divine promise. In the sense that the Oracle of Judgment is a two-part speech, this is a one-part speech. I suggest that any complexity added to the outlining of the structure of this genre which takes away from that basic point distracts damagingly from the fundamental uniqueness of the Oracle of Deliverance. Now, we do not merely have generic promises of better times. *The divine proclamation has three major thrusts.* They are quite specific and distinct in their themes, and in their characteristic expressions. The three thrusts are closely honed to have relevance to the particular historical situation to which the Oracle of Deliverance was delivered, and the three directions which God's initiative takes have an organic theological interconnection with one another. Let us consider now these three ways in which God's saving plan is brought to expression.

A. Structure in Prophets from Amos through Ezekiel

1. Deliverance

The promise of Deliverance is the starting point and presupposition of everything else. God's "I will" is where the oracle centers, where it usually begins. "Behold, I will gather them . . ." (Jer. 32:27; so also "gather" appears in 29:14; 31:8, 10; Ezek. 11:17; 20:41; 34:13; 36:24; 37:21; 39:27) with *qābaṣ* ("gather") as the verb. Another frequent image is "I will restore your fortunes" with a double use of *šûb* ("restore") some seven times. But there is richness as well as repetition in the language of Deliverance.

One gradually comes to be amazed at what is not said in this promise. There are no preconditions to be met before God's action is to take place, and there are no explanations following the announcement of the divine action. It is altogether characteristic of the Oracle of Deliverance that we learn nothing of God's motivations for saving his people out of Exile, no justification of the timing of his act, no details as to the means by which it will be accomplished. Gradually it becomes clear that what is *not said* makes an important positive statement in its own right. In the Oracle of Judgment, by contrast, God is not arbitrary, illogical, tight-lipped, or mysterious. Yet in the Oracle of Deliverance God is arbitrary, illogical, and unfathomable.[3] The whole structure and choice of words in the characteristic Oracle of Deliverance underscore this point. Since it is clear even in some of these Oracles of Deliverance that the Exile is an attestation of God's *anger* (Jer. 32:37), we must conclude that deliverance from Exile is an attestation of God's *love.* There is much implied, theologically, in the Deliverance section. It speaks in a very concrete, nontheoretical way about *God's disposition* toward his people at this time. The sign that the era of judgment is over and a new era of love has begun is the promise that God will return them from Babylon to their homeland, Judea. This Deliverance is sometimes elaborated by words spelling out the changed conditions of restoration. The restoration is part of the implementation of the Deliverance thrust. This is not a time, however, when the familiar institutions of the theocracy are renewed. The judgment has created a changed reality and a discontinuity which goes much deeper than that. But the *stage setting* for the next two thrusts in the Oracle of Deliverance is God's powerful intervention into history as its Lord, to bring his people back to their land to which their religious aspirations are still so closely tied. As in the original Exodus there is a very concrete spatial movement—revelatory of God's unpredictable love—before new theological developments come to expression.

In Diagram C we see that the Deliverance component is normally the one which appears first. (The letter symbols, D-T-R, show the sequence of the major elements in each passage.) It is the only one which ever stands alone. And only in two out of thirty-nine oracles (Jer. 31:31–34 and Ezek. 16:59–63) is its express articulation omitted.

DIAGRAM C
THE PROPHETIC ORACLE OF DELIVERANCE

D = God Intervenes to *D*eliver his People (from Exile)
T = God Creates a *T*ransformation
R = God Reinitiates a *R*elationship with his People

Three Components	*Two Components*	*Two Components*
Hos. 2:16–20=T-D-R	Amos 9:11–12=R-D	Ezek. 36:6–15 =D-R
14:4–7 =T-R-D	9:13–15=D-R	36:33–36=T-D
Jer. 24:4–7 =D-T-R	Hos. 2:21–23=D-R	37:11–14=D-T
32:36–41=D-R-T	Mic. 4:6–8 =D-R	37:24–28=D-R
33:6–9 =D-T-R	Jer. 3:15–18=D-R	
50:18–20=D-T-R	16:14–15=D-R	
Ezek. 11:16–21=D-T-R	23:3–4 =D-R	
20:39–44=D-R-T	23:5–6 =R-D	
36:22–32=D-T-R	29:10–14=D-R	*One Component*
37:19–23=D-T-R	30:3 =D-R	
39:25–29=D-R-T	30:8–9 =D-R	Mic. 2:12–13=D
	30:18–22=D-R	Jer. 31:2–6 =D
	31:7–9 =D-R	31:38–40=D
	31:10–14=D-R	32:42–44=D
	31:31–34=R-T	
	33:14–16=R-D	
	Ezek. 16:59–63=R-T	
	34:11–16=D-R	
	34:20–24=D-R	
	34:25–31=D-R	

2. Transformation

Part of the mystery about the timing of God's dramatic shift from a plan of judgment to a plan of deliverance is penetrated in the transitional section between "Deliverance" and "Relationship." Within this particular thrust we find the assumption that the people *have not basically changed.* And so, because God's will for the redemption of history can no longer tolerate the imperfection of this people as his revelatory vehicle, he says: "I will give them a heart to know that I am the Lord" (Jer. 24:7); "I will put my law within them" (Jer. 31:33); "I will put the fear of me in their hearts" (Jer. 32:40); "I will take the stony heart . . . and give them a heart of flesh" (Ezek. 11:19); "A new heart I will give you, and a new spirit I will put within you"

(Ezek. 36:26).[4] The same thrust also comes to expression in declarations about a thoroughgoing cleansing, or a regenerative forgiveness (Jer. 33:6–9; 50:18–20; Ezek. 20:39–44; 36:33–36; 37:19–23).

Looking at the people in a very inward, spiritually sensitive, theologically probing way, the prophets insist that God cannot move from outward acts of help to a renewal of the relationship on a new basis without first dealing with the inward condition of the people. This concern calls forth an unexpected, unprecedented promise that God will take the initiative in this area too, and make Israel both want to obey and *capable of obeying.* God is now asserting his Lordship over his people's humanity, their human religiosity. Something of the self-determination of his creatures is placed in abeyance as the Creator God works a deliverance in the very heart of man.

This thrust most often appears as a preliminary act to the promise of the establishment of a God-Israel relationship on a new level for a new day. It links the outward act of deliverance to the forging of a new covenant. Already here we see God acting on three fronts: D=the people with relation to their external circumstances and what those circumstances imply; T=the people with relation to themselves (the contradiction between moral intentions and immoral actions is now resolved by God's giving them resources to rise to his expectations); R=the people with relation to God.

What is remarkable is not that we find the "Transformation" element in only fifteen out of thirty-nine Oracles of Deliverance. What is remarkable is that we find it at all. It is a profound look into the inner soul of mankind, and an initiative by God which challenges the basic optimism about man within the orientation of Israelite theism. Its appearance in ten out of the seventeen Oracles of Deliverance with greatest claim to authenticity in Jeremiah and Ezekiel makes it impossible to ignore this element. (See Diagram C.) One could deal with it as an addition to the normal pattern of the genre, but I prefer to claim that oracles without it are abbreviations of the full deliverance message—in some cases merely presupposing this element (the twenty out of thirty-nine times where there is a movement from "Deliverance" to "Relationship" without dealing explicitly with this consideration), and in other cases ignoring it or not penetrating to this depth of theological awareness.

3. Relationship

In thirty-three out of thirty-nine passages there is either a direct promise that the God-people relationship will be reinitiated, or an implied promise with the use of some other language. The emphasis on "Relationship" shows that this is an area of anxiety as real as whether or not the people would ever return from Babylon. Continuity of Relationship is not presupposed. Quite the reverse: discontinuity is assumed.

In some cases it is enough for God to take the people back to the land which he promised them as his sign of election given to the Patriarchs. That may be strongly stressed as in Amos 9:15: "I will plant them upon their land, and they shall never again be plucked out of the land which I have given them. . . ." Sometimes it deals with the resumption of the Davidic Covenant. But it is clear in other sources that the breach in God-Israel relationship, indicated by the express preaching of rejection, is very much in mind: "I will not hide my face any more from them" (Ezek. 39:29). This is the reverse of the saying, "I will turn my face from them . . ." in the rejection saying of Ezek. 7:20–24 (cf. Jer. 15:1 and Ezek. 15:7). To the concern about rejection there needed to be addressed a new election within the same tradition-historical framework of the Exodus under which the rejection took place. This, I feel, is especially communicated by the so-called Covenant Formula ("They will be my people, and I will be their God") which in these oracles takes on quite a distinctive counter-balancing import. This formulation is found eleven times in the Oracles of Deliverance represented on Diagram C, and in my estimation it is the single most important and effective way of expressing a new era in the God-Israel relationship (see in Hos. 2:21–23 [modified]; Jer. 24:4–7; 30:18–32; 31:31–34; 32:36–41; Ezek. 11:16–20; 34:20–24 [modified], 25–31; 36:22–32; 37:19–23, 24–28).

As will be seen in the chapter to follow, I think that the real meaning of the Covenant Formula in this context is the communication of a new act of election. Another very important and explicit statement of the reinitiation of Relationship comes in those passages in which God promises a "new" or "eternal" covenant: Jer. 31:31–34; 32:36–41; Ezek. 16:59–63; 34:25–31; 37:24–28. In the remainder of cases where we find the Relationship thrust it comes in quite a variety of circumlocutions indicating the resumption of a close relationship rapport between God and people. We can give only a few examples of these. Hos. 2:16–20 contains three repetitions of "I will betroth you," as that prophet brings the husband-wife imagery for God and Israel full circle. In Jer. 31:7–9 it is "I am a father to Israel," and in Ezek. 34:11–16 it shifts to "I myself will be the shepherd of my sheep. . . ."

If the first word that those experiencing God's judgment by being estranged in Babylon needed to hear was the promise of deliverance from Exile, the concluding assurance must be that God yet had a use for them and would intimately relate to them, in however different a fashion. In twenty-four out of its thirty-three appearances the Relationship thrust comes as the conclusion to the oracle. At this time, while languishing in Babylon, the people of Israel could scarcely conceive of a new beginning with God. But there is a profound sense that the problem uncovered in the judgment episode is not cured simply by planting the people back in Jerusalem and its environs. "Deliverance" shows that the stigma and the suffering of the past are over; "Relationship" provides some indication of the basis on which God and Israel will move into the future.

4. Conclusions

Therefore, the structural components which we suggest as normative for this genre, the passages in which they occur, and the sequence of their initial statement are shown in Diagram C. Our only claim is that this is a typical, complete Oracle of Deliverance from the period down through Ezekiel. There is no reason to claim that the prophets had to construct, with prescriptive force, their Oracle of Deliverance in relation to this norm. But the passages which have all three major elements are full, vigorous expressions of this genre, and all but one or two of them have claim to being authentic words of the prophet in whose book they occur.

Taking the thirty-nine oracles as a whole, we discover that it is a very common characteristic that a structural component (D, T, or R) stated early in the oracle will be repeated later. For instance in Jer. 32:36–41, which I take as an outstanding illustration of this genre, the actual pattern is: D - R - T - R - T - D. Ezekiel's oracles, in particular, often have this fuguelike construction. With this phenomenon we are not speaking of a mechanical repetition of the same promises in the same terms. Rather, there is a repetition within diversity, a reinforcement, a building, a cumulative impact. The impression gained from Jer. 32:36–41 and present elsewhere is that *each* of the major theme-components is important enough to warrant special stress. Each serves, in its own way, to bring forward the singular, unified emphasis: that in each of these oracles we encounter a definitive promise of God's intervention to save his people.

B. Structure in Second Isaiah

Issues in the Application of the Method to Second Isaiah

Up to this point our study of the Oracle of Deliverance genre is unique in that we have found a definite pattern, and its implied ideology, for this type of message without any reference to Second Isaiah. I hope that we have thereby demonstrated that it is both viable and natural to study this speech-form by beginning with the early exilic and pre-exilic prophetic literature. It now becomes desirable to ask: Does the pattern carry over into Second Isaiah? Since Second Isaiah has the most instances of a salvation oracle type of speech, and since it is those occurrences of a deliverance message which have received almost all of the scholarly study up until this time, it would be fruitful if we could extend our analysis into the writings of this later prophet.

We can move in this direction, however, only in a very

limited and tentative way. Second Isaiah confronts us with a type of language and thought for which research on Jeremiah and Ezekiel is almost no preparation at all. God's "I am," it would seem, is more frequent in this book than his "I will." Vocatives like "Jacob, my servant, Israel whom I have chosen" or "the Lord your God, the Holy One of Israel, your Savior" carry much of the communication. One is never quite sure whether he is reading divine proclamations to a specific audience or the hymnic soliloquies of the Almighty. It is outside of the scope of the present study to explain all those unique portions of Second Isaiah's oracles which nevertheless might bear some comparison with the Oracles of Deliverance in Jeremiah and Ezekiel.

I have made a preliminary attempt to delineate Second Isaiah's

DIAGRAM D

D = God Intervenes to *D*eliver	s.p. divine self-predication
T = God Creates a *T*ransformation	cn. consolation
R = God Reinitiates *R*elationship	v.g. vindication against gentiles
	ad. admonition

Isaiah	41:8–13	= R - cn. - D - v.g. - cn.
	41:14–16	= cn. - D
	41:17–20	= cn. - R - T - s.p.
	42:5–9	= s.p. - R - s.p.
	42:14–17	= T - D - R - ad.
	43:1–7	= s.p. - cn. - D - R - D - s.p. - c.n. - D
	43:14–21	= s.p. - D - s.p. - D - T - R
	44:1–5	= R - cn. - T - R
	44:21–22	= ad. - R - T - D
	44:24–28	= s.p. - D
	46:3–4	= R - D
	46:8–13	= ad. - s.p. - ad. - D
	48:17–20	= s.p. - ad. - D - R
	49:5–7	= R - D - R - D - R - v.g.
	49:14–21	= R - D
	49:22–23	= D - v.g. - s.p.
	51:4–6	= ad. - T - D - T - D
	51:7–8	= ad. - cn. - D
	51:12–16	= s.p. - D - R
	54:4–10	= cn. - s.p. - R - D - R
	54:11–17	= T - D - v.g. - R
	55:10–13	= s.p. - D - T - R

Oracles of Deliverance and show their structure. The reader is referred to Diagram D. It must be admitted that because there is so much deliverance language throughout the book and because Second Isaiah exercises such freedom in inventing new speech-forms and transforming old ones, the units shown in Diagram D are singled out with much less sense of assurance than was the case with the speech units shown in Diagram C. For the most part I have followed J. Begrich and H. von Waldow in determining the pericopes,[5] but the listing contains additions and deletions made on my judgment. I have attempted to show the components in Second Isaiah's deliverance oracles in a quite descriptive way.

New Elements in Second Isaiah's Oracles

In addition to "Deliverance," "Transformation," and "Relationship" there is a series of other types of communication in Second Isaiah's salvation oracles. In almost every oracle there is an apparent concern which incites God to protest his identity, his titles, his powers, and prerogatives. There is substantially more divine self-predication in Ezekiel than in Jeremiah, but Second Isaiah totally outstrips Ezekiel in this matter. Exactly what the presence of this element means for the Oracle of Deliverance is not clear, because as in Ezekiel the divine self-predication is found throughout the book and not limited to the Oracle of Deliverance. Some scholars have found a place for this within the genre structure.[6] I think that it is important within the genre—especially as it moves into a theophanic dimension—but I am not convinced that it helps set this genre apart from other speech-forms in Second Isaiah.

Much the same thing could be said about the element of "consolation." Even in other genres of speech this book is full of words of consolation (note 40:1–2, 11, 27ff.; 48:14; 49:8; 50:2, 7–9; 51:3; 55:3). The note of consolation is not lacking in the deliverance oracles of Jeremiah and Ezekiel. One wonders whether "Fear not, I am with you" or its equivalent is a rhetorical feature characteristic of Second Isaiah—one of many ways in which he expresses consolation inside and outside of deliverance oracles—or is this a definitive structural feature of the Oracle of Deliverance genre, as a whole series of scholars have overzealously urged?[7]

God's self-justification or vindication against the gentile nations was a more prominent concern in Ezekiel than in Jeremiah. Here in Second Isaiah there is no separate block of Oracles against Foreign Nations such as we find in Jeremiah 46–51 and Ezekiel 26–32. Thus, this theme finds its way into a variety of genres in Second Isaiah. Does its presence tell us something significant about the Oracle of Deliverance, or are we to see it more as part of the total flavor of Second Isaiah's expression?

Seemingly, in Jeremiah and Ezekiel the bare proclamation of divine intervention to deliver was enough to overwhelm the people with joy and hope for the future. Second Isaiah, at the end of the Exile, seems to be speaking to a very despondent, lethargic audience. He admonishes them to listen, to hope. To some extent his admonitions seem to function to preserve the promised salvation as standing in a relationship of integrity with the time of judgment and the threat of its recurrence—a note otherwise carried in Second Isaiah only to a fractional degree from what Jeremiah and Ezekiel did with this theme.

I would urge restraint in moving to the conclusion that Second Isaiah has an Oracle of Salvation source different from that of Jeremiah and Ezekiel. Perhaps the differences are more apparent than real. Some of them are a matter of Second Isaiah's rhetoric and style. As we have shown, some of them fall in with patterns of concerns generic to the book as a whole. Still others reflect the development of prophetic thinking into this latter half of the sixth century and were already anticipated to some extent by Ezekiel.

1. Deliverance

Our diagram shows that this element occurs in nineteen out of twenty-two passages. It has strong and explicit expression in 43:1–7, 14–21; 44:24–28; 48:17–20; 49:5–7. Quite frequently God speaks of or promises his "deliverance," "salvation," "redemption," "help," without being specific about the Exile situation and return to the homeland, although that application seems supplied by the context: 41:10, 13, 14; 44:21; 46:4, 13; 51:5, 8. Sometimes there are images and metaphors which recall the Exodus or wilderness wanderings, and suggest that Israel is about to come through an analogous experience again: 42:16; 49:19–20; 55:12–13. Repeatedly throughout the book, one of the appellations by which God is made known is "your Redeemer": 41:14; 43:14; 44:24; 48:17; 49:7; 54:5, 8. Again with this term we have the association with the Exodus. Thus here, while we learn to appreciate Second Isaiah's creativity in style of expression, we also recognize through these types of sayings a content whose history is rooted in Jeremiah's and Ezekiel's development of the Oracle of Deliverance tradition.

2. Transformation

With 44:3 we have one of the strongest expressions of this component: "For I will pour water on the thirsty land, and streams on the dry ground; I will pour my Spirit upon your descendants, and my blessings on your offspring." The same progression in thought from a Transformation of nature to a Transformation of God's people is also found in 42:15–16 and 43:19–21. We already see here a shift in emphasis in the Transformation thrust as it is found in Second Isaiah. As has often been noted, this book is decidedly more universalistic in its horizons than its prophetic predecessors. The redemption has cosmological dimensions. God's act of Transformation is amplified so that God as Creator stands forth in bold outlines, perfecting and refashioning all of nature as well as Israel's inner condition.

Beyond those passages shown in Diagram D where we find a description of God's *action* to transform, there are five additional units in which we see some image testifying to God as Creator (42:5–9; 43:1–7; 44:24–28; 51:12–16; 54:4–10). In this book the confession of God as Creator has become an important affirmation in its own right. What was present only in germ in Jeremiah and Ezekiel now receives dramatic affirmation: because God has the power to create, to create anew in nature, one can trust that he has the power to redeem, to create new situations in history (41:17–20; 42:5–9, 14–17; 43:1–7, 14–21; 44:1–5, 21–22, 24–28; etc.) God not only creates a way through the desert, he creatively transforms Israel's homeland so that it will be as green and lush as a paradise (41:17–20; 43:14–21; 54:11–17; 55:10–13). This component is handled differently in Second Isaiah in that there is less of a moral concern about the inward condition of the people—perhaps explicable because Second Isaiah did not participate in the judgment preaching—so that their Transformation is a prerequisite to the reinitiation of Relationship. The Transformation is more fully integrated into the whole saving act. As an answer to the restricted alternatives faced by theodicy, God brings about an eschatological improvement in both the human and nonhuman parts of his creation.

3. Relationship

Language of election and Relationship, reaffirmed or reinitiated, is remarkably rich and repetitive throughout these oracles. This component appears almost as frequently as the Deliverance element; we see the two thrusts here in about the same ratio of frequency they had in Jeremiah and Ezekiel. While the Covenant Formula as such never appears, we have its parts separately, "I am your God" in 41:10; 43:3; 51:15; "you are my people" in 51:16. Six times God reminds his people that he has chosen them, using the maximum term for this, *bāḥar*: 41:8, 9; 43:20; 44:1, 2; 49:7. Three times God denies that he has rejected or will reject them: 41:9, 17; 42:16. The theme receives a poignant expression in 49:15: "Can a woman forget her suckling child . . . these may forget, yet I will not forget you." The consciousness of rejection, and its healing, are the major concern of the oracles in 54:4–10. The pivotal saying is in verse 7: "For a brief moment I forsook you, but with great compassion I will gather you." The Relationship anxiety which calls for such frequent and powerful Relationship affirmations is grounded in historical events and in the community's faith-interpretation of it. The very names used to identify who speaks in these oracles, and who is addressed, carry important statements about Relationship. Six times Israel is addressed as "my servant": 41:8, 9; 44:1, 2, 21; 49:6. Often God identifies himself as "the Holy One of Israel" or as "the Lord, your Redeemer": 43:14; 44:24; 48:17; 49:7; 54:8. Beyond this, there is a wealth of other images and metaphors by which Second Isaiah reaffirms the God-Israel relationship.

What we conclude from the evidence is that Second Isaiah shows profound continuity with the major structural and thematic components of the Oracle of Deliverance in Jeremiah and Ezekiel. This is not to overlook that Second Isaiah brought innovations. His language and thought carry a very distinctive stamp. Since the differences between Second Isaiah and Ezekiel are greater than those between Ezekiel and Jeremiah, I would not want to exclude the possibility that Second Isaiah was influenced by some new sources. But our evidence says that he transformed, and in many ways further strengthened, a time-honored prophetic genre, rather than shifting to a new form of speech to bear his salvation message.

C. Suggested Structural Elements Which We Have Not Included

1. A "Reason" upon Which God's Help Is Grounded

Not surprisingly, there has been an early and recurrent pattern of suggestion that the Oracle of Deliverance fits a new content into the basic outline of the earlier, and very common, Oracle of Judgment. As we saw in our survey of this speech-form several chapters earlier, that genre has an altogether convincing two-part structure in which a "reason" explains why God is about to judge the people in terms of the sins they have committed, and then this is followed by the "announcement" that the judgment is indeed coming in such and such a form. Using the example of the judgment oracle in Isaiah 29:13, H. W. Wolff long ago explained: "Here reason and threat are tied together tightly: Because—therefore. Thus the prophet makes understandable to the people how each event is the necessary result of a cause."[8] This is what is important to see: the "necessary" connection between cause and effect. Before he announces what he will do God explains, makes logical, justifies, or accounts for his intervention through the other main component of the speech-form. This two-part pattern has made such a tremendous impression on the way much of the prophetic message has come to be understood that it would be remarkable if nothing comparable to the "reason" section found its way into the Oracle of Deliverance. (In Chapter 1, p. 17, I called this half of the Oracle of Judgment the "Accusation"; but, with Wolff, it still holds good that the "Accusation" supplies the *Reason* for what I designated there as the "Proclamation" [of judgment] half.) Thus many scholars do find a "reason" structural component in the genre of speech used by the prophets to proclaim deliverance.[9]

What would the "reason" for deliverance out of Exile look like? If God punishes according to the people's sins, why does he save? In Psalms of Lamentation grounds for God's compliance are frequently attached to pleas that God show mercy and deliver out of trouble. No "reason" appears more often in that context than appeal to God's *ḥẹsẹd,* his "steadfast love" or "covenant faithfulness" (in private laments: 6:4; 31:16; 40:11; 69:16; 109:21; in public laments: 44:26; 89:49; 90:14).[10] In other Psalms the appeal is made to God's covenant or to any institution which represented God's tendency to show mercy toward his people in the past. There are assumptions here about a *continuity* in God's "relationship maintaining love" (*ḥẹsẹd*) toward them. There are assumptions about *continuity* of religious institutions, *continuity* in God's propensity to show mercy toward his people. The people assume that there are threads which link them to God, on which they can pull, in times of trouble, to bring his mercies nearer.

The expression "steadfast love" (*ḥẹsẹd*) never appears in the focal six oracles in Jeremiah and eleven in Ezekiel which have the greatest claim to authenticity. Indeed, in only four instances out of the sixty-one Oracles of Deliverance does the term "steadfast love" appear. In two cases it appears as a *result* of God's saving action (Hos. 2:19; Isa. 54:8), and in two in a use which might possibly let it be taken as a "reason" (Jer. 31:3; Isa. 54:10).[11] References to "covenant" and to institutions like the line of David all come forth as benefits and gifts *resulting* from the saving action, and not as causes of that action. The pattern we find again and again is that God's promise of intervention is preceded by the bare statement of the Messenger Formula ("Thus says the Lord"), or some words like "Behold," or "The days are coming when . . ."; and it is followed by additional promises of gracious intervention, not by "reasons" or explanations. I know of no instance in Jeremiah or Ezekiel where the *kî* or *'āl-kēn,* "for, because; therefore," so commonly providing the causal connection of the "reason" to the "announcement" ("Accusation" to "Proclamation" in our terminology) in Oracles of Judgment stands after any of the three thrusts of the Oracle of Deliverance to introduce a "reason" for the action.[12] Ezekiel's frequent "then you shall know that I am the Lord" can hardly be a distinctive reason for a saving action because: 1) it appears seventy-two times outside of this genre in Oracles of Judgment and in Oracles against Foreign Nations, thereby revealing itself as a peculiar rhetorical and conceptual distinguishing mark of Ezekiel's message taken as a whole; 2) a "reason" rooted simply in God's Godness is just a way of making explicit what is implicit when there is no "reason" given at all: that God does it for his own reasons, and not out of consideration for any obligations or institutions tying him to Israel.[13] The same thing can be said for the much less frequent expression "for my name's sake," which occurs a few times in Ezekiel.[14]

The important thing to see is that *the threads* which the Psalmists thought existed between themselves and God's assured mercies are all *broken.* There is *discontinuity* between all of the institutions through which God's mercy operated in the past, and the condition of the present.

Another source of a "reason" might be a change in the people

Israel such as was encouraged in the "Admonition" section of the Prophetic Summons to Repentance. But we never find such a statement preceding or following the proclamation of gracious intervention of the sort as: "Because my people have repented," or "Because Israel has been cleansed through its suffering in Exile."

I hope that the reader recognizes that some of the most important theological understandings of what the Oracle of Deliverance is all about arise out of the surprising discovery that *the genre has no "reason" to explain or justify it.* This means:

There is nothing which provides a logical transition into the announcement of divine intervention.

In human terms, that intervention is not founded upon anything reasonable.

There is nothing human beings have to do or can do to prepare for this intervention.

The statement of intervention does not lean on any other part of the genre to make sense of it or complete it.

The nature of the communication imprints an abruptness, an unexpectedness, which the prophet let stand.

God's intervention is its own explanation.

On his own timetable, for his own reasons, God has acted or will act. What he does is unexpected. There is more mercy, more power; there are more elements of a new dispensation for history than could have been anticipated. Any effort to explain that or make it reasonable cheapens it.

One does not explain Deliverance (D) in terms of Relationship (R), or Transformation (T) in terms of Deliverance (D). Each of these is a unique act of divine initiative. Both in meaning and arrangement they stand, as we have seen, in parallel or co-ordinate relationship. In terms of Begrich's, Wolff's, Von Waldow's, or Westermann's[15] analyses of the structure there would be, in our view, a reduction of two or three major *different* elements to just one element, so that we have:

I. Divine Intervention	**1. Deliverance** **2. Transformation** **3. Relationship**

Everything else is strictly secondary so that there is no Roman numeral II. This throws in sharp relief the unconditional, unqualified, and certainly unexpected character of this oracle. God's initiative, God's prerogative stand alone. It is very important to see the full nature and extent of the *difference* between the Oracle of Deliverance and either the Oracle of Judgment or the Summons to Repentance. *With this speech we have crossed a watershed in the history of Israelite religion.*

2. "Goal"

There have been a number of suggestions that the genre which contains the deliverance message has as one of its most basic component structural parts a "goal" toward which the action moves.[16] This suggestion seems reasonable; it does not betray a carry-over of expectations from other genres.

What does the textual evidence show? If we take the concluding verse of an oracle to be the most likely place to find the "goal" expressed, we discover a tremendous freedom for variation of elements which occurs there. This is perhaps most readily seen in Diagram D, where I show repetitions of themes as well as their initial statements. And the situation is not really different in Jeremiah or Ezekiel from that in Second Isaiah. It is a very common format for an oracle to begin with a promise of Deliverance (D) and end with a repetition of that theme (Jer. 3:15–18; 29:10–14; 32:36–41; 33:14–16). But there are greater numbers of times in which the Relationship (R) component comes last (Hos. 2:16–20, 21–23; Jer. 30:18–22; 31:7–9; Ezek. 34:20–24, 25–31, and more). One sometimes finds an ending with a word about forgiveness (Jer. 31:34; 50:24; Ezek. 16:59–63; 37:23). There may be a final stress on some theophanic element (Ezek. 36:33–36; 37:11–14). And, in several cases the whole oracle ends with some note of admonition (Ezek. 11:16–21; 36:22–32).[17] We should recognize that whatever is last, if it is expressed with any emphasis at all, has a tendency to sound like a "goal." Here, however, I think it is essential to distinguish between a "goal" *function* and a "goal" *structural component.* In the sixty-one Deliverance oracles as a whole there simply is no "goal" component beyond the elements which we have already described. Depending upon the particular rhetorical features of a given oracle unit, any of the components already described can seem to function as a "goal." This statement holds equally if one moves farther inside the oracle and looks for a "goal" in an earlier part of the sequence. Perhaps then our criteria for determining what is the "goal" would be that it receives particular stress, and that other dimensions of the intervention seem to lead up to the statement of this part as the culminating purpose. But this leads us back to the discovery we found earlier. In one oracle the central emphasis will be on Transformation (T), in another Relationship (R), in another Deliverance (D). Apparently there was no feeling of the need for an additional "goal" if each of these parts could be an end in itself.

In a recent article on methodology in form criticism, R. Knierim suggested that the researcher should ask "what is the principle of structuring in this genre"?[18] I would say that if the Oracle of Judgment was structured to convince people that their sins justified God's punishment, and the Summons to Repentance was structured to apply maximum motivational leverage, then the Oracle of Deliverance was structured out of dramatic considerations to highlight the decisiveness and power of the divine intervention, the unconditional character of this action, the unexpectedness of the divine prerogative expressing itself in what is about to happen. The whole thing is God's show! The genre is basically a proclamation of the *intervention* of divine grace. Anything added to that is a footnote.

STANDPOINT

A. Context

In an article referred to above, Knierim has warned, "We should not be surprised if the intention or the function or the context of a text may play a role equally as important as formal and stylistic arguments have in the past."[19] I will try to summarize the important elements that define the context in which the Oracle of Deliverance was spoken and heard.

1. The context is the Babylonian Exile. That is no longer an image in judgment preaching, a threat, but a "historical reality." As I argued in the preceding chapter, these oracles may have been spoken by Jeremiah in Jerusalem, but the promises were applicable only to those in Exile.

2. Theologically speaking, the judgment is no longer in the future, but takes its place in the past and continues up into the present until the Oracle of Deliverance is heard.

3. The threads are all broken. These are the threads of "steadfast love," covenant, continuity of the *Heilsgeschichte,* the theocracy, and every precedent of God's acting in mercy on which the lamenting Psalmists drew when they gave reasons why God should grant their petitions. Even for Ezekiel, knowledge of the desecration and demolition of the temple nullifies, for the time being, any cultic assurances built around the election of Zion. The break in the Davidic line, the absence of any Israelite ruler on that throne, yes, the absence of the throne itself cut the people off from assurances clustered around the election of David. In the chapter on "Rejection" we have already given evidence that the Mosaic Covenant was now abrogated. That forgiveness is not available for covenant violations was made explicitly clear in such covenantal texts as Josh. 24:19; Deut. 29:20; and Exod. 23:21. This principle was accepted by the prophets, and reinforced when they used the denial of the possibility of forgiveness in their Oracles of Judgment; see this in Hos. 1:6; 8:13; Jer. 4:28; 5:1, 7; 6:20; 13:14; 14:10; 15:6; 16:13; Ezek. 5:11; 7:4, 9; 8:18; 9:10; 24:14. *Thus the Sinai Covenant contained the terms for its own dissolution, but not the terms for its own restoration.*

4. Not one word in Jeremiah or Ezekiel suggests that the people of Judah have been transformed by the experience of Exile. These two prophets address the same audience, in nearly the same moral condition which evoked the Oracles of Judgment.

5. Similarly, in the time of Jeremiah and Ezekiel, there is no

historical ground for hope. There is no sign of Cyrus. The end of the Exile is not in sight.

6. The words of deliverance had to address communal despondency.

7. They had to differentiate themselves from false prophecy.

8. There was extremely little precedent in the prophetic tradition for the deliverance message that was proclaimed.

9. Compared to the word of judgment or the call to repentance, the prophet is almost invisible in the Oracle of Deliverance. The authority of the prophetic word introduced by the Messenger Formula, developed in judgment preaching, substantiated by the factuality of the Exile is clearly presupposed and built upon. But the prophet's own contribution is circumscribed even more here than in the Announcement portion of the Oracle of Judgment. The word in this oracle is focused on God's initiative from beginning to end. It is a breakthrough from the beyond.

10. The message creates a turning point in Israel's history, opens the door to a dramatically different era.

B. Intention

The main considerations can best be sketched in outline. The intention of the Oracle of Deliverance is:

1. To show that God has seen the people in Exile, taken the dimensions of that situation seriously, and addressed a new word to it.

2. To give the people hope and build a new foundation for their religious faith.

3. To demonstrate that the God of judgment is also the God of deliverance, that the God of wrath is also the God of love. The propensity in God toward mercy, which he had to restrain all through the judgment episode, now bursts forth and wants to express and confirm itself.

4. To affirm that after the judgment is a new era, the beginning of a new relationship between God and his people.

5. To show that God acts for his own reasons, is not bound by the logic of institutional structures or precedents in the past, and sometimes shows grace far beyond any deserving.

6. To demonstrate that Israel's failures do not defeat God. This and other points are to be developed more fully in the chapter which follows on the content of the deliverance message.

SETTING

From the beginnings of form criticism to the present day the two dominant concerns have been to determine the structure of a genre and then its *Sitz im Leben* or "setting in life."[20] The traditional idea is: "Each genre originates in a particular setting . . . and this setting can be recovered through a study of the genre itself."[21] There is an assumption here that just as "form and content are inextricably related,"[22] so each genre is fashioned by the type of occasion which gave it birth. According to K. Koch:

> A setting in life is a social occurrence, the result of customs prevailing in one particular culture at one particular time, and which has granted such an important role to the speaker and his hearers or the writer and his readers, that particular linguistic forms are found necessary as a vehicle for expression.[23]

We should not miss that there is some expectation of sociological determinism in these assumptions about what impact a setting has upon its genre: "The regulations and needs of a particular sphere of existence *determine* and form the respective manners of speech. . . ."[24] Or in G. M. Tucker's words: "The term ["setting"] refers to the sociological situation which *produced* and *maintained* the various genres. . . ."[25]

Along with the continued importance attached to setting, in the last decade there has developed an increasing awareness that its determination is deceptively difficult. R. Knierim has said that "it is here that the work of form critics seems to have had its most grievous weaknesses."[26] Knierim illustrates his point by showing that until recent years there had been much naiveté about how "settings can change." Before this, "one could presuppose tacitly or expressly, that he knew automatically the setting as soon as he was able to define the *original setting* of the genre. . . . This presupposition was based uncritically on the assumption that a genre is always related to its setting in the genuine sense, wherever the genre occurs."[27]

Obviously we all would like to know the "inside story" behind the Oracle of Deliverance. I feel certain that in many cases there was something shared between speaker and audience in various genres of communication which supplied the rationale by which that message was understood, the framework against which it was to be interpreted. But much as we would feel more secure if we had a definite social-institutional niche into which we could fit the Oracle of Deliverance, we have to be realistic about anything authentically prefiguring the situation and message which received form in Jeremiah's and Ezekiel's Oracles of Deliverance. Certainly some human shaping was inevitable. To find the sources drawn upon for that shaping is undeniably important. But we need to look for a setting which liberates and illuminates this speech-form, and not settle for one which locks it into something with narrower horizons than the message we have already found within this genre.

A. Established Positions on "Setting" of This Genre

1. Setting as an Answer to a Cultic Lament

a. The Thesis Initiated by Begrich

It would be impossible to exaggerate the influence which the work of Joachim Begrich in the 1930s has had on subsequent interpretations of the Oracle of Deliverance. The two major studies of this genre since his, those of H. E. von Waldow and C. Westermann,[28] both take Begrich as their starting point and never break out of his pattern of assumptions. And there are perhaps a dozen scholars who have accepted his views largely uncritically and applied them to related studies in the prophets and beyond.[29]

Begrich did not begin dealing with the genre in question by an inductive study of its occurrences in the prophets, or even within Second Isaiah. He came to it fresh from his notable success in partnership with Hermann Gunkel in working on the Psalms. And his original 1934 article, "Das priesterliche Heilsorakel," was written to solve a problem which had arisen in their Psalms research. Noting the striking shift in mood from near despair to a final verse or two filled with confidence and thanksgiving in the Lament Psalms, Gunkel and Begrich had surmised that something actually had taken place which was the basis for this shift. Perhaps the priest had assured the supplicant that God had heard his complaint and would take favorable action. But where then was the attestation for this priestly oracle of favorable hearing? It is not contained, as such, within the Psalter. Begrich claimed to find that missing oracle in Second Isaiah. Not too surprisingly, when Begrich later wrote a study on Second Isaiah and was looking for the setting of that prophet's oracles of salvation, he decided that they originated from the priestly oracles of favorable hearing in the cult. Thus the circle was complete.

EXCURSUS

Summary of Begrich's Position on Setting of Second Isaiah's Salvation Oracles

Begrich sees the priestly oracle of favorable hearing attested in: Isa. 41:8–13, 14–16; 43:1–3a, 5; 44:2–5; 48:17–19; 49:7, 14–15; 51:7–8; 54:4–8.[30] He discerns in it the following structure: a) It begins with the words "fear not!" (cf. Lam. 3:57). b) Then the one addressed is designated (singular form of pronouns). c) This is followed by a "motivational clause" introduced by *kî*—"for I am with you." d) Then there are expressions that Yahweh has heard (the lament) together with specifications of how he will help. It is important to note that these clauses are usually in the perfect form of the verb. e) The last element consists of further promises of how God will help, contained in the imperfect form of the verb.[31]

A second major part of Begrich's description of the "priestly oracle of salvation" involves a correlation of images, phrases, and themes in the oracles with either the same or similar language to that found in the Lament Psalms. This builds up to his basic affirmation that "form-wise and also content-wise the oracle is nothing other than the answer granted to the song of lament."[32] Most scholars find this part of Begrich's article very convincing. I have some misgivings. He is dealing with catch-words and ignoring context. The tremendously wide range of concerns expressed in Psalmic laments perhaps makes pairing with phrases and themes in these selected oracles in Second Isaiah more a matter of painstaking effort than proof. Begrich rounds off his description of the priestly oracle of salvation by urging that it was originally and properly spoken in the cult by a priest, acting out the priestly office in response to the penitent person's lament.[33] Begrich then returns to the second level on which his article is written, and tells us once more that Second Isaiah has taken over the fixed form of "the priestly oracle of salvation" "verbatim."[34] The prophet uses this genre, according to Begrich, because it would have been widely known among the people through the pre-exilic cult, and because it ties the God who announces historical salvation to the God of mercy so often encountered in worship.[35]

By exploiting Second Isaiah's oracles to give the attestation and model for the "priestly oracle of salvation," Begrich predetermined that Second Isaiah's deliverance message would *necessarily* be expressed in a genre with the closest possible ties to a cultic setting. The next step was to shift from a primary interest in the Psalms to a primary interest in this prophet, and in particular to draw very broad implications from that linkage for Second Isaiah's message as a whole. This step was taken by Begrich himself in his 1938 monograph *Studien zu Deuterojesaja.*

In the second study the list of oracles has grown from eight (1934) to twenty-four units. The additional ones are: 41:17–20; 42:14–17; 43:16–21; 45:1–7, 14–17; 46:3–4, 12–13; 49:8–12, 14–21, 22–23, 24–26; 51:12–16; 54:7–10, 11–12, 13b, 14a+13a–17; 55:8–13.[36] Begrich explicitly presupposes his 1934 article as the basic description of the genre.[37] He also argues for the same correspondence with Psalms of lament as in "the priestly oracle of salvation." In fact he says that these units in the prophet "copy the simple [priestly] salvation oracle for the individual."[38] However, he now offers a different structure for the genre as it appears in Second Isaiah: a) An expression of Yahweh's intervention with help; b) result of the intervention and the way distress is turned aside; c) the goal toward which this activity moves.[39] We receive no explanation why elements of the 1934 structure were dropped, what their absence does toward changing the meaning, nor any awareness of inconsistency in that those elements are still as present as they ever were in the eight passages of Second Isaiah which supplied his evidence for the existence and structure of "the priestly oracle of salvation." Clearly Begrich has changed the structure of the genre so that it will better fit the additional sixteen passages without reconsidering his commitment to the cultic setting.

In the latter chapters of his monograph where Begrich goes into aspects of the content of Second Isaiah's salvation message, several additional considerations come forward which are important for us: a) He makes quite a point that Second Isaiah stands in the line of the prophetic tradition. But in this regard he thinks in stereotyped terms of the influence of the earlier "doom prophets" on Second Isaiah's judgment message and never considers that his prophetic predecessors had a salvation message which might have been a source of influence also.[40] b) Begrich assumes that there is no genre available out of the prophetic tradition which could have suitably framed Second Isaiah's message of salvation. He thinks that nothing would make salvation so convincing to the exiles as a word from Yahweh in the genre of a priestly oracle of salvation.

> Deutero-Isaiah's message finds its expression in most cases in the oracles of salvation. He wants them to make the exiles as secure as the "favorable-hearing" which the priest imparts to the lamenters. Therefore he chooses this speech to the individual man in order to make it entirely vivid what he knows out of the answer of Yahweh to the entreaty. The intention is to make clear that the same gracious and ready-to-help God stands behind the promises of Deutero-Isaiah.[41]

c) Begrich finds the same radical dimension of salvation preaching in these oracles which I see. He explicitly says that the two sources of the forgiveness which give Israel new hope are election and eschatology.[42] Begrich gives no evidence of a willingness to rethink his position on the derivation and setting of the *genre* out of consideration for this content which has moved so far from what one might expect a priest to say in assuring a lamenter that God gives him a favorable hearing.

Within the last decade or two Von Waldow[43] and Westermann[44] have restated Begrich's basic position, albeit with a few significant refinements in each case.

b. Critique of "Setting" as Answer to Cultic Lament

Additional points in Begrich's method and results, as well as objections to them, will be seen in what follows.

1) Errors in Method

Begrich reversed what would be the normal direction both in working from setting to structure, and even worse in moving from Psalms to a prophetic speech-genre. He seemingly backed into his theory of a cultic setting of Second Isaiah's oracles. First the evidence in Second Isaiah was used to solve a question in Psalms research. Then the same passages were taken as evidence of a cultic setting for the prophet's salvation oracles. This is a flagrant example of a circular or self-validating argument. The *same passages* are made to prove two separate things: a) that there was a "priestly oracle of favorable hearing" as conjectured from Psalmic research; b) that Second Isaiah got the form for his prophetic message of salvation to the exiles from an extremely literal and direct dependence on the "priestly oracle of favorable hearing."

What we still need, if part of Begrich's thesis is to be salvaged, is a realistic assessment of the full dimensions of adaptation made when a consoling word to an individual was taken over to address an exiled community. There is more than sickness to be healed; there are broken institutions, a broken relationship with God, all graphically symbolized in the painfully obvious separation from the homeland. For God to break the silence following judgment and speak means that God's initiative is not confined to giving a favorable answer to someone's lament and petition—there were plenty of those which went unanswered back in Judah (as in Jer. 14). Now, in this situation, there is a dramatic intervention, and a highly unexpected turn in God's initiative. God does not respond favorably because there is that "connecting thread" of institutional continuity tying him to Israel. *Begrich deals wtih the salvation preaching as though the judgment proclamation and the attestation of it in the exile had never taken place.*

What seems credible is that Second Isaiah grafted on some rhetorical elements from the hypothetical "priestly oracle of favorable hearing" to give a specially tender, personal, and consoling tone to his message—but grafted that onto the genre he inherited from Ezekiel and Jeremiah. Perhaps it is best seen in just this way, as a sub-genre added to *some* oracles of *one* prophet to achieve a special rhetorical effect: giving the message a tone that was immediate in its assuredness, very direct, personal, and consoling. Until Begrich's thesis is adapted to take account of the fact that "settings change," his preoccupation with cultic needs and ideologies will leave the conjectured "priestly oracle of favorable hearing" largely irrelevant to Second Isaiah's deliverance message.[45]

2) Theological Problems

The burden of the message of the prophetic Oracle of Deliverance is a proclamation that God is, by an act of his own will and without human prerequisites, bringing about the restoration of a (covenant) relationship which has been abrogated. In light of this it is facile to talk about the rationale for the genre of speech communicating such a message coming within the optimistic belief of cultic lamenters that their entreaty would receive a favorable hearing. It was indeed part of the earlier judgment preaching that just such an attitude prevailed, that the masses of people wanted to offer sacrifices when they had not kept the basic requirements of covenant justice. Is an Exile which began by the terms we have described in Chapters II-IV, which even in its early deliverance preaching took judgment as seriously as we showed in Chapter V, finally to come to an end by the prophets' promising a turning point in history through a speech-form still closely attached to the cultic expectation that lament petitions would receive a favorable answer? Even to make such a suggestion involves a serious lack of perspective. By the standards of Jeremiah, this would be "false prophecy" of the most flagrant sort. It would be a cheap and very restricted answer to a historical and theological dilemma of unexpected proportions.

In Chapters III and IV of his 1938 monograph, Begrich urged that the two most basic beliefs expressing the content of the "oracles of salvation" in Second Isaiah were election and eschatology. This, however, leads to the paradoxical result that the more successful Begrich was in showing the origin of the *form* in the priestly and cultic oracle of favorable hearing, the less he was thereby enabled to explain the distinctive *content* of Second Isaiah's deliverance message. And the more perceptive he was in describing the unique *content* of those oracles, the less sense those themes made in the context of his described original setting of the *form.* Begrich all but totally ignored this problem. If unresolved, the relationship between form and content would become so loose that the genre's setting would not necessarily tell us anything significant about how to understand the prophetic employment of the "oracle of salvation."

3) Omissions

For the purposes of the present study, the most dramatic omission made by Begrich was in ignoring the possibility that the salvation oracle was not original in Second Isaiah within the prophetic tradition, but built upon a deliverance oracle tradition from Ezekiel, Jeremiah, and earlier prophets. Begrich betrays a very dated, stereotyped perception of prophetic roles when he speaks of prophets before Second Isaiah as "doom-prophets."[46] And Begrich raises a basic issue when he assumes that Second Isaiah had to go outside the sphere of prophetic authority and prophetic speech-forms to find a rationale and linguistic vehicle sufficient for his message of salvation.[47] He does not seem to have seen the latent grace, frustratingly withheld grace of the earlier prophetic ministry, or with any precision the terms by which it could at last become freely expressed. In other words, he failed to see that *salvation prophecy has an integral connection with doom prophecy* and has no need for a change to exotic institutional settings (the cult) in order for a convincing word of deliverance to become possible. The problem is not that Begrich gave Second Isaiah too broad a base—that prophet does draw upon a wider range of traditions than any of his predecessors—but that he gave earlier prophets too narrow a base and consequently underestimated Second Isaiah's continuity with them.

Moving from earlier prophets through Jeremiah and Ezekiel to Second Isaiah's Oracles of Deliverance we are not at a loss to understand what we see there. Most of the structure and most of the content are already familiar to us at least in a generic way. The differences in his language and conceptions may be greater than between Jeremiah and Ezekiel. Some of this is due to the thirty to forty years between Ezekiel and Second Isaiah, whereas Jeremiah's and Ezekiel's ministries came back to back. Some of the difference is due to language adopted from the cult. But the point is that in moving forward in time we are not hard put to understand Second Isaiah's salvation oracles as a development on the earlier prophetic Oracle of Deliverance. He has refashioned that genre according to his own literary genius, the needs of his time, and his sense of theological priorities. I think that he has grafted onto perhaps a third of his uses of that inherited prophetic genre some elements of a conjectured "priestly oracle of favorable hearing" to give his message a unique pastoral twist and poignancy.

However, if we take Begrich's "priestly oracle of favorable hearing" and try to move backward with it to Ezekiel or Jeremiah we get nowhere. Why, especially, did not Ezekiel, the priest-prophet, use this conjectured genre? The answer is that Ezekiel knew that the cult was cut off, symbolized by God's willing the defilement of his own temple and the prophet's refusal to suggest that any hope would come out of Jerusalem. This is also seen in that God promises to restore the cult as a *second consequence* of his deliverance intervention (Ezek. 40–46). Therefore, *Ezekiel's understanding of what the Exile means for the cult moves toward repudiating the position of Begrich and those dependent upon him.*

2. A Setting in the Israelite Tradition of Blessing

Because God's blessing is a widely attested and deeply rooted benevolence within Israel's history and its institutions, some scholars have adopted the position that prophetic promises of salvation arise out of the context of blessing.

H. G. Reventlow has taken the position that the prophetic word of deliverance originates from the sort of covenantal blessings one sees in a text like Leviticus 26, parallel to the way the word of judgment can be seen to originate out of the covenant curses.[48] For similar or independent reasons several other scholars have located the origin of the prophetic salvation oracles in some enactment of blessing.[49] Since there is a certain inevitability that this suggestion would be made, it is good that it has been raised. In a substantial fraction of the deliverance oracles *some* of the promised help sounds like a blessing.

We need, however, to be clear about the distinction between "blessing" as something which God gives after the people are re-elected to relationship with him and returned to their homeland and "blessing" as the overarching rationale or conceptual setting and springboard for the Oracle of Deliverance as a whole. Blessing as we find it in such covenantal texts as Deut. 7:12–16; 11:13–17, 26–29; 28:1–14; 30:1–10, 15–20; and Leviticus 26 *is altogether conditional on keeping the terms of the covenant.*[50] Blessing is something Judah can expect from God when it is living on its promised piece of land and when its relationship with God is healthy.[51] Blessing might well be a *consequence* or a *sign* of the successful reversal of the situation of alienation between God and Israel. In such a framework a word of blessing would attest that the curse had been removed; it would betoken that a renormalization of the relationship had been accomplished. But it has struck me that blessing never initiates a relationship. Like "steadfast love," it operates *within* a healthy relationship as one of the benefits of the relationship. Within covenant the curse is more powerful than the blessing.[52] The curse can destroy the covenant relationship and seal that fate by denial of forgiveness (Exod. 23:21; Deut. 29:20; Josh. 24:19). Yet I know of not a single suggestion of forgiveness being mentioned within the context of God's blessings, covenantal or otherwise.

This fits in with what one finds in an examination of the root *bārak,* the only significant word for "bless" in Hebrew. It is centered on the physical aspects of life. It becomes a virtual synonym for human fertility; it is manifest in rain, good crops, productive flocks. It involves good luck, success, power, material prosperity, health: everything that supports staying alive and living in the security of abundance and power.

The only points where blessings approach the kind of concepts found in the Oracles of Deliverance appear in Genesis, where the blessing is historicized into a promise that the Patriarchs will be blessed with offspring and a land of their own to possess (Gen. 12:2–3; 28:3–4; 49:25–26).[53] Some of the oracles in the prophets which we have been discussing promise the people a land of their own to possess, and promise that God will multiply their numbers. Does this mean that these are blessings? Here, as with the "priestly oracle of favorable hearing," *it is of crucial importance to understand the status of the people and their institutions at the time that deliverance is promised.* I maintain that coming in the context of the Exile, following the judgment, these promises are no simple blessings. *Nothing is normal.* God has to change that through an intervention; he has to reverse the situation; he has to reinitiate the relationship. To migrate slowly out of the desert into the more fertile environs of Jerusalem may be seen as a blessing, but to be granted a sudden return from Babylonian Exile to Jerusalem is a *Deliverance.* It is thus simply out of perspective to say that the prophesied salvation roots itself in the "blessing." That is a small, very materialistic, highly conditional source of weal out of which to extrapolate a definitive turning point in Israel's history and religion.

B. New Sources for the Setting of the Oracle of Deliverance

1. Reflections on Methodology and Limits on the Results We Can Expect to Achieve

Why have serious efforts to explain the setting of the prophetic Oracle of Deliverance met with so little success? Why has a nagging incongruence between the actual dimensions of the message-content and the social-institutional home proposed for this speech-genre undercut the credibility and relevance of the proposed settings?

Perhaps the problem has been that both the "cultic answer" approach tried by Begrich and his followers and the "covenantal blessing" position represented by Reventlow among others were undertaken on fairly traditional form-critical methodological assumptions, whereas the prophetic Oracle of Deliverance confronts us with a speech situation in which those methodological paths are simply not productive. Let me try to point out a few stumbling blocks which suggest that the Oracle of Deliverance is largely an exception to the kind of genre whose setting can be discovered within the established institutions of Israel.

a. Precedents for the Context

When before the latter part of the ministries of Jeremiah and Ezekiel was there ever an occasion for God to announce that he was restoring a lapsed covenant, reinstituting a defiled cult, bringing home an exiled people? There is no preprophetic analogy to such a stiuation. And outside the distinctive prophetic interpretation of events, there was no discernment of a predicament in such terms. Inasmuch as Amos, Hosea, or Micah accepted the fall of Samaria in 722 as a *fait accompli*, they could have spoken to just such a context.[54] But it is nearly impossible to give evidence of an early date for their Oracles of Deliverance. In any case, their use of the Oracle of Deliverance is of one fabric with its appearances in Jeremiah and Ezekiel. We seem to be talking then about a *sui generis* prophetic genre[55] as likely as not beginning with Jeremiah. This would be the case, in no small part, because the situation which called forth this kind of message was not a recurrent social-institutional phenomenon, but historically unique. And of course *the whole idea of an institutionally determined speech-form collapses if the genre in question characteristically communicates the reestablishment of a series of institutions whose efficacy and operation had lapsed.*

b. Institutional Rootage

Cult, as understood by the prophets, is an institution which rests on the more comprehensive and basic institution of the covenant. "No covenant justice, no cultic expiation," says Amos 5:21–24; Hos. 6:6; Mic. 6:6–8; Isa. 1:10–17; and Jer. 7:2–7. To employ cultic expedients as a leverage on God's grace when the basic requirements of the covenant were being ignored elicited God's wrath toward what otherwise might have been very acceptable cultic acts. Yet, we must understand in turn that the covenant was an institution with its limits, its conditionality. Through the curses, and their historical actualization in the proclamation of judgment, the covenant could self-destruct. This we argued at length in Chapters II and III.

Our diagram below shows that cult rests upon and operates within what was sanctioned by the Sinai Covenant. The Sinai Covenant in turn has foundations, but they are *not* institutional foundations. The prophetic Oracle of Deliverance was spoken to a situation in which the cult and covenant were no longer operative as formerly. It is basic to the positions symbolized by

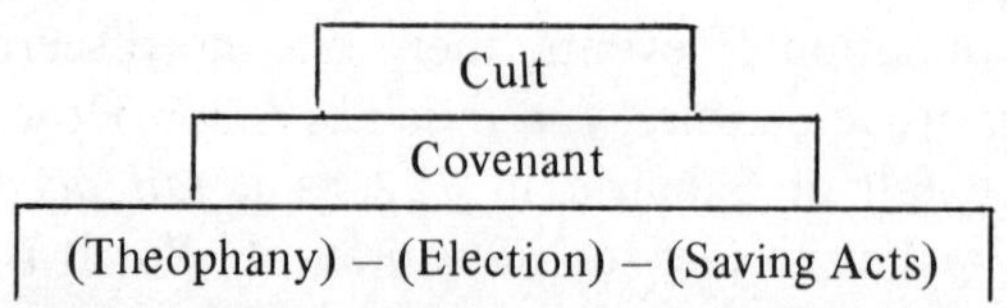

Begrich and Reventlow that they failed to realize this. To what institution does one then appeal for a word of deliverance if the cult and the covenant were made null and void through the exile-judgment? *What institution is more comprehensive and basic even than the covenant?* The answer is: none. In that case we can only ask, "What faith elements were the foundation on which the covenant institution was built?" One thinks of: 1) God's self-revelation; 2) God's election of a people; 3) God's initiating a sequence of "saving acts," later to be recited in a credo, in which his plan to redeem all history through Israel's instrumentality gradually unfolds. We need to look for oracles declaring God's initiatory actions. We need to find affirmations that deal with the presuppositions of covenant. What does Israelite faith perceive to be God's most fundamental initiatives? What can be said to be God's most enduring intentions and modes of action in the Old Testament? Are they ever given voice?

The *content* of a speech-genre finally becomes the criterion by which one judges whether the *form* and its origin have been meaningfully described. This realization, and the issues just raised, give us a new sense of direction. But even with election initiating promises, which seem to bear valuable structural and conceptual comparison with the prophetic Oracle of Deliverance, we must recognize how different is the *context* in which such Pentateuchal promises were spoken and the context to which the prophetic Oracles of Deliverance were addressed. Each is at a different end of a long road. I would therefore caution the reader that with this speech-genre especially it is self-defeating and misguided to expect *too much* in terms of finding a wholly satisfying setting to explain the form and its message. Early, initiatory communications will probably offer only *analogies* to elements in the prophetic Oracle of Deliverance, from which it was later constructed, and not a prepackaged institutionally shaped speech which Jeremiah and Ezekiel had only to pick up and utilize for their own purposes.

2. Possible Early Strata Sources or Analogues for the Prophetic Oracle of Deliverance

a. Deuteronomy

Even though this book is full of reflection on election and God's saving acts, it turns out not to be fertile ground for finding antecedents to the prophetic Oracle of Deliverance. This is so because Deuteronomy betrays its lineage as a covenant renewal document dating only a little before the main part of Jeremiah's ministry. Very little of it is cast in the form of oracular speech from God. The book is shot through with endless admonitions and sharp conditional statements. It does not contain the kind of speech which stated what happened to Israel before covenant could come into being. Any thoughts along those lines are adapted here toward speeches which will help bring about the changes needed to renew the existing covenant. This is seen in Deut. 7:6–11 which comes closer than anything else in Deuteronomy to the prophetic Oracle of Deliverance. Here election is explained (7:6–7) rather than announced. God's saving act is presented only as a historical remembrance (7:8). Deuteronomy is shaped toward a different need from that addressed by Jeremiah and Ezekiel.

b. "J" and "E" in Genesis

In Genesis there is no shortage of initiatory promises given by

God to Abraham and his descendants. But not one of them in the old narrative "J" and "E" strands uses any term like *bāḥar* (the specific verb for "choose, elect") or expressions anticipatory of the Covenant Formula which would make it clear that the beginning of a relationship is being depicted. Seen in light of other Old Testament material, this situation is rather strange. In Ezekiel (20:5), Second Isaiah (41:8–9), and Psalms (105:5–10) it is quite clear that later faith thought of the election relationship as beginning with God's calling of the Patriarchs.[56] However much later faith saw the God-people relationship beginning with the Patriarchs, the actual textual evidence afforded us in Genesis by "J" and "E" does not support this in a way that provides useful antecedents and analogies to the "Relationship" component of the prophetic Oracle of Deliverance. Part of the problem, of course, is that Israel has not yet emerged as a corporate religious community. At best it is only implict that in singling out an individual Patriarch for a special mission, the promises and the commission given him pass on to his posterity.

There are some dimensions of God's promises to the Patriarchs which do seem to prefigure aspects of the type of speech found in the prophetic Oracles of Deliverance. In Gen. 12:1–3; 13:14–17; 26:2–5, 24; 28:13–15; and 46:2–4 we find oracles with God speaking as "I," addressed directly to one of the Patriarchs, and promising him help. These are abrupt and unexpected; the promises are unqualified and unconditional; they initiate something which heretofore did not exist. The help which they promise again and again is land and progeny.[57] In some cases this is explicitly formulated as a kind of historicized blessing (12:1–3; 26:2–5, 24; 28:13–14); in other passages the same basic things are promised, but without any reference to blessing (13:14–17; 46:2–4). There can be little question but that the promise of a land of their own is basic to an election or covenant tradition attached to the Patriarchs.[58]

The "I will gather you back to your land" of the prophetic Oracles of Deliverance could be seen as containing a twofold promise: 1) Exile is ended; 2) the Patriarchal covenant is reinitiated. Although it does not deal with important dimensions of the rejection preaching and the requirements of reinstituting a lapsed Exodus covenant tradition, perhaps for many of the Israelites whom Jeremiah and Ezekiel addressed the *sine qua non* of re-election would be God's bringing them back into their own homeland, their inheritance.

At the same time we must recognize that the help which God promises to give the Patriarchs is not "Deliverance" from captivity or distress, not the reversal of a bad situation, not the healing of broken institutions. So here again, as with the Relationship issue, the divine oracles of promise to the Patriarchs provide no more than quite limited analogies to the prophetic Oracles of Deliverance. Although they may have been drawn on as one of several sources of influence, we can hardly say that these oracles to the Patriarchs constitute the setting by which the prophetic Oracles of Deliverance can be understood.[59]

c. "J" and "E" in Exodus

There are several very important promises of God's deliverance in Exodus 3. Each of them occurs in a speech-form which has been called "Theophany," meaning God's Self-revelation. (For an examination whether the Oracle of Deliverance genre could have developed out of the Theophany genre see the excursus at the end of this chapter.) The first comes in 3:7–8. With the relational motif struck in verse 7 ("my people"), and the foundational promise of God's initiative to deliver from captivity in Egypt, in verse 8, we have something comparable to the two most widely attested parts of the prophetic Oracle of Deliverance. And certainly the promise that God will intervene to deliver his people from Egypt comes closer toward the scope of the "Deliverance" component in the prophetic Oracle of Deliverance than the promise of land and progeny in the Oracles to the Patriarchs.

However, these promises hardly stand out alone as altogether abrupt and unexpected, even though they truly are unqualified and unconditional vows to save. What surrounds the promises compromise and diminish somewhat their parallelism with the prophetic Oracles of Deliverance.[60] Thus the words from God here, taken as a whole, do not create the impression of any *stylized pattern of speech* such as might have been the case if a promise to initiate a saving act had achieved the status of a definite speech-form. Any tendency to structure God's message seems quite subordinated to the need to address the concerns of the particular historical situation. That is much the same situation that we find in Exod. 3:13–22. The particulars of Exod. 3:7–9 and 3:16–17 *in their contexts* do not offer elements of structure or concept sufficiently close to the prophetic Oracle of Deliverance to argue a strong line of direct influence, as though this were *the* setting.

I am impressed by a second pair of declarations from God appearing in Exod. 19:4 and 20:2. We must recognize two limitations at the outset. Neither of these words is a promise; both are historical reminiscences, and both of them are followed immediately by terms of covenantally based conditionality. But in either case it is absolutely clear that covenant requirements, and thus the covenant institution, *presuppose* the prior unconditional, unexpected, decisive, divine intervention in God's deliverance of his people from Egypt. *The saving act initiates a new era,* and the covenant stands in a secondary position as the way of structuring the God-Israel relationship in that era. Our diagram on p. 162 asks "what is more foundational than covenant?" Clearly God's decision to exercise his divine prerogative and intervene in history in order to deliver a people is more basic than the covenant institution—is in fact, along with election, both a presupposition and a foundation of the covenant institution. The credo of "saving acts"—whether expanded or terse—always seems to be put immediately before an oath which Israel is expected to take (in Exod. 19:5 the "if" implies both oath and law; cf. Josh. 24:2–13 with Josh. 24:14), or a law they are expected to keep (Exod. 20:2 with 20:3ff), as though that is the natural beginning point and maximum motivation for entering upon new (institutionalized) obligations.

It perhaps is not too much to say that the prophetic Oracle of Deliverance was *conceptually* grounded equally in the remembrance of this event (Exod. 19:4; 29:2) as in the promise of it (Exod. 3:7–8, 16–17). I want to argue that the paradigm we see in such terse, classical, powerful form in Exod. 20:2 is the same paradigm on which the prophetic Oracles of Deliverance are founded. "I am the Lord your God" states *Relationship.* "Who brought you out of the land of Egypt" articulates *Deliverance.* Relationship↔Deliverance—this is the paradigm at the core of the *Heilsgeschichte* or "saving acts" credo.[61] It is repeated in the Pentateuch again and again as a foundational perception of the meaning of Yahwism. With little alteration in wording we have those same two components repeated as rationale or motivation in Exod. 29:46; Lev. 11:45; 22:33; 25:38; 26:45; and Num. 15:41. "Relationship↔Deliverance" is also the paradigm, the pairing of reciprocally supportive divine actions, which frame the prophetic Oracle of Deliverance.

In either setting, Exodus or Exile, we see in this paradigm the pairing of *word* and *event,* God and history, *divine purpose* and *human destiny.* In either historical setting, Exodus or Exile, this is the twofold action which initiates a new era. With their direct and indirect promises of a new convenant Jeremiah and Ezekiel anticipate Second Isaiah's announcement that the deliverance from Exile actually constitutes a new Exodus, a second and new beginning to the relational and redemptive events of Moses' time. It is assumed in either context, Exodus or Exile, that *election needs attestation in deliverance,* and that *deliverance is explained by election.* The double arrows show that the movement in fact seems to begin with either event of divine initiative and goes from there to the other. In the Book of Exodus as in the prophetic Oracles of Deliverance it is virtually impossible to sort out which event is the presupposition or precedent for the other. From the outset they seem to have been understood to dovetail in a supportive way. Although the words of Exod. 20:2 do not not give us a literal prefiguring of the formal structure found in the prophetic Oracle of Deliverance, the situational parallel is sufficiently strong, and the conceptual pattern so distinctive, that we must be encouraged to see here one primary preprophetic resource employed to shape the word of deliverance for a time of exile.

d. The "P" Source in Exodus

The position toward which we have moved in the preceding section finds a surprising and strong support from the post-exilic source of Pentateuchal material known as the "Priestly Code." "P" has its own version of God's foundational promise of the Exodus deliverance. Exodus 6:2–8 shows resemblances to the themes which preceded God's promises in Exod. 3:7–8 and 3:16–17. But the actual promise of deliverance in 6:6–8 manifests some striking shifts from those earlier strata promises. In outline this is what we find. 1) "Say therefore" (6:6) is equivalent to the prophetic Messenger Formula, "Thus says the Lord." 2) "I am the Lord" (6:6) reminds us of the "recognition formulas" in Ezekiel and the self-predications in Second Isaiah. 3) "I will bring you out . . . I will deliver . . . I will redeem" (6:6) are the language of *"Deliverance,"* just what we would expect to find in component *D* of the prophetic Oracle of Deliverance if that genre were used in the context of the Exodus. 4) "I will take you for my people, and I will be your God" (6:7) is a variation of the Covenant Formula so often found as the strongest way of articulating the *"Relationship"* component (*R*) of the prophetic Oracle of Deliverance. 5) "I will bring you into the land" (6:8) is the same wording that we might find for the familiar prophetic promise that God will return Judah to its homeland—another aspect of the "Deliverance" component. Here that appears as a Patriarchal type covenant promise, updated and closely incorporated into promises given through Moses. 6) "I am the Lord" (6:8) comes at the very end; it is exactly the same wording that we noted under *2* above, repeated here for emphasis and symmetry.

When we looked at God's promises to the Patriarchs, and then again at God's promises to his people through Moses in Exodus 3, I said that I saw no indication of these being cast into a stylized or patterned form. Each appeared to be an *ad hoc* message shaped specifically for the situation to which it was addressed. That, by contrast, is *not* the case with Exod. 6:6&8. Both in structure and in content the speech which we examined in points *1* through *6* just above is one which we have seen many, many times in the prophetic books of the sixth century. It is the genre which we have called the "prophetic Oracle of Deliverance." We have learned to understand and recognize that speech-form by a comparative exegetical survey of relevant passages in Jeremiah and Ezekiel. Now here it unexpectedly, but unmistakably, appears as the way the Priestly Code chose to formulate God's promise through Moses that he would deliver the people of Israel from bondage in Egypt and take them "for a possession" (Exod. 6:8). It is used by "P" in classic and spare style, with all of the main elements we found in this genre in the prophetic books, and with no extraneous elements beyond those required to adapt it to the Exodus situation.[62] What is it doing here? What does it mean that "P" employed this genre at this precise point in the Exodus narrative? What does its presence tell us about the origin and setting of the prophetic Oracle of Deliverance?

Let me offer two alternative explanations at the onset. 1) In its original form this passage was much earlier than the post-exilic Priestly Code. From some earlier, quite possibly pre-prophetic, date it stood as an alternate way in which the foundational Exodus traditions formulated the promise of redemption from Pharaoh's slavery. In this case it could have had a direct linear and formative influence on the structure and content of the prophetic Oracle of Deliverance. 2) The passage dates to the early post-exilic era along with the rest of the Priestly Code. It is an appropriation of the prophetic Oracle of Deliverance genre and retrojection of it back into the Exodus situation as the appropriate and effective way to express an unexpected, unconditional divine intervention to deliver and initiate relationship between God and people. In the absence of any direct evidence to support alternative *1*, I think we must view alternative *2* as the more likely explanation. But in either case, we have evidence here that the Priestly Code saw the Exodus situation as a kind of natural home for the Oracle of Deliverance, and a context in which the employment of this genre to express God's initiatory promises to Israel through Moses made even more sense than the way JE had formulated those promises (JE meaning J and E considered together, or passages where J and E have so coalesced as to be indistinguishable). At least in a theological and situational sense, "P" saw Exodus as the historical setting for the prophetic Oracle of Deliverance.

It is furthermore important to note that Exod. 6:7 is the only appearance of the Covenant Formula in the whole series of promises running through Genesis and Exodus. Commenting on the appearance of this formula in Exod. 6:7 R. Smend states:

> The passage shows that the Covenant Formula has already grown quite inextricable with the Moses tradition. For, the full word sequence of the formula, as well as the very fact of its appearance in this passage, are anything but self-explanatory in the Priestly source. Otherwise, the Priestly source knows only half of the formula, and moreover does not admit any covenant sealing in the time of Moses. If it takes up the formula in spite of this, then it is obviously because the formula has become so much the essence of that which happened through the person of Moses, that it necessarily must appear in this context.[63]

To clarify the implications of Smend's remarks, we should point out that the full Covenant Formula appears seven times in Jeremiah (7:23; 11:4; 24:7; 30:22; 31:1, 33; 32:38—five times within Oracles of Deliverance), five times in Ezekiel (11:20; 14:11; 36:28; 37:23, 27—four times in Oracles of Deliverance), and only six additional times in the rest of the Old Testament beyond Exod. 6:7 (Lev. 26:12; Deut. 26:17–18; 29:13; 2 Sam. 7:24; 1 Chr. 17:22; Zech. 8:8). Through what Smend thinks of as the nearest attestation to its original setting, Deut. 26:17–18, it has strong covenantal associations.[64] But Smend recognizes that the negative construction of the formula in Hos. 1:9 (cf. Hos. 2:23) presupposes that the Covenant Formula already existed well before Deuteronomy.[65] He thinks it probably originated in the terminology of adoption or marriage formulas.[66] With this lineage, its employment in Hosea to depict rejection (1:9) and re-election (2:23), and the nine uses in Jeremiah's and Ezekiel's Oracles of Deliverance to express re-election, we should see that the Priestly Code's employment of it in Exod. 6:7 carries strong election-salvation associations. And this is what it seems to connote in the six instances in which the Priestly Code employs half of the Covenant Formula together with a remembrance of the deliverance from Egypt in Exod. 29:46; Lev. 11:45; 22:33; 25:38; 26:45; and Num. 15:41. And with those passages we come to a convergence between the JE credo of Exod. 20:2, the prophetic Oracles of Deliverance, and "P's" oracle in Exod. 6:6–8. Exod. 20:2 seems to have set such a strong conceptual model for the prophetic Oracles of Deliverance that the articulation of those beliefs in the later, but analogous situation of the Exile created the basic Deliverance↔Relationship structure of that speech-form.

The Priestly Code, in turn, *seems then to have looked back at the Exodus events through the more proximate pattern by which the sixth century prophets interpreted the need for God's deliverance and (re-) election in the Exile situation. We propose that the reason the Priestly Code worked a prophetic pattern of speech into Exod. 6:6–8 was that this source recognized that the situational and conceptual foundations of the Oracle of Deliverance were set in that context.* This then would also be seen in the Priestly Source's combining the abbreviated credo of Exod. 20:2 with the "I will be your God" half of the Covenant Formula in six passages running from Exod. 29:46 through Num. 15:41 (see above). In its reworking of tradition, as in combining an exilic prophetic pattern of speaking about deliverance and (re-) election with a JE perception of the meaning of those events in the Exodus context, the Priestly Code offers us some of the most significant evidence we have for discovering the roots of the prophetic Oracle of Deliverance.

e. Conclusion

We have risked taking the position that the prophetic Oracle of Deliverance does not have *a* setting. It does not stand in a cause and effect relationship to any Israelite institution as its logical product. We observe instead that there is no precedent for this historical situation to which the Oracle of Deliverance was directed. We are dealing then with a genre which is *sui generis* with the sixth or seventh century prophetic literature.

We conclude that there are limited but significant lines of influence between foundational promises in Genesis-Exodus and the prophetic Oracles of Deliverance. The innovativeness, scope, and theological significance of the divine initiative in the Exodus and Exile situations invite close and favorable comparison. Bearing the promise of a second new beginning, the prophetic Oracles of Deliverance both deny deterministic shaping from any earlier setting, and at the same time point back to the pivotal Exodus confessions of God's saving intervention as their strongest precedent.

EXCURSUS

Did the Oracle of Deliverance Develop out of the "Theophany" Genre?

Since so many of the foundational promises of salvation in Genesis and Exodus come in the midst of theophanies (Self-manifestations of God), we need to ask whether the genre "Oracle of Deliverance" is an offshoot or sub-species of the genre Theophany. The reader would profit by consulting J. K. Kuntz's excellent book, *The Self-Revelation of God,* which is a form-critical study of the Theophany genre. According to Kuntz a "typical" Theophany has the following components: 1) "Introductory description"—such as "and then the Lord appeared to . . ."; 2) "Divine self-asseveration"—"I am Yahweh, the God of Abraham . . ."; 3) "Quelling of human fear" —"fear not" is the repeated injunction; 4) "Assertions of gracious divine presence"—"I am with you"; 5) *Hieros logos,* meaning "holy word"—this is the specific message for the situation; 6) "Concluding description."[67] Obviously when the *hieros logos* is a promise of election and deliverance, the Theophany bears tremendously close resemblances to the prophetic Oracles of Deliverance. In that case one could take elements 2 through 5 above, and one would already have the familiar form and content of Second Isaiah's salvation oracles. That recognition further undercuts any need to explain Second Isaiah's salvation oracles by reference to a priestly oracle of favorable hearing to a cultic lament.[68] When Kuntz calls the *hieros logos "the very purpose of divine self-disclosure,"*[69] the dominant feature of Theophany, often comprising most of its extent,[70] the possibility is always close at hand that when the *hieros logos* is a word of grace and the other components are abbreviated, we are very close to an Oracle of Deliverance.

Having outlined the prospects for this line of influence, we need now to balance the situation by summarizing the problems. There is no intrinsic relation between a passage being in the genre Theophany and the issue of whether or not the *hieros logos* will be a promise of divine help and favor. Kuntz repeatedly says that the *hieros logos* is specifically shaped for the concrete historical situation to which God grants a theophanic disclosure.[71] The eighteen theophanies in Genesis have *hieroi logoi* of such widely varying contents that one can make no generalization about them. This impression is further borne out as we see the *hieroi logoi* of 1 Kgs. 19:15–18 and Isa. 6:8–12 consisting of commissioning words to a prophet together with God's promise of judgment on the people.[72] We can only conclude from this that it is primarily when a Theophany addresses a historical moment with a divine word of hope and the situations are comparable that it is similar to an Oracle of Deliverance. But there then would seem to be no intrinsic relation between the Theophany genre *as such* and the Oracle of Deliverance genre.

As we move from Jeremiah's to Ezekiel's and then Second Isaiah's Oracles of Deliverance, we do find that theophanic motifs become a more evident part of the *content* of this prophetic genre.[73] This is no doubt due to an intentional effort by these two prophets to strengthen their words of promise by creating links back to the great revelatory and salvation initiating acts of Israel's Patriarchal and Exodus periods. It is at this point, and through this process, that we see some convergence between the Theophany and the Oracle of Deliverance.[74] But here we are talking about Theophany being exploited as a way of strengthening the dramatic and decisive quality of God's Exile deliverance. It is thus *serving* the Oracle of Deliverance, rather than providing an unavoidable historical-linear and deterministic influence on this prophetic genre.

Chapter VII

THE CONTENT OF THE DELIVERANCE MESSAGE

If we did not have the actual words of at least six authentic deliverance speeches from Jeremiah and eleven from Ezekiel it would be impossible to suggest that they had ever expressed such beliefs. What logic is there in pursuing a retribution theology down to such depths of judgment that a theodicy is called forth only to follow that with a proclamation of God's breakthrough to a new era in which almost all the old necessities are left behind? By any reasonable institutional standard or norm of piety accepted by Jeremiah and Ezekiel during the time of their judgment preaching, the claims of their deliverance proclamations are simply *illogical!* And that is only part of the problem. As we have shown, these two prophets gave vent to a judgment preaching with implications radical beyond comparison. But what we have found is that they *followed* a radical judgment preaching with a deliverance proclamation so radical that it ruptures the mind to think about the sequence, let alone the combination, of these two seemingly diametrically opposite communications. Perhaps this situation is enough to explain why the problem has been glossed over so often in earlier treatments of these prophets.

We are calling attention, once more, to what is remarkable in the material we are studying. By a logic which is difficult to grasp, Jeremiah and Ezekiel combined in their sayings an uncompromising message of judgment and an unconditional message of deliverance. We are moving toward an understanding that in their view judgment and deliverance neither negate one another, nor contradict one another, nor provide in the case of the one the framework in which to understand the other, nor mollify the impact of the other in the time in which it is proclaimed. Yet, these two messages are combined by the integrity of God's justice, and by the incisive historical appropriateness of the different forms in which God expressed his will.

As preparation further to understand the intriguing relationship between deliverance and judgment, we need now to deal more comprehensively and systematically with the conceptual structure of the deliverance message. Most of the important theological motifs within the deliverance preaching have already been touched on in the preceding two chapters. We will not reiterate what we already have shown. I ask now whether there is a cohesive pattern or discernible configuration of themes within the deliverance message. For example, what does one have when motifs like "transformation of man," "forgiveness," "re-election," "new covenant" are brought together? What is the significance of the *sum* of them? How do they relate to one another? Only when we have seen this sum can we begin to understand the *level* on which these affirmations communicate.

We have suggested that the speech-genre which communicates the deliverance message is unprecedented, and *ad hoc* invention of the sixth century prophets. If that is true, then the contents of this genre cannot be evaluated adequately by norms from any of the ideational structures existing prior to this time. Are the rules by which God operates really changed? What are the decisive elements of continuity and discontinuity between the deliverance message and its antecedent judgment message? *We need to find out whether the deliverance messages of Jeremiah and Ezekiel introduce us into a new era.* What are the criteria for determining the beginning of a new era for God's plan within history? Should a term like "eschatology" be used to describe whatever is new in the deliverance messages of Jeremiah and Ezekiel, or can that content of faith be better discussed under other terms?

A. Transformation

Many deliverance oracles deal only with God's helping the people in regard to their outward condition. This is a fundamental and nearly universal part of the deliverance message. But we are offered a much richer insight into the theological meaning of deliverance in those oracles which move to a second level and depict the healing of God's people with regard to their inner condition. Such oracles are found predominantly in those six passages in Jeremiah and eleven in Ezekiel which were the focus for our inquiry about the transition from doom to salvation in Chapter V. The present chapter will focus on that significant, but limited, group of texts.

Three times in Jeremiah and three times in Ezekiel a promise that God is going to create a transformation within the nature of his people appears as what makes re-election possible. This transformation is an indication that salvation does not consist in a reinstitution of the old conditions, the old alternatives. *From creation until the end of the judgment preaching it was assumed that man is fully responsible for his own sin, and that natural man is wholly capable of the complete obedience which God requires. But in the era which deliverance inaugurates this is no longer assumed.* The shift is subtle, but far-reaching in its significance. Man is still evaluated by his actions in relation to the norm of the law. That in itself is a strong line of continuity, and it rebukes any overzealous Christian appropriation of these promises. Here, however, the man who is evaluated by the norm of the law is no longer natural man left to his own power and his own instincts toward goodness. In the depths of their judgment preaching, in some perceptions of man which we described under "Failure of the Repentance Episode" (Chapter II), Jeremiah and Ezekiel despaired that unaided or unimproved human nature could ever meet what God expected. And in neither case was this a momentary despondency. Rather, it was an ongoing, painfully sober realism about the possibilities and limits of the capacity for goodness within human nature.

Jer. 24:4–7

We are attracted here to the beginning of verse 7: "I will give them a heart to know that I am the Lord." In the Hebrew view, the heart (*lēb*) is the center of willing and acting; with A. Johnson "it is here that a man's real character finds its most ready expression."[1] Jeremiah uses this term, "heart," more often than any other prophet. It figures very prominently in his explanations of the causes of God's judgment: "this people has a stubborn and rebellious heart" (5:23); "the sin of Judah . . . is engraved on the tablet of their heart" (17:1); "your ways and your doings have brought this upon you. This is your doom and it is bitter, it has reached your very heart" (4:18). With a frequency for which many of us are unprepared, Jeremiah talks about the people's "evil hearts": 3:17; 7:24; 11:8; 18:12 (cf. also 4:14; 17:9; 22:17). This type of saying is a measure of how far Jeremiah has moved toward seeing Judah's problem as intrinsic, and not merely extrinsic. It is a radical understanding of sin, and it requires a radical conception of salvation.

What is said about transformation of the heart in 24:7 must be compared with similar "heart" sayings in 31:33; 32:40; Ezek. 11:19; 36:26. It is perhaps the earliest formulation in a development of unique deliverance sayings which grew in explicitness, power, and significance. Jeremiah picks up on a motif frequently used by Hosea: the people do not "know" Yahweh (Hos. 2:8; 4:1, 6; 5:4; 6:6; 11:3; cf. Jer. 4:22; 5:4, 5; 8:7; 9:3, 6). In effect this says that the people have little capacity for right religion. They must be given a heart for that. It fits a pattern in Jeremiah's judgment preaching that he would speak of the heart and of the importance of knowing God. And as deliverance oracles develop the "heart" sayings, this development comes to fit into a pattern. But are there earlier precedents for the idea of God transforming someone's heart? The weight of the evidence seems to be that this is a new hope, a new level of God's promised saving activity. There are many types of expression about the heart in the Old Testament, but this is the first time that God promises to transform the heart of his whole people as part of a new and unconditioned scheme of salvation.[2] It is easy to miss the full impact of what Jeremiah says God will do to the people's heart in 24:7; that becomes clearer in passages which build upon this initial statement of a new beginning in man's humanity.

As this passage is structured, the "heart to know" seems to be the prerequisite for re-election, because the Covenant Formula follows immediately. The saying "know that I am the Lord" is interpreted in part by the closing phrase of the oracle: "for they shall return to me with their whole heart." Thoroughgoing repentance is the prerequisite for re-election, but God's giving "them a heart to know" is the precondition for that kind of repentance. *Deliverance creates a transformation which produces the repentance expected of God's elect.* God delivers the people from Exile (24:5–6); he saves his people from a condition of alienation to a state of re-election (24:7). And, as if to underline the unconditional character of this salvation and the enduring difference it will make in the era about to be inaugurated, God also transforms the people so that they can readily meet his expectations.[3]

Jer. 31:31–34

The first part of this oracle deals with repeated promises of a new covenant. On what is this new covenant based: repentance, knowledge of God? No, it is based on an amazing new initiative which God takes, which rests on the same assumptions about the hopelessness of natural man as underlie God's initiative in 24:7. Here we find, "I will put my law within them, and I will write it upon their hearts" (31:33). The sense of this is closely equivalent to the "I will give them a heart to know that I am the Lord" of 24:7. Can we not say that each formulation helps explain the other? And, exactly as in 24:7, we go immediately from this transformation to the re-election promise of the Covenant Formula (final phrases of 31:33). There is obviously a movement toward that promise, but is it not clear in both passages that this promise would be meaningless or be misunderstood if it were to stand alone? To know God is to live obediently. When people are brought to that level, then re-election is possible. But God brings them to that level by himself. God creates both salvation and the preconditions for it, both repentance and the preconditions for it, both forgiveness and the preconditions for it, both a new election relationship and the preconditions for it.

The amazing thing in these passages is the tenacity of holding together both the salvation era sign-marks of election, forgiveness, deliverance, and the refusal to compromise away the necessity of moral preconditions, even if those moral preconditions are fulfilled by God as an arbitrary act of his divine prerogative. As we saw already in Chapter V, *the deliverance stands in a position of moral integrity with the judgment.* God's standards have not changed, and ultimately what he expects of his people has not changed. But the source of initiative and the divine strategy are so radically transposed that we sense that we have been brought to the beginning of a new era.

From the structuring of Jer. 31:31–34 it looks as though the following equivalents are set out:

$$\frac{\text{“put my law within them”}}{\text{“I will be their God . . .”}} = \frac{\text{“they shall all know me”}}{\text{“I will forgive their iniquity”}}$$

The sequence in each pairing shows the tenacity of the traditional idea that God responds with mercy to human goodness. But in the irrational logic of this salvation thinking, we see that the kind of act which recreates election goes a step further and creates the context in which a new election could have ongoing fruition and fidelity. Knowing God and obeying him are shown to be similar in meaning. Forgiveness is a healing back into relationship with God. We sense that there is a design here, with interlocking components. Never before has the Old Testament presented such a comprehensive structure of deliverance; never before has it dealt so profoundly with the inner condition of man; never before was deliverance articulated not merely as temporary relief, but as a full ongoing plan for the future.

Man's freedom, accountability, self-determination here at last take a back seat. At this point God will no longer wait on man. Man's freedom has cost God *his* freedom. Man's self-determination has brought things to a standstill. Just what can *follow* the kind of judgment which Jeremiah and Ezekiel preached? Only this can follow. That kind of judgment necessitates this kind of salvation. Human accountability is still present, and law is still the norm for ordering the relationship. But, the twin structures of *retribution* and the *conditionality* of God's alternate lines of action resting on a tension over what man will do *are utterly swept away and absent from this new era.* Retribution is past—irrevocably past. And it no longer matters what man does, *nothing* is any longer conditional on that. Anticipating Second Isaiah, God as Creator changes the situation (here an internal human condition), so that God the Redeemer can act fully, freely, and without thwarted intentions. Perhaps it is significant that A. Weiser and W. Rudolph each found it necessary to say that with this passage we have entered the sphere of eschatology.[4]

Jer. 32:37–41

The first thing we notice here is that the sequences are reversed from what we found in 31:31–34 and 24:4–7. In this passage God re-elects (Covenant Formula in 32:38), and then he promises, "I will give them one heart and one way, that they may fear me . . ." (32:39). A reprise of this thematic note comes in 32:40. First we see, "I will make with them an everlasting covenant," and then, "I will put the fear of me in their hearts, that they may not turn from me." Here it is quite clear what was only implicit earlier: the moral "prerequisites" are not literally prerequisites. God's intervention to deliver is the beginning of this chapter of history. That is true in terms of Judah's outward condition, but it is also true in each case with regard to its inner condition. Jer. 31:31–32 begins with the announcement of a new covenant, and 24:5 announces that God "will regard as good the exiles from Judah." The moral preconditions do not function in a temporal or a cause and effect sequence. In either of those senses their mention is artificial and unnecessary. If the future is all based on God's grace, why should sayings about the human heart or about fearing or knowing God be mentioned at all?

There are several answers to this question. 1) We still see here, as we saw in the remembrances of the judgment episode discussed in Chapter V, that in the early stages of deliverance preaching the prophets were making a transition into a new frame of reference. In a formal sense there continued to be moral requirements to be met before merciful and relational initiatives by God would make sense without his sacrificing some of the integrity of his righteousness. But the moral rigor of the Mosaic Covenant is not abandoned in this new deliverance preaching, even though its conditionality has been wholly superseded. 2) The promises which are contained in the Oracles of Deliverance are intended to apply to natural, historical man. This may seem like a contradiction to points made earlier. But we are not dealing with grace to save man for heaven. We are dealing with grace to bring about a sweepingly changed situation in which historical, mortal man can live in right relationship with God on earth. To get from the point where we left man at the depth of Jeremiah's and Ezekiel's judgment preaching to this new goal, nothing is more pivotal in importance than an act which transforms man from one level of moral and relational capacity to quite a different level. It will not do merely for God to elect Israel and try it all again one more time; and it is not even enough for God thoroughly to cleanse them in an act of forgiveness. God has to deal with their proven and enduring tendency toward *waywardness.* Perhaps in this respect, above all else, the deliverance is truly radical in what it undertakes.

Ezek. 11:17–21

The main points which we have made in relation to the three Jeremiah passages are hammered home for us by this early word of deliverance from Ezekiel. It seems to presuppose and build upon those Jeremiah oracles and make their promises even more explicit. Here, instead of a transformation we have a heart transplant and an added, empowering gift of God's spirit for good measure (11:19). In congruence with what we said above, God is not transforming his people into saints. No, what he removes is a "stony heart," and what he gives them is "a heart of flesh." Human nature is being perfected only within the dimensions of what was originally intended for man. In this case, unlike the Jeremiah passages, the purpose of the transformation of man is stated immediately after that act and immediately before the Covenant Formula (in the three Jeremiah passages the purpose is always given after transformation and Covenant Formula). The purpose of transformation gains in power here not only by its position but also because it makes explicit what was only implied in the Jeremiah passages: "that they may walk in my statutes and keep my ordinances and obey them" (11:20). It is probably difficult for Christians to become adjusted to the idea of an eschatological-like era in which the law plays an absolutely central role, but that is clearly what we have to deal with in this whole series of passages. The same law *by which* the people were judged becomes the law *to which* they are saved.

The paradigmatic positioning of the promise of transformation before the announcement of election, here as in Jer. 24:4–7 and 31:31–34, betrays a relationship anxiety. The people have not changed, they have not done anything to deserve re-election, they are not fit for re-election. Yet Judah is lost as long as the relationship with God is null. Re-election presents a difficulty for God. The problem cannot be glossed over. It would be cheap and inadequate—given the terms by which judgment was preached—to suggest that election somehow continues or that it merely needs the boost of a reaffirmation. No, a bold, unconditional new election must be stated firmly and without qualification. And it is. But it compromises God to elect a defiled people into relationship with him. Hence we have the repeated stress on forgiveness in these passages. It also compromises God to elect a people of proven waywardness. If he did, that act of election would be as isolated a moment of overflowing compassion as was sounded in Hos. 11:8–9. Again we see that transformation has an absolutely pivotal place in the whole drama of deliverance. Only by it is integrity with judgment preaching maintained, and only because of it can there be any long-range hope for the future.[5]

Ezek. 36:22–32

Although this passage offers what is probably the most complete synopsis of deliverance themes in either of the two prophets of the beginning of the Exile, the wording of the statement about transformation is almost identical to 11:19. Other elements are added earlier and later, but from the statement about deliverance in 36:24 to the Covenant Formula in 36:28, the sequence of promises is what we have come to see as paradigmatic. The single exception to this is that there is a very strong statement about forgiveness in the imagery of cultic cleansing in verse 25, just before the "new heart," "new spirit" transformation saying in verse 26. In our discussion of Jer. 31:31–34 above we found a parallelism between election and forgiveness. Here in Ezek. 36:25–28 we receive the impression that forgiveness and transformation are mutually supportive actions. Both clear the way for re-election to be announced in integrity and power. It may well be that transformation presupposes forgiveness, or that forgiveness includes a transformation.[6]

Ezek. 37:21–23

This is the first of our six focal transformation passages and the only one not to include a "heart" saying. Otherwise the sequence of themes is one with which we have become quite familiar: deliverance from external distress (37:21–22), transformation (37:23a), Covenant Formula (37:23b). This is an abbreviated oracle, and such elements as a statement of the purpose or consequence of transformation are notably omitted. The transformation itself is put in a form we have not seen before. It is stated very definitely that "they shall not defile themselves any more. . . ." Obedience and ritual purity are imposed on the people by God's decision. This is followed by a forgiveness-like saying, "but I will save them from all the backslidings in which they have sinned, and will cleanse them." This sounds as though God is going to save them from their history of sinfulness and the stain of it. The saying really straddles the line between transformation and forgiveness, combining elements of both. Since this takes place in the context of the resurrection of the people, I think that it cannot reasonably be doubted that we have another in a line of transformation sayings leading up to the promise of election.

Summary Perspective

What Jeremiah and Ezekiel have to say about the transformation of man in the era of deliverance is not exhausted by what they communicate in these six passages. We find pieces, or components, of the pattern we have examined in still other of their oracles.[7]

In their strongest expression, the transformation sayings are unique within the Old Testament—probably its most radical perspective on sin and salvation. Second Isaiah shifts the focus of God's primary activity more to a universal and revelational thrust. In Daniel, God's intervention is meta-historical and cosmological. These later sources change the framework of the classical Old Testament understanding of sin and salvation; the distinction of Jeremiah and Ezekiel is that they move as far as they do clearly inside that classical framework. Their perspective is de-escalated, de-radicalized, or domesticated somewhat in later psalm, narrative, wisdom, and priestly sources (even in the vision of a new temple and new capital in Ezek. 40–48). God's deliverance is never again such a fundamental and *interior* act of creative change, because the judgment is never again dealt with so existentially, corporately, and in terms of internal causes. But here, for the first time, in the passages we have surveyed, we meet the affirmation that God can accomplish his will as Deliverer, only because he innovates a change in the nature of things through his power as Creator. And all of this change is to take place *within* history.

B. Forgiveness

As Judaism and Christianity have developed since the time of the great prophets of Israel, forgiveness has come to occupy a prominent place in each of them. Sometimes it is taken as virtually synonymous with "salvation." From this understanding we need to move to appreciate and comprehend how the possibility of forgiveness stood before the time of the deliverance preaching of Jeremiah and Ezekiel. Only then will we be able to see their words about forgiveness in Oracles of Deliverance in right historical perspective; only then will we see that what they added was distinctive and a contribution to the later developments with which we are more familiar. Declarations of forgiveness are found in two Jeremiah oracles among the six which are our focus of attention: 31:34 and 33:8. Among the eleven most credibly authentic deliverance oracles in Ezekiel, forgiveness comes to expression, in one manner or another, in 20:40, 41, 44; 36:25, 29; 36:33; and 37:23.

1. Forgiveness in Oracles of Deliverance vis-à-vis Its Earlier Expression

In a previous study on forgiveness in the pre-exilic period I wrote: "Forgiveness is not a simple possibility, and in the Old Testament it frequently denotes less of a change in the sinner's status than we are inclined to expect."[8] Since that time K. Koch published an article in which he claimed as a basic thesis: "The divine forgiveness of sins plays no role in pre-exilic Israel."[9] Koch overstated his case, and there are serious problems in his article, but his suggestion could never have been made unless the trend of evidence lent some support to it. Several decades earlier, in what I consider to be one of the few valuable studies on forgiveness in any language, J. J. Stamm wrote: "Mitigation of punishment belongs to the essence of forgiveness."[10] More often than not lessening of punishment is the most that we find in the pre-exilic period.

What kind of textual evidence lies behind the claims made above and indicates the dimensions in which forgiveness functioned in the pre-exilic period? Five features deserve our special attention. These have their corresponding points in the deliverance oracles of Jeremiah and Ezekiel. The distinctiveness of the teachings of the latter and the dimensions of the shift can be brought out if we juxtapose the two lines of thought.

a. In the pre-exilic period the normal understanding was that punishment is mitigated rather than swept away. For example, in Num. 14:20, God says, "I have pardoned (*sālaḥ*), according to your word," but the verses following (14:21–23) describe the level of *punishment* which will be exacted. A frequent image for forgiveness is *nāsā' 'āwōn* (Exod. 34:7; Num. 14:18; Josh. 24:19; Pss. 85:2; 99:8; etc.) *Nāsā'* is a common word meaning "lift up, bear, carry." *'Āwōn* is one of the three important words for sin, but it can also mean the guilt or punishment for sin, as well as the act of sin. After an earlier study of the uses of this image (*nāsā' 'āwōn*), I came to the conclusion that it means to lift up the weight of guilt and punishment arising from sin. It is relief from guilt-punishment conceived as a heavy burden pressing down ominously before the guilt-punishment sequence had moved its customary and inexorable way toward death.[11] An illustration of this use of "bear up" (*nāsā'*) where *'āwōn* or an equivalent word for punishment is presupposed is found in Gen. 18:24, 26. We read God's decision: "If I find at Sodom fifty righteous in the city, I will *spare* the whole place for their sake." To spare is not the same as to forgive. Here and elsewhere the main idea is averting total destruction.

In the deliverance oracles of Jeremiah and Ezekiel one never finds forgiveness carried under the image of "bear up the guilt-punishment" (*nāsā' 'āwōn*). Forgiveness in the latter texts is comprehensive and complete. It is not just mitigation of punishment, but on a level that Christians would be tempted to call "pure grace." Here, as elsewhere, as Stamm has noted, forgiveness carries with it "an external attestation."[12] What are the external attestations? They are: deliverance out of Exile, election following rejection, new covenant after lapse of the old covenant, closer fellowship with God than ever before, transformation of human nature to meet God's expectations. *Forgiveness becomes an integral part of a whole new era of salvation.* If *these* are the attestations of the level on which *this* forgiveness operates, then we have to say that it is a revolutionary understanding of an act which no longer merely controls or cancels destructive forces. Rather, *it is an act which liberates creative power and makes new things possible.*

b. In the pre-exilic period a heavy cloud of uncertainty always hung around whether or not God would respond favorably to a heartfelt petition for forgiveness. In Exod. 32:30, 32

Moses makes a concerted effort to obtain forgiveness for the people; in 32:33 we learn that Yahweh denies his request. Jer. 14:7–10 shows the same type of thing. There again sincere intercession by a notable leader is answered by God's declining to forgive.

In the deliverance oracles of Jeremiah and Ezekiel, by contrast, there is absolutely no uncertainty about whether God will forgive in the new era. There is no restraint. God is not petitioned; he moves to forgive on his own initiative. What was once a *very* predictable indulgence has now become a firm and dramatic part of God's plan for the future.

c. In the pre-exilic period forgiveness is held in sharp tension with God's readiness to punish. If anything has claim to being a normative statement about forgiveness in the pre-exilic period, certainly it is Exod. 34:6–7 and its echoes. But that formulation combines into one statement the promise that God is very ready to forgive and very ready to punish. The significance of the passage and its influence are seen in the many texts which stand in some relationship of dependence with it, five of which retain the tension of these two poles (Exod. 20:5–6; Num. 14:18; Deut. 5:9–10; 7:9–10; Ps. 99:9).

Once we are really into the promise aspect of Jeremiah's and Ezekiel's Oracles of Deliverance, what they say about forgiveness is set free from the alternate tension, the movement toward punishment. At this point the people are no longer threatened with that alternative. This could be because with the onset of the Exile the threatened punishment of the judgment preaching had become a fact. With this line of reasoning, the punishment would begin to satisfy the requirements of God's justice. The people's accountability for earlier sins would change once the Exile, interpreted as punishment, taught them what they had done and itself had extracted from them some payment for transgressions. Thus the punishment alone would have created an entirely new situation for the possibility of forgiveness. I think that this may have been part of the historical-theological reality.

But we are not yet at the end of the Exile, at a time when Second Isaiah could say, "She has received from the Lord's hand double for all her sins" (40:2). Although we cannot document the time at which the switch from doom to salvation took place, I have the impression with Jeremiah and Ezekiel that it actually overlaps the latter part of the judgment preaching (as in Jer. 24: 4–7 and Ezek. 11:17–21), although, as we argued in Chapter V, it was applicable only for Judah in exile. The relative earliness and suddenness of the change continue to astonish me. And we may not do justice to this phenomenon unless we allow the possibility that God simply willed judgment for one era; then he willed salvation as the beginning of another era. In a theological sense, and in terms of God's communicataing his will to his people, judgment simply ran its course, did what it could do, said all it could say, came to a blind alley. And long before the people were overpunished, Jeremiah and Ezekiel commenced communicating a revolutionary shift in God's will and plan for his people in history. *This new era did not exist under the threat of punishment in the same way as had been the case in every generation since the days of Moses.*

d. In the pre-exilic period forgiveness is contingent upon repentance as a prerequisite. Some people consider it to be a biblical axiom that forgiveness "always" requires repentance.[13] Such a generalization can be made only if this is the case the majority of the time. Texts indicating that forgiveness is forthcoming only in response to genuine repentance include the following: Deut. 4:26–31; 30:1–10; 1 Kgs. 8:46–53; Jer. 26:3; Ezek. 18:21–22.

But the total absence of prerequisites for forgiveness in the deliverance era is shocking. We breathe here new air. Nothing prepares us for this. Repentance or its accompanying signs, if mentioned at all, is shown as the product and not the precondition of forgiveness (Ezek. 36:31; cf. Jer. 24:7; Isa. 44:22). As we saw with the transformation theme (pp. 175–84), the composite deliverance act creates its own preconditions and requisite moral corollaries.

e. In what is said about forgiveness in the pre-exilic period it seems as though the hope for forgiveness is more often denied the community Israel than it is granted. We dealt with this topic in

Jeremiah and Ezekiel in Chapter II. If we take the entire pre-exilic period, including Jeremiah's and Ezekiel's judgment preaching, the most important texts are: Exod. 23:21; Deut. 29:20; Josh. 24:19; Hos. 1:6; 8:13; Isa. 22:14; Jer. 4:8, 28; 5:1, 7; 6:20; 13:14; 14:10; 15:6; 16:13; 23:20; Ezek. 5:11; 7:4, 9; 8:18; 9:5, 10; 24:14. It will be seen from this that no sources deny the possibility of forgiveness more often than Jeremiah and Ezekiel. When this fact is taken in context it has three dimensions: 1) there is present in those denials a polemical corrective of a shallow optimism among the populace about the ease and certainty of divine mercy; 2) the depth of the judgment and its inevitability are thereby underlined; 3) in these denials Jeremiah and Ezekiel show not that they despise forgiveness, but that they value it very dearly. Therefore, I cannot think of any books in the Old Testament in which the sweeping promise of forgiveness would be more striking, powerful, and revolutionary than in these two.

We suggested several times in the preceding section on transformation that "the rules have been changed." That seems to be a good criterion for determining whether we are in a new (eschatological) era. When one moves from the earlier material into the deliverance preaching of Jeremiah and Ezekiel, many shifts have taken place with regard to the workings of forgiveness. These shifts are not singled out and announced to us or explained to us, but they are real nonetheless. How can this be? I think that it is not too much to say that this can be because a new "game" or dispensation has begun. From the position on forgiveness in the *earlier era* in points *a* through *e* above to the position shown in the *deliverance era*, we have moved under new procedures. God is operating under a new plan. A tremendous number of serious restrictions are suddenly lifted. We find ourselves in a new frame of reference for which we are not adequately prepared. The forgiveness is not explained or justified in terms of any previously existing revelation or institution established by God: not out of consideration for his covenant, or his temple and its cultus, or any personal qualities of God like *love* or *ḥęsęd* previously manifested.

As we found in the chapter on the deliverance speech-genre (Chapter VI), the absence of a "ground" or "basis" component in these oracles is at once upsetting and yet one of the most significant things about them theologically. The forgiveness, therefore, is purely an act of God's intervention, an exercise of his divine prerogative, an assertion of his freedom, a way he takes to get for himself and his people an open-ended future. *Forgiveness is taken out of the sphere of religion and becomes once again part of the mystery of God.* In religion people think they can formulate an understanding of the terms of God's action, the cause and effect relationships, the preconditions of divine favor. But here, as in Hos. 11:8–9, *God is merciful because he is God.* This cannot be institutionalized. The whole deliverance message compels the recognition that God is now recapturing his God-ness, that God is reestablishing his freedom. It says that *God can transcend retributional, historical, relational, and institutional necessities.* This point comes out more clearly, it seems, in the forgiveness part of the Oracles of Deliverance than through any other of its constituent motifs.

EXCURSUS

Imagery and Concepts Associated with Forgiveness in Deliverance Oracles

If the deficiency in the expression of corporate forgiveness before the deliverance message of Jeremiah and Ezekiel was its restricted and problematic character, the weakness of the post-exilic expression of forgiveness was in a tendency to schematize and institutionalize an all too lenient sense of the possibility of divine forbearance.

This understanding comes out in a series of texts—many of them used in covenant renewal ceremonies—in which the pole of Exod. 34:6–7 expressing God's readiness to punish is dropped. At least some of the distinctive parts of the stereotyped language of the formula in Exod. 34:6–7 are kept ("merciful and gracious," "slow to anger," "abounding in steadfast love and faithfulness"), so that we can identify the lineage of these sayings: Neh. 9:17; Pss. 78:38; 99:8; 103:8–10; 106:45; Joel 2:13; Jon. 4:2; Mic. 7:18–19. Without the kind of supportive context which we find in the prophetic deliverance passages, these seem to express only an abstracted generic truth of Israelite piety and superficial reading of the universal availability of forgiveness.

Another type of forgiveness saying from the post-exilic period which is used frequently and in a stereotyped way comes in a series of passages in Leviticus. With next to no variation in wording we find this statement of what proper cultic acts effect: "the priest shall make atonement (*kippẹr*) for him, and he shall be forgiven (*nislaḥ*)." See in Lev. 4:20, 26, 31, 35; 5:10, 13, 16, 18; 6:7; 19:22.[14]

By contrast, the six deliverance oracles in Jeremiah and Ezekiel which contain explicit expressions of forgiveness *never borrow the stylized language of the formula in Exod. 34:6–7 and never echo or anticipate the cultic formulation of Leviticus. In every case one has the impression that what one finds is an ad hoc formulation which is a distinctive saying for a unique moment in history.*

A few examples will suffice. When Ezekiel was given the words to offer hope to Judah in 37:21–23 he broke all the rules. He did not limit forgiveness according to any of the five patterns found in pre-exilic statements; he did not fall into any of the "easy grace" formulas of post-exilic religion; and he refuted in advance the view of modern scholars that forgiveness is "properly" expressed only in one or two vocables like *kippẹr* or *sālaḥ*.[15] The first image out of God's mouth is: "I will deliver them from all their backslidings." "Deliver," *yāša'*, is used only in this sense in Ezekiel. It normally means "to save someone from an external threat." Then Ezekiel uses a very specialized word for cultic expurgation, *tāhēr*, to carry the promise: "and I will purify them." These sayings follow immediately upon God's unconditional statement that the people will no longer be permitted to sin (37:23a), and they in turn are immediately followed by the formula of election which concludes the oracles (37:23c). This is a forgiveness that knows the depths of sin, that wants to separate God's people from the habit of defection. It knows that sin stains, and that sin estranges people from God. Ezekiel is creatively stretching language here. The very depiction of forgiveness embodies elements of the inner transformation of man about which we spoke earlier, and it depicts the alteration of a human situation so that it is possible for God to come into an intimate relationship with these people once again. Coming in the context of a death and resurrection of the people (37:1–14), this forgiveness seems to play an integral part in a turning toward a new future.[16]

A new set of images confronts us in Ezek. 20:40–44. The less difficult one, in verse 44, says, "You shall know that I am the Lord, when I deal with you for my name's sake, not according to your evil ways. . . ." When God *does* deal with them according to their evil ways it is punishment. To move from that entrenched pattern is to change the rules. This change, opposite to retribution and punishment, sounds like forgiveness. W. Eichrodt explicitly says that it comprises an act of pardon and further interprets its meaning: "His forgiveness is not weakness which overlooks or ignores the guilt of the breaking of the covenant, but a creative act reshaping his people out of the depth of his unalterable will for fellowship with his elect. . . ."[17] The more difficult image occurs in verses 40 and 41. I have not found a commentator who is willing to equate it with forgiveness but I think that the possibility is there. The more suggestive use of "accept" (*rāṣāh*) comes in 20:41: "As a pleasing odor I will accept you. . . ."[18] Ezekiel throws us off guard by using both archaic and cultic language here. W. Zimmerli admits that it is not clear how to interpret this phrase.[19] Lev. 1:4 speaks of God's accepting (*rāṣāh*) an animal sacrifice to make atonement for a sinner. In Amos 5:22 God says that he will not accept (*rāṣāh*) thier offerings. The context of not accepting sacrifices in Hos. 8:13 makes it clear that forgiveness is thereby denied. In Jer. 14:10 the object of the verb *rāṣāh* is the people: "The Lord does not accept them, now he will remember their iniquity and punish their sins." Not "accepting" the people in that passage obviously means not forgiving them. Only Ezekiel uses *rāṣāh* as a positive act of God with Judah as the direct object of the verb (pronoun is second person plural). It is already clear that "accept" (*rāṣāh*) means to take a favorable attitude toward someone or something. In Isa. 42:1 and Ps. 147:11 it further suggests the idea of the Lord *relating* to those whom he regards favorably. The association with Ezek. 20:44 and the place of this saying in the oracle as a whole lead me to suggest that 20:41 is an extraordinary image in which the ideas of forgiveness and election are combined under one turn of speech.

We turn now to two passages in Jeremiah. The promise in 33:6–9 has three images for forgiveness: "heal" (*rāpā'*) in verse 6, "cleanse" (*tāhēr*) and "forgive" (*sālaḥ*) in verse 8. Their combination makes forgiveness the dominant emphasis of this oracle. We have not encountered "heal" (*rāpā'*) before. It is used in poetic parallelism with "forgive" (*sālaḥ*) in Ps. 103:3, so that its metaphorical application as a term for pardon cannot be doubted. Compare its earlier use in a repentance summons in Jer. 3:22: "I will heal your faithlessness," and in 30:17. One should notice that verse 6 of chapter 33 follows the saying in 33:5: "I have hidden my face from this city because of all their wickedness." Under our study of "rejection" in Chapter III we found God's hiding his face to be an integral part of the cutting off of the relationship. The way the passage is put together requires a twofold healing: 1) healing from dispersion, weakness, brokenness as a socio-religious community (33:6b and 7); 2) healing from the stain of that which causes God to turn his face from them. This defilement is also directly attached to the cultic image, *ṭāhēr* ("cleanse"), which we saw used in Ezekiel. Here it is used for the first time directly with the "proper" word for forgiveness, *sālaḥ*. The healing, cleansing, and forgiving taken together embrace some sense of transformation, so that God is now free to pour out his favor on Judah and Jerusalem. It is interesting that both Rudolph[20] and Weiser[21] see these words of mercy building upon what they consider to be the more definitive promise of forgiveness in Jer. 31:34.

The distinction of the oracle in Jer. 31:31–34 is not in the unusual imagery for forgiveness—the common and "proper" technical term for forgiveness, *sālaḥ*, is employed in 31:34—but in its association with other key elements in the deliverance event which are stated with unusual power and simplicity. As compared with the sixteen other oracles which are the central concern of this chapter, 31:31–34 is unique in its repeated emphases in the opening two verses that God is going to give a "new covenant." The forgiveness saying does not come in the middle of the oracle along with transformation as a preparation for election; instead, forgiveness comes at the end. New covenant and forgiveness are what frame this deliverance promise. The recognition of this forces us to ask: What has forgiveness to do with covenant? Is forgiveness part of the new covenant in a way unlike the case in the old? We need to distinguish between the mere statement that forgiveness is a part of covenant renewal, and a precise delineation of the kind of forgiveness found here in association with a new covenant. This need is underlined by the fact that most commentators find it impossible to speak about 31:31–34 without using the word "eschatology" to describe the level of God's action here.[22] Rudolph, who is not given to hyperbole, says that forgiveness is the climax of the whole oracle, the pivot to a new era:

> And for a sure sign that the old condition is finally removed, the disobedience on the people's side, the wrath on God's side, Yahweh forgives their sin (34b). This word stands at the conclusion not as a chance addition, but as the operative basis of the whole promise: under all that is prevailing hitherto, a line is drawn, a new life with God commences.[23]

Weiser has a similar comment: "The history of salvation in the past and the future rests on God's willingness to forgive sins as the fundamental part of God's covenant."[24] From this time on forgiveness does take on a more explicit and important position in the way God's people understood the covenant, probably in no small part under the impact of this passage.

One thing we learn from this excursus is that the prophets resisted attempts to regularize the understanding of forgiveness exemplified in later times, as much as they broke open restrictions in the understanding of forgiveness from earlier periods. Unless we see this we lose the prophetic insight that *what is theologically true changes as historical circumstances change. The word of God is always a particular word, and it is addressed to a particular event. Forgiveness happens when God in his sovereign prerogative wills for it to happen, not in relation to human religious institutions and not in general perceptions of how God operates. Forgiveness takes place as a very special event as one part of a decisive turning point in history.* The prophets expressed these beliefs in very innovative images for forgiveness, and in powerful constellations of interrelated components in God's redemptive action.

C. Relationship

To be among the exiles in Babylon, knowing that the Davidic line was cut off, knowing that the temple was defiled and dismantled, knowing that prophets had said through divine oracles that just such a calamity was the final curse for violating the Mosaic Covenant, seeing apparent evidence of the abrogation of that covenant, of God's rejection of his elect: this is the situation with which we need to empathize in order to feel the main thrust of the Oracles of Deliverance. The central message is: God turns his face toward his people, he comes to them, he accepts them, he creates the basis for a new future in the interaction between Lord and people, he brings them home. Perhaps that central message sounds as if it has separable parts. Actually, it does not. There is no suggestion of God's electing and covenanting with his people while they are left to languish indefinitely in Babylon. No. "Deliverance" brings the people out of the situation of punishment and into that homeland, where, and only where, it is possible to think about a new future in the God-people relationship. Deliverance is the dramatic and necessary attestation that God has turned toward his people and wills a new life for them and with them. Although God's initiatives in *transformation* and *forgiveness* offer us particularly valuable insights into the thoroughness and intended far-reaching consequences of God's revolutionary alteration in his historical mode of operation with Israel, neither stands alone. If there is any focus in all this, I think it has to do with the God-people *relationship.* Deliverance to the homeland sets the stage, as regards essential externals, for a new try at *relationship.* Transformation of the heart prepares for a new kind of *relationship.* Forgiveness breaks the stalemate of the past, cleanses toward a new being in the present, and opens the door to the future. But forgiveness, transformation of the heart, and deliverance are not justified if God and his people are to have in the future only that quality of relationship which they had in the past. That was a relationship leading to death, and Ezekiel 37 couches deliverance in the imagery of resurrection. Relationship is theologically central to the era of deliverance because only a new quality of relationship between God and Israel will justify all the other components of initiative in the comprehensive plan of salvation.

Because of the centrality of the relationship concern it has been impossible to avoid anticipating it. It would seem that *by definition* we have made the God-people relationship central to this part of the prophets' message; that has come about only because everything returns us to this point. Some of the primary questions remaining for us are: Are we dealing at a level at which it makes sense to say that election/covenant are renewed or reaffirmed, or are we talking about something essentially new after a time of discontinuity? How do the statements of election and covenant relate to one another, and to other themes within the deliverance message? What about the suggestion of those who say that Judah was judged under the Mosaic Covenant rationale, but saved under the rationale of the Abrahamic or Davidic Covenant?

1. Election

What our focal six oracles in Jeremiah and eleven in Ezekiel have to say about relationship within the context of the deliverance message is not primarily given expression through explicit reference to a "new" or "everlasting" covenant (*b^erît*). That term is only found twice in Jeremiah's oracles (31:31–34; 32:38–40) and twice in Ezekiel's (34:25–31; 37:24–28). Nor do we find here the situation of Second Isaiah in which the time of rejection is announced as ended (49:14–15; 54:4–8), or the people are told that they have been elected (using the maximum term *bāḥar*) as in Isa. 41:8, 9; 43:20; 44:1, 2; 49:7.[25] If we are correct in insisting that Jeremiah and Ezekiel speak to a relationship anxiety, then they accomplish that primarily through the so-called *Bundesformel* (Covenant Formula: "I will be your God and you will be my people") found in Jer. 24:7; 31:33; 32:38 and Ezek. 11:20; 34:30; 36:28; 37:23, 27 (compare adaptations of this formula and abbreviations of it in Ezek. 34:24; 37:12–13). When "covenant" does appear in their deliverance oracles it is always in passages where the *Bundesformel* is present, as though it were an addition to that more basic and widely attested assurance.

It therefore now must be asked: Precisely what does the *Bundesformel* mean when it is used in Jeremiah's and Ezekiel's Oracles of Deliverance? Surprisingly enough, there has been rather little reflection on that question by commentators on Jeremiah and Ezekiel, or by Rudolf Smend who coined the term *Bundesformel.* Smend gave longer ("they shall be my people, and I will be their God") and shorter ("Yahweh, the God of Israel . . . Israel, the people of Yahweh") attestations of this construction the title "Covenant Formula" or *Bundesformel* for several reasons. a) It designates what he sees as a more or less abbreviated way of expressing a two-sided relationship of the two covenant partners.[26] b) It appears several times directly with the term *b^erît* standing for covenant (Lev. 26:45; Deut. 29:12–13; Jer. 11:3–4); three additional times in promises for the future: Jer. 31:33, Ezek. 34:24–25; 37:26–27.[27] c) Smend thinks that we are closest to the possible original *Sitz im Leben* (setting) of the formula in the covenantal text of Deut. 26:17–18, which may be related to the covenant renewal occasion of 2 Kgs. 11:17.[28]

I would like to mention a number of difficulties with this theory: 1) It is not a careful or accurate use of the covenant concept to assume that, every time a two-sided relationship between God and his people is present, there is specifically a *covenantal* understanding of that relationship. While Smend has clearly called attention to a very significant formula of relationship, it is perhaps too specific and limiting to entitle it a "*covenant*-formula." 2) In connection with that fact, one needs to delineate between what happens in the process of formal covenant-sealing, then in covenant-renewal, and in whatever kind of affirmation is being made when the *Bundesformel* is expressed in prophetic Oracles of Deliverance. 3) It is far from self-evident that Deut. 26:17–18 is the "normative" or "original" setting for this formula, or that such a suggested setting continues to inform the content of the *Bundesformel* when it appears as a divine promise in Oracles of Deliverance.

I have found it increasingly natural to speak of the *Bundesformel* as communicating re-election and have used this as its apparent meaning in discussing "transformation" and "forgiveness" earlier in this chapter. I am not alone in finding meanings for the *Bundesformel* other than those contained under its title.[92] In his exegesis of Jer. 31:33, Weiser speaks of "the election of the people of God through Yahweh in the new covenant coming to expression in the *Bundesformel*."[30] In its position within 31:31–34, relationship with God seemingly is being *offered* or *promised* rather than being contracted or structured; thus the *Bundesformel* seems to function in relation to covenant as an election. I have also been struck by the interpretation which G. Fohrer gives to the *Bundesformel* in the middle of what is probably Ezekiel's most important Oracle of Deliverance, 36:28:

> But in contrast to the earlier time, there now even more materializes the true and genuine relationship between Yahweh and Israel, God and man: my people—your God! For Ezekiel there lies in this repeatedly employed expression (11:20, 34:30, 37:23, 27) more than the Bundesformel has originally intended. It is parallel to the turn of speech of Jeremiah of the new covenant (Jer. 31:31–34) and points to the closest and most

> far-reaching relationship between God and man. It purports the communion between God and the man newly created in his inner life, as the inner goal and result of the redemption.[31]

Fohrer seems to be saying that the *Bundesformel* in such a context is communicating the most inward, personal dimension of a covenant relationship, not the structured, institutional, formal part of a covenant arrangement. This is what I would think of as the "I-Thou" goal of election or any profoundly personal and spiritual God-man relationship. Something really transcendent and ideal along these lines seems to be what T. C. Vriezen has in mind when he says that the "basic content of eschatology is the prophetic word of God that Jeremiah as well as Ezekiel impress upon their people in their greatest distress: 'Ye shall be my people, and I will be your God'!"[32]

The full *Bundesformel* had much of its development in prophetic deliverance oracles. There it would fit the context for the formula to announce a new election, or to promise the accomplishment of that perfect communion between God and man which was always the ultimate goal of the inward part of covenant. There are only five out of nineteen occurrences of the full formula that could be earlier than the prophetic deliverance passages, and they are all in Deuteronomic or Deuteronomistic sources: Deut. 26:17–18; 29:13; 2 Sam. 7:24; and Jer. 7:23; 11:4.[33] An interesting feature which Smend apparently overlooked is that these uses of the *Bundesformel* come within three different covenant traditions: Deut. 26:17–18 is Mosaic; Deut. 29:13 is Patriarchal; and 2 Sam. 7:24 is Davidic. Since only the Mosaic Covenant is conditional, with laws and with specific contractual terms of initial or renewed entrance into its obligations and privileges, even the "D" sources do not permit a constriction of the meaning of the *Bundesformel* to the Mosaic framework. We must ask instead: what is the common thread between the Mosaic, Patriarchal, and Davidic covenants that would help us understand how the *Bundesformel* could be used in each of these contexts? The *Bundesformel* cannot be concerned with the *terms* of covenant; more likely it has to do with the presupposition of covenant (election) or the goal of covenant (communion with God).

An alternate *Sitz im Leben* to the one R. Smend suggests, Deut. 26:17–18, which has the possibility of being both earlier and of more direct influence on the use of this formula in Jeremiah's and Ezekiel's deliverance oracles, is found in the paired sayings in Hos. 1:9 and 2:23. The first of these announces rejection in the language of divorce: "Call his name Not my people, for you are not my people and I am not your God" (compare the language in 2:2). The second declares a new election in the language of remarriage: "I will say to Not my people, 'You are my people'; and he shall say, 'Thou art my God.'" Interestingly, Smend admits that the *Bundesformel* may copy the style of adoption formulas or marriage formulas.[34] The suggestion, and the evidence we see in Hosea, certainly finds a correspondence with what we have already learned about the emphasis on the *personal* dimension of God-people relationship as the *Bundesformel* is used in Oracles of Deliverance.

Since Jer. 31:31–34 begins with the promise of a new covenant, we know that the *Bundesformel* in verse 33 cannot deal with reaffirming the terms of the old covenant. And, framed before and after with words about transformation and forgiveness, it can hardly be an affirmation of the sure continuity of an election made at Sinai. Yet it builds upon the hope that the events of Exodus and Sinai brought to life. I think that the *Bundesformel* in such an oracle as this expresses election but is more; through a history of associations it connotes the inward, personal side of what is possible in a covenant relationship; yet it moves beyond election and covenant as they have been known in the past toward the fulfillment of what God can be for Israel and what Israel can be for God. It answers, but goes beyond answering, a relationship anxiety. The Israel of the future is not the Israel of the past. It is freed from its sin and changed in order to relate to its God in a new way. In such an atmosphere there can be a new covenant; certainly the old one will not do. There can be an everlasting covenant (Jer. 32:40; Ezek. 37:26). Such references as to how the relationship may be structured are helpful, but they are not necessary. The promise of Israel's future with God is complete in the assurance that the relationship *will be newly created from the inside outward.* The people will be changed internally, so that God can be wed with them (Jer. 24:7; Ezek. 11:19–20; 36:26–28; 37:23). It sounds like a very simple, basic hope. Only now it is mandated as a divine promise: "they will *really* be my people, and I will *really* be their God." In the fulfillment of this ancient longing, we approach the realization of the kingdom of God within history.

2. Covenant

The promise of a deep personal relationship contained in the *Bundesformel* carried as its corollary, in a limited number of passages, a word about the overall structure and historical plan for implementing this relationship. By this "word" I understand a reference to a *b^e^rît* or covenant. Of the four references to covenant within deliverance oracles, the one which has attracted by far the most attention is the "new covenant" passage in Jer. 31:31–34. How new is this "new covenant"? H. Ortmann says it is not very new at all; he sees this only as a proclamation of the renewal of the old covenant.[35] Most scholars see it quite otherwise. B. Anderson says, "He speaks of a new covenant, not a covenant renewal, and thereby assumes a radical break with the Mosaic tradition."[36] G. von Rad declares: ". . . the old covenant is broken, and in Jeremiah's view Israel is altogether without one. What is all important is that there is no attempt here —as there was, for example, in Deuteronomy—to reestablish Israel on old bases. The new covenant is entirely new. . . ."[37] Other scholars could be cited who have equally strong views on the newness of this covenant.[38]

A second challenge to the originality of this covenant comes from a few scholars who say that the problem created by the collapse of the Mosaic Covenant at the onset of the Exile is solved, in broad perspective, by a shift toward the unconditional, promissory covenant which God made with David, or by a synthesis of the Mosaic Covenant with this other tradition of unconditional, ongoing covenant.[39] This position is countered by those who insist of 31:31–34 ". . . the oracle stands in the northern Mosaic Covenant tradition, not in the southern tradition of royal covenant theology,"[40] or who make the same point in other words.[41]

These issues highlight for us what should be a primary concern: In just what ways is the covenant of Jer. 31:31–34 "old," and in what particulars is it "new"? It is old in that: 1) it is unilaterally initiated by God; 2) it requires of the people "knowledge" of God (31:34); 3) it carries "law" (*tôrāh*) as its central structuring norm (31:33); 4) it is made with "the house of Israel and the house of Judah" (31:31). To this extent it is clear that even though it is "not like the covenant which I made with their fathers when I took them by the hand to bring them out of the land of Egypt" (31:32) it remains a new covenant *within* the Sinaitic tradition.

In what ways is it new? 1) It will contain full and free forgiveness such as was never known under any of the pre-exilic covenant traditions. Many commentators see this as the single most distinctive feature of this new covenant.[42] 2) There is an employment of the *Bundesformel* in the same sense found in other deliverance oracles which look toward the fulfillment of the optimum possibilities in the inner relation between God and man. 3) The people are creatively transformed into a new humanity; accordingly, a new level of obedience and knowledge of God is required of them and made possible for them. 4) This covenant is therefore inviolable. 5) It *combines* an unprecedented grace with traditional law. 6) It is based on a new act of divine deliverance, a new intervention of God into the course of international events. 7) Contrary to the view of those who say that such new content as one finds obtains for itself no new form,[43] this covenant is promised in a distinctively new speech-genre which is quite unlike the covenant structures found in places like Exodus 20 and Joshua 24. 8) Not least of all, this covenant is new because God calls it "new." Many scholars regard the concept of a "new covenant" as the virtual touchstone of a national eschatology.[44]

What I see in Jer. 31:31–34 is a change in the balance between human initiative and responsibility under a covenant structure and divine initiative and responsibility. I see a shift in the balance between the conditionality of covenant and its eternality. Clearly this kind of covenant gives evidence of God's having modified or changed the rules. For God it announces a new mode of action, a new plan of operation, a different structure or dispensation by which God can succeed in fulfilling his purposes in the period of history newly opening.

As we turn to related passages we ask: To what extent are the things we have found in Jer. 31:31–34 normative for Oracles of Deliverance generally? In other words, is the "new covenant" idea normative for deliverance oracles with similar constituent elements, even if there is no explicit reference to a "new" covenant? The first text that requires us to deal with these questions occurs a chapter later in Jeremiah. Some scholars think that it is just a pale echo of 31:31–34, totally dependent upon it.[45] Is this oracle, 32:36–47, independent enough of 31:31–34 to provide fresh evidence for what was found there? Instead of "new" covenant this passage promises an "everlasting" covenant (32:40). Are those equivalent in meaning?

The suggestion that an editor wrote 32:36–41 with 31:31–34 before him as a prototype has been overworked.[46] In some ways the oracle of 32:36–41 is closer to 24:4–7 and 29:10–14 than to 31:31–34. It has a twofold "land" promise (vv. 37 and 41); these are totally lacking in 31:31–34 (but cf. 24:6; 29:10, 14). And it has a twofold declaration of God's intent and decision to do "good" to them (cf. 24:5 and 29:11), also with no analogous promise in 31:31–34. Von Rad's interpretation of the relation of the two passages is instructive:

> We can be certain that Jer. 32:37ff is not simply a copy or twin of Jer. 31:31ff. The phraseology of the second passage is too distinctive, and the distinctions occur at the central points of the argument. The best explanation is therefore that Jeremiah spoke of the new covenant on two different occasions, both times in a different way, and that each of the passages as we now have them has been subsequently worked over.[47]

We conclude that 32:36–41 is as independent and basic a statement of Jeremiah's deliverance proclamation as is 31:31–34.

Here we find the first use of *b^e^rît 'olām* ("everlasting covenant") in the Old Testament. The idea of a covenant in perpetuity existed already in the Davidic Covenant tradition (see 2 Sam. 7:16, 24), from which R. Clements sees it borrowed by the post-exilic "Priestly" source to give the covenant with Abraham the quality of perpetuity (Gen. 17:7).[48] In contradistinction to these models, it must be seen that Jer. 32:40 promises the *beginning* of an "everlasting covenant" and not the perpetuation of an unconditional covenant along Abrahamic or Davidic lines. It is all too clear from the explicit reference to severe judgment and exile (32:37), new election (32:38), transformation of the people so that they will "fear" God and "not turn" from him (32:39–41), that we are here within the Mosaic and Sinai Covenant tradition. An everlasting covenant in that tradition is unprecedented; this is the covenant of law, the covenant of conditionality, the covenant of jeopardy. It is the covenant that ended with the "Rejection" episode.

An everlasting Sinai Covenant is ipso facto a *new* covenant. In the hyperbolic and poetic language of deliverance, problems become overcorrected. A wayward people get a new heart and spirit; a semi-arid land becomes an oasis; and a defunct relationship becomes an "eternal covenant." This is not a "one shot" statement about covenant. It is picked up with affirmations of *b^e^rît 'olām* later in Jeremiah (50:5), twice in Ezekiel (16:60; 37:26), twice in Second Isaiah (55:3; 61:8).[49] The Torah covenant that begins with prophetic deliverance preaching is thus more normatively called an "everlasting" covenant than a "new" covenant. Why this emphasis? It seems to me to arise out of the depths of Judah's relationship anxiety. Re-election and "new" covenant heal the relationship breach, but only an "everlasting" covenant speaks to deep psychological anxieties that had arisen over Judah's life, identity, and purpose being rooted in its relationship with God at the time of rejection and Exile. At the same time since an everlasting covenant founded on unconditional forgiveness, structured around law, and made possible by the transformation of human nature is wholly without precedent, every important implication of the "new covenant" contained in

Jer. 31:31–34 is subsumed under the promise of an "everlasting covenant."

The particular context in which "everlasting covenant" is promised in Jer. 32:40 places this as an example of God's "doing good to them." One has the flavor here of God's dedicating himself to a new pattern or mode of action. I think that one could argue that *it promises a new dispensation more than a new institution.* The verbal idea predominates. God is going to relate to Israel in a new way. The relationship is closely tied to his transformation initiatives which are perhaps the most decisive elements in the shift to a new era. God shifts gears, tries new things. As the dispensation changes we see that the definitive events creating for God an open-ended future are to be part of an ongoing process. The "everlasting covenant" is simply a label to help mankind understand this new quality of action.

To what extent does what we have found about "new covenant" in Jer. 31:31–34 and "everlasting covenant" in Jer. 32:36–41 carry over and find expression in Ezekiel? Both W. Eichrodt[50] and G. von Rad[51] feel that the notion of a new covenant is present by implication in Ezekiel's great promise contained in 36:22–32. Von Rad even suggests that Jer. 31:31ff. and 32:37ff. were used in a rather literal way as the prototypes of that great speech.[52] Apparently it is the combination of the use of the *Bundesformel* with elements like promise of transformation, internalization of the law, and God's forgiveness which leads to the conclusion that in everything but literal word we find the new covenant there once again (so also to a slightly lesser extent with Ezek. 11:16–21).

While I agree with this suggestion, it seems odd that apparently no commentator has raised the issue of parallelism between Ezek. 37:26 and Jer. 32:40 where we find the identical formulation: *kāratî lāhẹm . . . bᵉrît ʻôlām,* "I will make for them . . . an everlasting covenant." Leading commentators like G. Fohrer[53] and W. Zimmerli[54] even fail to raise the issue of a possible continuation here of the thought in Jer. 31:31ff., and 32:36–41. It must, however, be recognized that Ezek. 37:24–28 is a striking passage even within the uniquely creative imagery of Ezekiel. We see here a tremendous synthesis of tradition lines: a) 37:24a ("My servant David . . .") rests on Davidic promises; b) 37:24b ("They shall follow my ordinances and . . . statutes . . .") is out of the Exodus circle; c) 37:25a ("They shall dwell in the land . . . that I gave to my servant Jacob") is based on promises to the Patriarchs; d) 37:25b is Davidic; e) 37:26a ("covenant of peace . . . everlasting covenant") the tradition line is to be determined; f) 37:26b–27a ("I will set my sanctuary in the midst of them . . .") relates to the election of Zion; g) 37:27b, *Bundesformel* is out of the Exodus tradition; h) 37:28 ("when my sanctuary is in the midst of them . . .") again derives from the Zion circle. Certainly this oracle comes forth like a veritable fugue of election tradition motifs.[55]

One also finds an accent on the Davidic tradition along with the promise of a *b^e^rît šālôm* ("covenant of peace") in Ezek. 34:23ff. In the midst of this richness of allusion, von Rad yet finds the dominant emphasis in Ezek. 37:24ff. and 34:23ff. to be the Exodus Covenant tradition. To this end he comments on the placement of the *Bundesformel* in each of these passages and then says: "Ezekiel fuses the Sinai tradition and the David tradition. . . . But the Sinai tradition dominates his thought—under the new David, Israel will obey the commandments (Ezek. 37:24)."[56] Eichrodt emphasizes the *newness* which he sees in mention of the covenant both in Ezek. 37:26 and in Ezek. 34:25 by translating *b^e^rît šālôm* a "covenant of salvation" in each case.[57] The suggestion may be that, if we understand the context, we will see that the whole emphasis is on what can come in the future, rather than on links to what has happened in the past.

These lines of evidence suggest that we should not read the oracles in Ezek. 34:25–31 and 37:24–28 in isolation from oracles like 36:22–32 or 11:16–21. The oracles containing covenant sayings are not exceptional within Ezekiel's deliverance message. There is a consistency of pattern here including recurrent emphasis on promise of transformed human nature (11:19; 36:25–27, 33; 37:11, *23*), the centrality of God's law (11:20; 36:23; *37:24*), and perhaps most important of all the promise of a new election-relationship through the *Bundesformel*

(11:20; *34:24* modified, *30*; 36:28; 37:23, *27*). What was said about "transformation," "forgiveness," and "election" in the earlier parts of the present chapter provides the conceptual background for reading and understanding Ezek. 34:25–31 and 37:24–28. To put it another way, those two oracles stand in integrity with Jer. 31:31–34 and 32:36–41. The source and pattern of Ezekiel's hope for deliverance are the same as Jeremiah's. But onto the dramatic, painstakingly thorough revolution announced in the other authentic oracles in Jeremiah and parts of Ezekiel, Ezek. 34:25–31 and 37:24–28 *add* the extra and enriching components of Davidic Covenant hopes. In this way the promise for the future is broadened. In this way Ezekiel moves beyond Jeremiah and closer to Second Isaiah in pulling upon various covenant tradition lines, as he sees a convergence of Israel's and Judah's election traditions in the acts of God which open toward a new era in the future.

D. Eschatology

1. Orientation to the Issue

I believe that the distinctive emphases which we have been discussing thus far in this chapter come into a pattern which is best designated as eschatology.[58] What we find inside of the Oracle of Deliverance is not explicable in terms of the logic or the terms of the Sinai Covenant. It is not understandable in terms of any of the election traditions, institutions, or frameworks of interpretation known to Israel's religion prior to 587. What the Oracles of Deliverance foretell signifies a break between everything which has happened and that which is about to happen. And yet what God is going to bring to pass will occur within the context of this world, in history and not in heaven: and it will be created within the foundational structure of Israelite religion. Clearly what those oracles promise is not the end of the world; we have here no apocalyptic. Not apocalyptic, but not covenantal; not alien, but wholly unprecedented: how is one to conceptualize such a development? We do best to follow the lead of those scholars who take a term of much later origin, "eschatology," and introduce it here to delineate a pattern of belief which needs to be appreciated and seen clearly in its vigor and uniqueness.

By any definition "eschatology" consists in a particular kind of theology of history. Since Israel's faith dealt with *history* as the primary category to be interpreted (rather than with God's nature, or man's psyche), we need to be as precise as possible about distinctions and developments in Israel's theological statements about history. Just as I have argued that a "covenant theology" model of history was the predominant frame of reference during Jeremiah's and Ezekiel's judgment message, I want to urge that an eschatological model of interpreting God's activity in history superseded covenant theology throughout their salvation preaching. If we do not recognize this distinction, the mistake will be perpetuated that deliverance preaching operated within the logic of the covenant theology, or had to adopt a rationale from the cult for making grace convincing. The complex interrelationship between Jeremiah's and Ezekiel's judgment preaching and their deliverance preaching is missed if we do not see this progression and point of division.

2. Alternatives for Perceiving Eschatology in the Old Testament

The term "eschatology" has meanings ranging from the very broad to the very narrow. We can best determine the appropriate implementation of the concept in the framework of the present study if we examine and sift through some of the prominent applications of "eschatology" to Old Testament thought.[59]

a. Eschatology as Endism

Since *eschaton* is Greek for "end," there are those who take the view that eschatology must be restricted to refer to passages which announce the absolute end of the world as we know it.[60] There is little ambiguity about this position, and that is one of its attractions for those who hold it. But even within this perspective, what are the important features? Does emphasis fall upon changes in the external stage-setting, or upon the more internal developments and changes in God's plan? If the latter, then we will be able to show that many of the qualities which are important to eschatology in apocalyptic dress are also present in sixth century prophecy: God alone is Lord; God is the sole source of the consummation; the division between eras is definitive; nothing more is expected after the "end." It is an unnecessary sacrifice to restrict eschatology to apocalypticism.

b. Eschatology Found throughout Prophecy

The restrictiveness and rigidity of the former position appear to have stimulated some studies concerned to show an early and intrinsic origin for eschatology in Israelite faith. One source seemingly equates eschatology with "future hope," and says that "the principal theme of eschatology is the destiny of Israel."[61] Another urges that "eschatology is the part of the history of salvation which is still in prospect." When one talks in terms like this, or about eschatology having as its central theme "the coming of Yahweh," or the sign-mark of eschatology being "a new, entirely different state of things," then the examples of passages adduced to demonstrate these criteria cover a dismayingly wide range of material including both judgment and deliverance promises.[62] Yet a third investigator ties everything to the "conclusiveness" or "finishing-off aspect" of eschatological predictions. But when he starts finding that quality widely attested in Amos, Hosea, Isaiah, and their successors, one suspects that the "conclusiveness" of their proclamations is not being singled out with enough selectivity for the results to be meaningful.[63]

A fourth source broadly equates eschatology with "the prophetic expectation of salvation."[64] If that is so, how then does one distinguish between widely attested Yahwistic expectations and distinctively eschatological expectations? The final contributor to this perspective which we consider wants precisely to eliminate that distinction. He says, "The prophets . . . were not the creators of Old Testament eschatology."[65] For him the source of eschatology is generated in the fundamental orientation of Yahwistic faith. For our purposes it is very important to see *when* eschatology begins and *why* it begins. If it is basic to Yahwistic faith from the beginning or to future hope or to judgment/deliverance successions in prophecy generally, then eschatology does not help us set apart and understand what we found and described earlier in this chapter.

c. Eschatology Applied Selectively to the Prophets

The scholars whom I have found most helpful are those who have sifted through the evidence and come up with a pattern of criteria which allows the eschatological element in prophecy to be marked out from other prophetic sayings on a quite selective basis.

1) *J. Lindblom's* widely influential 1952 article was the first to take really seriously the issue of discontinuity as marking off the eschatological from the noneschatological. He wants us to take the thought of two eras in time as our point of departure.[66] To this he adds the idea that the future era will be "wholly different" from the present era—out of "the context of *normal* historical events," but not out of the context of time or this world.[67] His basic, composite, criterion is then put together in this form: "Those expressions are to be designated as eschatological, in my opinion, which show the way to a future, where the circumstances of history, or of the world, become so altered that one can truly speak of a new condition of things, of something 'wholly different.' "[68] In an important qualification, Lindblom is quick to warn us that the term eschatology may be too widely applied within the prophetic writings.[69] Not all theophanies, not all ecstatic visions, not all symbolic sayings are eschatological. Eschatology is recognized by specific conceptions and not by high-strung rhetoric.

Lindblom is one of the very few scholars who ever raise the question whether promises of judgment on the nation meet the criteria for being considered eschatological. On Amos he insists:

> I would scarcely designate as eschatological the thought of the complete rejection and of the national ruin of the Israelite people, which we find with Amos. The annihilation of the national existence of Israel is for Amos an experience which decidedly falls within the context of normal history.[70]

Lindblom is one of the very few scholars who ever raise the Judgment in his survey of passages from Amos through Ezekiel as he examines what typifies "national eschatology"; but in those passages, all but a few of the passages which we cited as the earlier examples of the Oracle of Deliverance do appear.[71] There seems little question, then, that for Lindblom "national eschatology" is all but, if not exclusively, salvation eschatology. I think Lindblom moves us forward in careful application of terms, by tightening up, in this way, the criteria for the presence of eschatology, and by reducing the number of passages to which that designation is applied.

Another of Lindblom's strong points is that of those we have considered he is the first scholar relating these theological structures to real, historical events of the times. His sense is that national eschatology is closely focused on and around the Exile. "In the years right before the demolition of Judah, during the Exile, and in the time after the return, the national-eschatological hope stirred within the prophets and their disciples in much stronger degree than with the earlier prophets."[72] At another point it becomes quite clear that "this judgment-catastrophe," which national eschatology as least presupposes, "coincides with the Babylonian Exile."[73]

As must already be evident, I am much helped by Lindblom and have rather few criticisms of his work. One wishes that he had gone further in seeing how individual motifs within passages which he thinks are eschatological relate back to his general criteria for the presence of eschatology. I think it is significant that Lindblom avoids discussions of "finality," "futurity," and "conclusiveness"; he does not put the emphasis on the time reference. He works out criteria for the presence of eschatology in prophecy without leaning on the norms which characterize apocalyptic eschatology. Thus his argument is at once independent and fresh, but also very judicious. We do well to accept the major part of this statement.[74]

2) In some ways *E. Rohland's* 1956 dissertation, "The Meaning of the Election Traditions of Israel for the Eschatology of the Old Testament Prophets," moves us forward beyond Lindblom's study, but in other ways it blurs the issues and introduces unnecessary problems.[75] Rohland's strength is that he adds new identifying conceptions to determine the presence of eschatology and reformulates others. For the sake of brevity I will simply list

some of the explicit or implicit criteria by which Rohland understands eschatology: a) "nothing more decisively new can be expected";[76] b) the matter at hand is a "new aeon";[77] c) "a new beginning of Yahweh with his people";[78] d) "the eschatological renewal of the people is promised here";[79] e) "eschatological renewal of *Heilsgeschichte*";[80] f) "expectation of the end of the existing and beginning of a new history of Yhwh";[81] g) "new election";[82] h) stress on the "exclusivity of the activity of Yhwh in that eschatological event" [renewal of the people and their history];[83] i) "the fulfillment of the election";[84] j) "the tension between promise and fulfillment . . . abolished";[85] k) "this always means a deep incision in the history of the people."[86] One can see from these emphases that Rohland is in agreement with Lindblom on the importance of the distinction between the two eras and the discontinuity between them. I see it as an improvement that he moves from Lindblom's strict statement of criteria to a more inclusive constellation of characteristic eschatological beliefs. I agree that those beliefs which Rohland singles out *are* central to prophetic eschatology.

There are, nevertheless, problems with Rohland's approach. Unlike Lindblom, Rohland does not establish a criterion for eschatology and then test its validity by an analytical application of it to various passages. With other scholars who are primarily interested in the *sources* of eschatology, Rohland includes too many passages as eschatological, and does not point out what is not eschatological. Within this he moves from a reject→re-elect paradigm to a more generalized judgment→salvation pattern. He sees the two phases as organically united, so that a passage like Ezekiel 20 (which has both) exemplifies eschatology better than either an especially powerful judgment or an equally forceful deliverance speech.[87] His position ends up taking either a judgment or a deliverance speech only as an abbreviation and incomplete representation of what he urges is the normative eschatological pattern. Thus, he completely misunderstands the independent sources of the Oracle of Judgment and the Oracle of Deliverance. In spite of these problems and limitations, I have found Rohland's dissertation to be the second best and most helpful source on prophetic eschatology.

3) *G. von Rad* adds a few important ideas to the ever stronger set of criteria for eschatology which we have been sifting and accepting. He works inside the two aeons' view set out by Lindblom and others. From there, he offers what I consider to be an outstanding statement on discontinuity as a hallmark of eschatology:

> To my mind, it is far more important to realize that there is this break which goes so deep that the new state beyond it cannot be understood as the continuation of what went before. It is as if Israel and all her religious assets are thrown back to a point of vacuum, a vacuum which the prophets must first create by preaching judgment and sweeping away all false security, and then fill with their message of the new thing.[88]

This explanation helps to clarify what is meant by the division between the two eras. But it is not clear to me whether Von Rad sees the preaching of judgment as *included* within eschatology, or merely *presupposed* by eschatology. Von Rad says that "with Jeremiah, the gulf between old and new is far deeper than with any of his predecessors among the prophets."[89] But then with Ezekiel, Von Rad sees this taken yet a step further: "no other prophet tore open so deep a gulf between doom and salvation, or formulated it in so radical a fashion."[90]

One might also be tempted to include Fohrer among those scholars who apply "eschatology" to the prophets on a selective basis, but since he dogmatically excludes all eschatology before Second Isaiah's and casts eschatology in the light of being a deterioration of the rigor of early prophecy, his study does not warrant further consideration.[91] From Lindblom, Rohland, and Von Rad, however, we have obtained the essentials of a working definition for eschatology. What we need to do now is see how that relates to discoveries already presented as a result of our own study.

3. Application of Perspectives on Eschatology to Jeremiah and Ezekiel

a. *National Deliverance Is Eschatological*

We need now to see how what we have learned about eschatology applies back to our inductive-exegetical study of Jeremiah and Ezekiel. From that textual study I have found some additional criteria to suggest for determining the presence of eschatology. Once these are seen we then must determine what eschatology shows about the relationship between judgment and deliverance.

On an initial level I accept the combined criteria suggested by Lindblom and Rohland as valid for delineating the presence of eschatology. By their standards it is now explicitly clarified that, in effect, *the earlier portions of this chapter have already shown the eschatological character of the deliverance message of Jeremiah and Ezekiel.* We see by looking back over the exegetical portions of this chapter that we have inductively come to a recognition that these two prophets' deliverance messages were repeatedly focused on affirmations which marked out "two eras within history" and the signs of discontinuity which set them apart (see above, pp. 175–80, 182, 186–90, 194–95, 198–99, 201–6). Some of these points can be summarized in the following diagram.

Old Era	*New Era*
1. Expected standard of righteousness achieved by human efforts at obedience, and by repentance	1. Expected standard of righteousness created by God's intervention to transform the people's natures: "heart to know," "new heart and spirit"
2. Forgiveness conditional, partial	2. Forgiveness unconditional, total
3. Election grounded in events dating back to David, Moses, Abraham . . . followed by total rejection	3. New election a future event, direct between God and people, more of an idealistic "I-Thou" quality
4. Old covenant	4. "New covenant," "eternal covenant"
5. The norm for faith is events in the past.	5. The norm for faith shifts toward events in the future.

The diagram is not meant to suggest that God's act of delivering the people out of Exile and restoring them to their homeland is of no importance in the deliverance message as we find it in Jeremiah and Ezekiel. But deliverance or restoration does not delineate the contrasting elements of discontinuity between the two historical eras so clearly as the items listed above. One might ask: Have we understood the prophetic Oracle of Deliverance genre in such a way that its message will necessarily be characterized by an eschatological content? I am not ready to concede that. Jer. 31:2–6, for example, contains only the deliverance and restoration elements (see Diagram C, Chapter VI, p. 132). It gives voice to lyrical promises. But the emphasis on God's "everlasting love," his *ḥęsęd* (covenant faithfulness), and the three repetitions of "again" strike a note of continuity through distressful conditions rather than a note of discontinuity between two eras. Mic. 2:12–13 might be another example of an Oracle of Deliverance which we find little justification to designate as eschatological. Factors like the particular combination of deliverance motifs, what the sum of them adds up to, the extent of the judgment preceding this that is presupposed, and the level of intensity and dramatic newness in which the deliverance events are announced, are what determine whether an Oracle of Deliverance can be called eschatological. Thus, the genre (or speech-form) is neither intrinsically or by definition the container for an eschatological message. But *as it was given its coinage* by Jeremiah, Ezekiel, and Second Isaiah it became an extremely effective vehicle for expressing an eschatological level of God's action.

Nevertheless, we can be confident that the heart of Jeremiah's and Ezekiel's deliverance oracle message is eschatological. Inasmuch as all the scholars surveyed above, except Fohrer and the three who equate eschatology with apocalyptic, specify individual passages, they find eschatology in my six focal Oracles of Deliverance in Jeremiah and in the eleven in Ezekiel. In fact, these passages are looked upon as some of the strongest, most vital, and paradigmatic examples of deliverance eschatology in all of the prophetic literature before Second Isaiah.

b. *Suggested New Criteria for the Presence of Eschatology*

This leads me to the question: Have all the criteria that are valuable for determining the presence of eschatology been laid out, or can we add to those from our own study of texts in Jeremiah and Ezekiel? I offer to the reader, in a tentative way, my own list of criteria for eschatology which I have discovered. This enumeration comes with the warning that these categories may fit Jeremiah and Ezekiel better than other sources, but I think they deserve to be considered for wider application.

1) Often we find, within the Oracle of Deliverance, that the announcement *within itself* contains assumptions about new terms and conditions of God's action not previously revealed, understood, or accepted. In other words, that kind of proclamation is not merely the implementation of existing expectations such as would fit within established religious institutions. Rather, that kind of proclamation *both* promises a dramatic new act, but also *breaks ground* for a new understanding of the sphere, level, extent, and terms of God's activity. We would suggest that *eschatology is the search for and discovery of a frame of reference to explain events which are not understandable in terms of any previously existing tradition.* Within apocalyptic writings we find that world cataclysm, end of history, end of this order, universal judgment are not explainable in terms of conceptions in pre-apocalyptic or extra-apocalyptic sources. Analogously, a national rebirth under different terms than existed when the national death took place is not understandable in terms of eighth century prophecy and even less in preprophetic or extra-prophetic sources. Deuteronomy 30 and Leviticus 26 are good examples of passages which offer hope of a reversal in Israel's misfortunes, but in neither of them is there offered or seen as needed a breakthrough to a new frame of reference essential to understand such a hope. The echoes of conditionality, retribution, a "tit-for-tat" basis of operation in those two passages mark them off sharply from sixth century prophetic promises of eschatological deliverance.

2) One of the indications that one has broken through into a new framework in an eschatological proclamation is the discov-

ery that in the dawning era there are new rules, people are in a different game, God has shifted gears. One is naturally drawn to the idea that *God's mode of operation, "game plan," dispensation, when changed in the new framework, are as definitive of the watershed between the two eras as anything could be.* One has to ask, What is different in the two eras? Is it different most of all from God's point of view, or from man's? I think that the external changes for Israel are not the heart of the matter; that may be only the tip of the iceberg. We wonder what has changed in terms of *God's* attitude, *his* criteria for evaluating Israel, *his* plan of attack for fulfilling his purposes in history from this point forward. The sense of having entered a new dispensation arises from several indices, but carries implications beyond any one of them: a) shift in the relationship between human initiative and divine initiative; b) accessibility of forgiveness in the era; c) goals, hopes, expectations of the era; d) changes in normative or identifying conditions of human life; e) whether time moves forward *toward* a goal or norm in the future, or moves forward *from* a goal or norm that has already been established in the past.[92]

3) To a remarkable degree the strong emphasis on God as *Creator,* God creating a new world, God improving nature, God creating salvation which we find in Second Isaiah is already anticipated in Jeremiah and Ezekiel. In Jeremiah and Ezekiel it comes, of course, through the expression of the *transformation* motif: "give them a heart to know" (Jer. 24:7), "will put my law within them" (Jer. 31:33), "put a new spirit within them" (Ezek. 11:19), "will open your graves and raise you from your graves" (Ezek. 37:12). The purpose of these and other acts of new creation mentioned in Jeremiah and Ezekiel is further to perfect the people so that they are fit to be God's. It is the shift from the arena of history to the arena of nature and a fundamental improvement in nature which calls attention to itself as an eschatological act. It strikes me, as noted above, that quite often when the Old Testament gets into deep trouble over God's governance of history so that a theodicy is elicited, the problem in providence is resolved by shifting to God's power or new activity

in nature. This is how the theodicy issue in the Book of Job ends. And, I would suggest that the ultimate resolution to the theodicy articulated in the depths of Jeremiah's and Ezekiel's judgment message is the new historical possibilities which God creates in his eschatological intervention by further perfecting his original fashioning of human nature.

4) Finally, I want to suggest that the basic underlying theme of prophetic eschatology is the freedom of God. In eschatology God's freedom is reasserted. Israelite religion was enslaved to the retribution logic of the Sinai Covenant until that "vacuum" which Von Rad spoke about[93] came with the onset of the judgment of the Babylonian Exile. Between Israel's misdeeds, and Babylon's aggressions, and a covenant structure which brought the two into a correlation, God no longer had any freedom. Eschatology arose to provide that freedom. As has often been said, a fundamental theme of eschatology is the Lordship and Kingship of God. With *transformation* God is freed from Israel's weakness; with *forgiveness* he is freed from the burden of past sin; with *new election* he is freed from the alienation and separation from his people; with *new covenant* God is freed out of one restrictive framework into a liberating new framework. By these initiatives, taken out of consideration for his own prerogatives as much as out of pity for Israel, God is once again radically free. He stands facing an open-ended future. *In relation to Israel's past institutions eschatology never makes sense. In relation to God's freedom it always does.* In the apocalyptic judgment God got free of the burden of history, the threat posed by foreign nations to his chosen people. In the apocalyptic Kingdom of God in Heaven we have the ultimate fulfillment of that search for freedom which is at once always a reassertion of absolute divine Lordship over events that had become unproductive for God's purposes. The entirety of this liberating, forward-looking thrust in biblical eschatology has rich implications for some of the ways theology is being formulated today.

c. *National Judgment Is Not Eschatological*

If doom and salvation are linked together as twin parts of a two-act eschatological drama—which is what most scholars seem to assume—then we are back to having a patternism determining the relation of doom to salvation. Nothing other than the requirements of eschatology is needed to explain why the doom is so radical, or why a sweeping salvation follows it.

We urge that this cannot be the case. The present study differs from those primarily focused on eschatology in several ways. We have given attention to the form-critical genres carrying the judgment and deliverance messages. The two genres have nothing to do with each other. Each has its own setting, tradition-history, rationale, structure. Each is shaped to deal with different communication problems vis-à-vis the situation of the audience it addressed. No one who has searched for the setting of the Oracle of Judgment has suggested that it stems out of "eschatology." It is most often seen as some kind of formulation of a "covenant lawsuit." One can understand full well what an Oracle of Judgment is up to, and why it says what it does, without reference to eschatology. It is also within the particular nature of our study to attempt to understand the relation between the judgment and deliverance messages and the particular historical events taking place at the time in which they were spoken. We saw the Oracle of Judgment becoming more harsh as the Babylonian noose tightened around Judah's neck. There was no theological necessity for the radicalization of the judgment message (as would be the case were it governed by an eschatological patternism). That message was adjusted out of a discernment of God's will in relation to the condition of Judah and the international-political signs of the times. Following that, if salvation were assuredly *known* to be following the judgment, as the second part of a two-part drama, *theodicy* as we have seen it in Jeremiah and Ezekiel *would never have arisen.*

I think we have demonstrated that doom-rejection-annihilation preaching did not involve a theophanic revelation of a "new plan for history," but was the last act of an old plan, theophanically revealed to Moses. It did not involve a shift to a "new dispensation," but was completely understandable if not also necessitated by a dispensation known for centuries. It did not involve a "breakthrough in God's freedom" or in his initiative, but operated within the integrity of the prevailing pattern of divine initiatives. What happened in 587 was not "radically new," because it had already happened in 722. The judgment oracles from Amos and Hosea which helped Israel accept their fate in 722 stood alone, without paired words of salvation.

Following another line of criteria for the presence of eschatology, we wonder what discontinuity would set apart the beginning of the eschatological era of doom. What era precedes the time of national doom? At that time we are in a period of conditional blessing, conditional curse, calls to repentance, jeopardy, retribution, words of doom used as negative summonses to repentance, chastising punishment used to elicit repentance. It all slides slowly and erratically over many centuries into an annihilatory level of doom and rejection. So, nothing about this is new. Jeremiah and Ezekiel manifest no sharp discontinuity in their message of judgment from that proclaimed by Amos and Hosea. And Amos and Hosea are prefigured in the words of Elijah and Elisha. *In contrast to this, the deliverance era is clearly marked off.* But I would not say that the deliverance message is developed under any kind of deterministic influence from eschatology. *National eschatology of salvation is the child of an exilic deliverance message which first of all struggled to make sense of real historical events in terms of the movement of God's will.* Eschatology is *discovered* here, not presupposed.

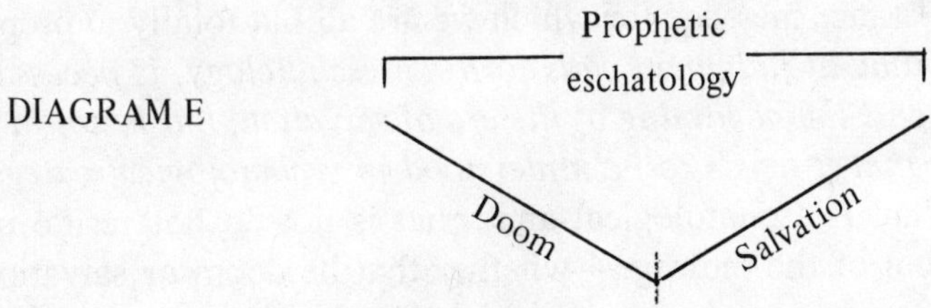

The position which I reject is shown in Diagram E. The line of history is on a downward decline in the era of doom as the people's fortunes and God's purposes through them fall. There is a turning point, shown by the vertical line, and in the era of

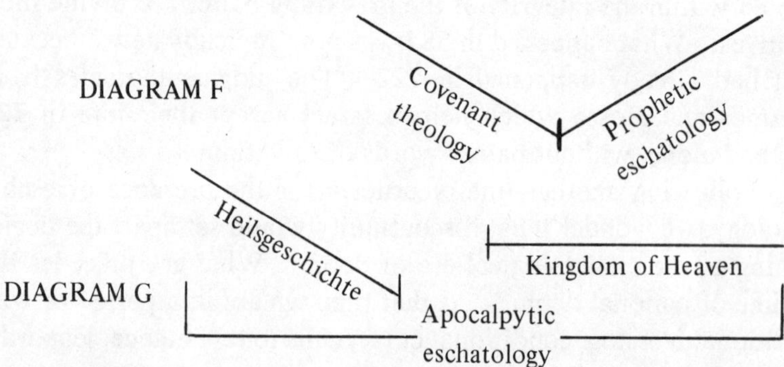

salvation Israel's fortunes and God's purposes take an upturn. The whole thing, taken as an organic unit, is seen to be the outline of prophetic national eschatology. *Instead of this* I say that the time of decline is characterized by the covenant theology which supplies the rationale for the Oracles of Judgment (Diagram F). Then with no causal connection whatever, this is superseded by the era of deliverance which finds its characteristic rationale and frame of reference in prophetic eschatology. Oracles of Judgment in Hos. 4:1–3; Jer. 5:1–6; Ezek. 24:6–14 do not evidence a breakthrough into a new frame of reference, do not put us into an era where conditions are "wholly different." Therefore, these passages are not eschatological. But I do hold that when covenant theology runs its course at the depth of the judgment preaching, it is usually superseded by an eschatological deliverance message for which we are all but totally unprepared. *The time of judgment calls forth an eschatology, is necessary to set apart the beginning of the era of salvation, but is not in itself such that it needs to be understood in eschatological categories.*

What is eschatological and what is not do not reside in the content of the message—whether that be doom or salvation, as we see when we look at Diagram G. Neither the end of God's plan for redemption and self-revelation in and through history (*Heilsgeschichte*), nor his shift to a wholly new setting outside this history and this world could be understood in terms of any normative Israelite expectations before this time, or in terms of any Israelite institutions. Therefore in this context *both* the era in which God gives up on *Heilsgeschichte* and the era which inaugurates the Kingdom of Heaven are eschatological.[94]

Perhaps the most important thing about the kind of eschatology I see in Jeremiah and Ezekiel is that there is such a thoroughgoing change within the bent but *unbroken line of history.* It is a change which resists schematic interpretation. As I perceive the eschatological dimension of these prophets' deliverance message, it accents and defines the change in eras, but without either moving away from the essential foundation of the prophets' faith or changing their understanding of God's basic goals.

d. Continuity/Discontinuity

In his book *Torah and Canon,* J. A. Sanders says that the miracle of the Exile is not radical discontinuity, but the achievement of continuity in the midst of radical discontinuity.[95] He suggests that other nations which lost as many tangible supports of identity and security as Judah lost in 587 simply went under and were no more. Is the theme of continuity in the midst of discontinuity part of the content of the deliverance message, part of eschatology, part of our basic concern to understand a theology of Exile?

Within the spectrum of Old Testament sources which deal with the Exile, Jeremiah and Ezekiel are perhaps unique in that they give a theological rationale for total discontinuity, and do that at the very time the break is taking place historically. But matters do not end there. A whole new plan of God's action begins again, within their lifetimes, within their ministries. No one takes discontinuity as seriously as they do, and yet they end up with reaffirmation of hope and purpose for Israel. Let us suggest that *this embodies discontinuity in religion,* but *continuity in God's power and purpose.*

Several levels of meaning must be discerned in order to grasp the full significance of the Exile. Viewed from the horizon of the people, what physically happened to them, what resources they had to understand the event in terms of God's will, there is no continuity whatsoever. I see absolutely no causal connection, no theocratic connection, no institutional connection between the judgment and the deliverance. It is dishonest, and compromising of the drama of the shift, to use our hindsight to say that this kind of death caused the ensuing kind of rebirth. The death stands alone, and there is a hiatus between the death and the rebirth. It is on the empirical, historical level, most of all, that there is an eschatological separation between the two eras. Jeremiah and Ezekiel are loath to mollify that or to cheapen it.

We must, however, balance this point by attempting to look at the Exile from God's horizon. God's nature does not change, and his overarching intention and purpose do not change. God's hope and intention for Israel at the Exodus-Sinai events in 1275 and during the Josianic reform in 621 are never lost, never destroyed. It is precisely that hope and that intention which come back to expression, after temporarily being held in abeyance, in Jeremiah's and Ezekiel's deliverance message. It is part of the identity of the God revealed in the Old Testament to work toward redeeming the world through an elected community. While the Exile seems like a defeat to Israel, it liberates God from some religious baggage which was actually hindering his redemptive purpose. Through it he strips Israel, streamlines it, renovates it from the inside out, and sends it on its mission anew. *Exile is a time of victory for God.* In the eschatological fabric there are some absolutely new threads, and there are previously existing threads, if "threads" stand for elements of tradition-history. But the pattern woven is new, and the meaning of the earlier tradition-history threads (obedience, forgiveness, election, covenant) drawn upon is new in this changed context. So, God gives a new revelation of an old plan. He reintroduces himself to his people after they are prepared, at bitter pain, better to understand him. The crisis of Exile is not God's, it is Israel's. It is a crisis of faith amidst wrenching historical change and unprecedented "gear-shifting" in the *mode* for actualizing God's enduring plan. Jeremiah and Ezekiel deserve our admiration for having the faith to live through these times and to deliver God's word on both sides of the watershed. Would that we might have the faith to live through our own experience of Exile, when it comes.

CONCLUSION

ISSUES RAISED BY THE STUDY: A PERSONAL STATEMENT

A. A Perspective on Jewish-Christian Relations Obtained from the Theology of Exile

We learn something new from the deliverance preaching in Jeremiah and Ezekiel. And it cuts two ways in terms of how Judaism and Christianity have commonly understood, and misunderstood, each other. What we have seen indicates that the Hebrew Bible goes further toward a theology of human failure and sheer unmerited grace coming into the vacuum created by the elimination of human alternatives than most of us have realized. It is hard for a Christian who takes the depth of Jeremiah's and Ezekiel's judgment and deliverance preaching seriously not to see a death and resurrection pattern: the death of human institutions, human alternatives, human possibilities—and the unexpected resurrection of human possibilities, alternatives, and institutions by an act of totally unmerited and unconditional divine mercy. Let it be clear that I am not saying there is anything here which one can talk about on a historical level which requires Jews to look to the crucifixion and resurrection of Jesus to find the fulfillment of their faith. What I am saying is that as Christians look back into this earlier part of Scripture, they find within the theology of exile some of the same basic, generic theological structures that are invoked to interpret the "Christ Event": the death of useful human initiatives, a caesura in the man-God relationship, a resurrection of human possibilities by a creative act of divine grace.

Let me warn the overzealous that there remain striking differences between this aspect of the theology of exile and the theology of the "Christ event" in its normative context. This act of deliverance: 1) is for the people Israel, not for individual believers; 2) opens a new era under the law, not an era in which the requirements of the law are superseded; 3) operates in a framework in which the act of forgiveness is historical and repeatable, not cosmological and once for all time. It is as though at this point God recreates on a new and better level a man-centered, history-centered, communal religion. Christians therefore have a heavy stake in the theology of exile and can learn and profit a great deal from it even though they should be warned against overappropriating or over-Christologizing the paradigm offered there.

At the same time I would emphasize that the theology of exile demonstrates something which Christians have been reluctant to recognize within Judaism, and which Jews themselves have known but perhaps underemphasized. This is that there is Good News within Judaism. There is total, unmerited, eschatological grace within Judaism. As I read the Talmud and the Midrashic literature I find no evidence of the Pauline and frequent Christian caricature of Judaism that in it a man must save himself by total obedience to the law. Rather, man must do all he possibly can to meet the norm for human life and human community established by the law, but ultimately God's mercy and forgiveness make the saving difference between what men can do and what God expects. One might speak here of the reliability and inevitability of grace within Rabbinic Judaism and its antecedents.

Just when did this belief in an assured presence of mercy and forgiveness closing the final gap between God and man originate within the stream of Israelite-Jewish faith? Clearly it is not there within the judgment preaching of Jeremiah or Ezekiel or in earlier sources. It begins with the deliverance preaching of these two prophets! In that situation grace serves as first cause in a hopeless, stalemated situation. As Judaism of later generations incorporated that revelation, the pendulum swung back somewhat toward a more man-centered perception of right religion. But from the theology of exile the model is established for the development of the view that man cannot realistically be expected to be morally perfect; and the model is there for the growth of the conviction that forgiveness is not necessarily contingent upon repentance or any other prerequisite which man must meet.

On these matters Judaism and Christianity would do well to understand one another better. It seems to me to be within the distinctive historical identity of Judaism to be a relatively humanistic faith, with a large role for human effort in obedience, and a smaller, but vitally important role for unmerited divine grace. Christianity, on the other hand, is more pessimistic about man and invests the major part of hope in a set of meta-historical, cosmological symbols of salvation centered around the "Christ event." I think it is much to be desired that, between these faiths, we reduce malicious exaggeration of differences as well as facile glossing over of distinctive emphases. I hope that what I have been able to say about the theology of exile will open new understandings of this common heritage and resource, given us by Jeremiah and Ezekiel, as well as prompt some reflection on how the two faith communities have, in quite different ways, appropriated and built upon the model offered in the theology of exile.

B. Historical Revelation, unlike "Truth," Is Mutable and Alive

I am struck that the dramatic movement from a message of judgment to a message of deliverance, in Jeremiah and Ezekiel, and the shaping of those messages for changing historical events do not augur well for the idea of a closed sacred canon of Scripture. If God acts *against* religious institutions as much as through them, if what is theologically "true" changes, if the revelation is situationally directed, then it seems to me that *canonization may contradict a principle operating within the Bible itself.*

On the other hand it is increasingly clear to me that the Old Testament keeps reinterpreting itself. It would rather have seemingly contradictory traditions standing side by side than reject the one over the other. In a sense the covenant with Abraham reinterprets the covenant with Noah; the covenant with Moses reinterprets the one with Abraham; the covenant with David reinterprets the one with Moses; the covenant envisioned by various pre-exilic sources (prophets from Amos through the judgment phase of Jeremiah and Ezekiel plus Deuteronomy) reinterpret all the previous expressions of covenant; and finally in the deliverance messages of Jeremiah, Ezekiel, and Second Isaiah the covenant traditions are once again reinterpreted. So, there is a progressively clearer focus on certain faith affirmations. One gradually receives a clearer picture of what beliefs stand at the center of Israelite faith. This means that there are norms, however often revised or restated. And that can be taken along with other pieces of evidence as a movement in the direction of a canon.

These various tendencies: 1) centering on fundamental affirmations, 2) reinterpretation of those affirmations, and 3) a strikingly new word from God for a new situation are inadequately represented by either of the present-day alternatives: having a canon of Scripture, not having a canon of Scripture. Since canonizing a body of literature as sacred carries with it the canonization of the history when that Scripture was composed and the culture lived by the community that produced the sacred collection of literature, we have against us the value judgment that we are living a post-canonical existence. We have sub-canonical theology, sub-canonical institutions, sub-canonical culture, and sub-canonical events in history.

So, the canon can function in a very negative way in suggesting: God no longer speaks in the way he spoke through the biblical witnesses; God no longer acts in the way he did in the events recorded in the Bible. The practical failure of belief in the Holy Spirit throughout much of Protestantism is a direct consequence of the "Midas touch" quality of the act of canonization. By Midas touch I mean that with the touch of canonization this body of literature turns to gold, thereby exaggerating the contrast between this literature and all other religious literature written under inspiration or revelation subsequently. But what is gold is also solidified, dead, impermeable.

One can say of Scripture that it is a revelation sufficient unto salvation, or that it contains the paradigms needed for salvation. I accept that. And as we have shown, a theology of exile can function as a paradigm in relation to which many contemporary experiences can be better understood. But there is also a singularity in what we have studied that is violated if it is reduced to a general principle that is repeated. We would do violence to the judgment/deliverance preaching of Jeremiah and Ezekiel if we were required to interpret it only in relation to earlier developments in Israelite religion, or only in relation to the turn of things in our own time. Part of the lesson of those events is that man cannot predict what God will do. Man does not know God's reasons. Man does not know how far judgment will go. He does not know whether judgment will be followed by a deliverance; if it is, he does not know how radical a deliverance it will be. So there is that sense in which the paradigm tells us about the *uniqueness* of events, the radical freedom God exercises to do what he will, the ultimately impenetrable mystery of the relation between God's propensity to bring judgment on sin and his propensity to deliver those on whom he will have mercy. Other times when the people of Israel were in great distress do not necessarily fit the pattern we have found: not the religious persecution around 167 B.C. under Antiochus Epiphanes, not the destruction of Jerusalem in 70 A.D.

Since the application of biblical precedents to contemporary events is so problematic, necessary but so shot through with variables as to be extremely difficult, it is important that we be ready to receive a new word for a new situation. God may say something to us that he has never said before, because events may do something to us which has never happened before. In this sense, it would be better to have an open-ended canon rather than a closed canon. Finally it is a choice between a principle which has its most natural ideological home in Greek philosophical perceptions (unchanging "Truth"), and a living God resident in all history whose story is begun in the Bible. Of the two I think Jeremiah and Ezekiel would clearly opt for the latter.

C. The Necessity of an Experience of Exile

It was good for Israel to go into Exile in 597 and 587. Exile purged the corporate psyche free of the idolatrous connection between God and Zion, God and temple, God and the Davidic dynasty. The Exile was a time for the liberation of God, for the awesome power and the holy heat of God's Godness to shatter through all the limiting structures of Israel's religious conceptions and religious institutions.

Prophetic faith at its best is always anti-religious. Or to put it another way, its experience of God is so intense that religion is shattered from the inside out, and then reconstructed on a wider foundation. If God elected Israel, Zion, the Davidic line once again, in Babylon, after the wreckage, then this shows that his doing so has *absolutely nothing* to do with intrinsic merit. There is no natural basis for the relationship whatsoever.

Exile is a good experience for the community of Christian believers in the United States. It purges them free from the idolatrous connection assumed to exist between Christianity and any of several visions of the "American way of life." In a state of exile the community of Christian believers realizes that it is blasphemy to identify the Body of Christ with the institutional church. God in Christ has no natural, necessary, or intrinsic connection with "churches." It is tremendously liberating to realize that God is in the whole arena of history and not just in churches. This means that believers in Christ can meet God anywhere: on the job, across a table on which a meal is spread, at the crossroads of brutal historical events. I think that this fundamentally means that human belief and God's initiative meet in unpredictable events more than in predetermined structures.

What is crucial to realize is that we have no institutional claims on God. We are not an elect people. Persons who take their Christianity with consistent seriousness will soon be cultural exiles within American society. Believers who are not ideologically pluralistic usually find themselves to be exiles within the churches. Exiled people are attractive to God. They know that the events of the past are a judgment. By that judgment they are stripped of facades. They are forced to be mobile, to travel light, to stand naked before God. They have no enduring worldly roots, no enduring worldly security. They are vulnerable. When God comes to these exiles, he is perceived in his Godness. With them he has an open-ended future. No agenda binds him. God loves exiles. They are ready to receive him as he is. They are a good risk. He gives them the transforming power of his Spirit; he heals their broken and depleted humanity.

Let us be quite specific as to why exile is good, necessary for believers. 1) Adversity is accepted. We learn not to expect winds of change always to blow in our favor. Reversals do not drive us to despair. In all things we confess God as Lord.

2) An exile has to learn that God's love is not absent when events speak judgment. One learns to see God present as much in judgment as in times when things go favorably.

3) Everything which is tragic and a source of self-pity in exile from a human point of view is a source of freedom and celebration from God's point of view. The dominant note in Second Isaiah is hymnic, and that is very appropriate. It is the time both of exile and its resolution. That is not the time of the exaltation of Israel, but the time of the exaltation of God.

4) We learn that God's love stands as much outside what we consider rational, what falls within our conception of religious logic, as his judgment. The unpredictability and power of God's love are an awesome thing. God's love is a kind of judgment. It creates where we thought nothing could be created. It gives life where we thought we had seen the finality of death. It refuses to give up on us when we had given up on ourselves.

5) Judgment (justice) gives deliverance (love) its integrity. Our condemnation is that we must die to all rebelliousness and to all notions of the efficacy of past human initiatives at doing "religion." Our salvation is in God's hands and subject to his

initiative alone. God may create a deliverance for reasons that dwarf those that motivate our pleas and prayers. He may turn around our minds with a new self-revelation, may inaugurate a new era and plan, may buy freedom for an open-ended future for himself and for us. Exile is the cradle for theodicy and eschatology, death and resurrection, a trusting end and a new beginning. It is the vacuum that precedes a second era of creation, a deeper construction out of faith elements that existed previously. The possibility of authentic faith is once again put in front of man. This possibility is his, but not to grasp with his hands. And so, amidst painful change, there is rejoicing for the opening to the future which God has created.

ABBREVIATIONS

AB	Anchor Bible
ATD	Das Alte Testament Deutsch
BKAT	Biblischer Kommentar: Altes Testament
BWANT	Beiträge zur Wissenschaft vom Alten und Neuen Testament
BZAW	Beihefte zur *Zeitschrift für die alttestamentliche Wissenschaft*
CBQ	*Catholic Biblical Quarterly*
CBSC	Cambridge Bible for Schools and Colleges
EvTh	*Evangelische Theologie*
FRLANT	Forschungen zur Religion und Literatur des Alten und Neuen Testaments
HAT	Handbuch zum Alten Testament
IB	*Interpreter's Bible*
ICC	International Critical Commentary
IDB	*Interpreter's Dictionary of the Bible*
Int	*Interpretation*
JAAR	*Journal of the American Academy of Religion*
JBL	*Journal of Biblical Literature*
KAT	Kommentar zum Alten Testament
OTL	Old Testament Library
SBT	Studies in Biblical Theology
TB	Theologische Bücherei
TBC	Torch Bible Commentaries
VT	*Vetus Testamentum*
WMANT	Wissenschaftliche Monographien zum Alten und Neuen Testament
ZAW	*Zeitscrift für die alttestamentliche Wissenschaft*
ZThK	*Zeitschrift für Theologie und Kirche*

SELECT BIBLIOGRAPHY

(The brackets contain abbreviated references used after the first citation of the work in each chapter.)

Ackroyd, P. R. *Exile and Restoration: A Study of Hebrew Thought of the Sixth Century B.C.* Philadelphia: Westminster, 1968. [Ackroyd, *Exile and Restoration*]

Baltzer, K. *The Covenant Formulary: In Old Testament, Jewish, and Early Christian Writings,* translated by D. E. Green. Philadelphia: Fortress, 1971. [Baltzer, *Covenant Formulary*]

Begrich, J. "Das priesterliche Heilsorakel." *ZAW* 11–12 (1935): 81–92. [Begrich, "Das priesterliche Heilsorakel"]

———. *Studien zu Deuterojesaja.* TB 20. Munich: Chr. Kaiser, 1963. [Begrich, *Deuterojesaja*]

Bright, J. *A History of Israel.* Philadelphia: Westminster, 1959. [Bright, *History of Israel*]

———. *Jeremiah: Introduction, Translation, and Notes.* AB 21. Garden City, N.Y.: Doubleday, 1965. [Bright, *Jeremiah*]

Brueggemann, W. *Tradition for Crisis: A Study in Hosea.* Richmond, Va.: John Knox, 1968. [Brueggemann, *Tradition*]

Clements, R. E. *Abraham and David: Genesis 15 and Its Meaning for Israelite Tradition.* SBT 5 (Second Series). Naperville, Ill.: Alec R. Allenson, 1967. [Clements, *Abraham and David*]

———. *Prophecy and Covenant.* SBT 43. London: SCM, 1965. [Clements, *Prophecy and Covenant*]

Cooke, G. A. *A Critical and Exegetical Commentary on the Book of Ezekiel.* ICC. Edinburgh: T. & T. Clark, 1936. [Cooke, *Ezekiel*]

Eichrodt, W. *Ezekiel: A Commentary,* translated by C. Quin. OTL. Philadelphia: Westminster, 1970. [Eichrodt, *Ezekiel*]

———. *Theology of the Old Testament II,* translated by J. A. Baker. OTL. Philadelphia: Westminster, 1967. [Eichrodt, *Theology II*]

Eissfeldt, O. *The Old Testament: An Introduction,* translated by P. R. Ackroyd, New York: Harper & Row, 1965. [Eissfeldt, *Introduction*]

Fohrer, G. *Ezechiel.* HAT 13. Tübingen: J. C. B. Mohr (Paul Siebeck), 1955. [Fohrer, *Ezechiel*]

———. *Introduction to the Old Testament,* translated by D. E. Green, New York: Abingdon, 1968. [Fohrer, *Introduction*]

Freedman, D. N. "The Book of Ezekiel." *Int.* 8 (1954): 446–72. [Freedman, "Ezekiel"]

Gottwald, N. K. *Studies in the Book of Lamentations.* SBT 14. London: SCM, 1962. [Gottwald, *Lamentations*]

Heschel, A. J. *The Prophets.* New York: Harper & Row, 1962. [Heschel, *The Prophets*]

Hyatt, J. P. "Introduction, Exegesis," *Jeremiah. IB* 5. New York: Abingdon, 1956. [Hyatt, *Jeremiah*]

Kaufmann, Y. *The Religion of Israel: From Its Beginnings to the Babylonian Exile,* translated by M. Greenberg. Chicago: University of Chicago Press, 1960. [Kaufmann, *Religion of Israel*]

Knierim, R. "Form Criticism: The Present State of an Exegetical Discipline," presented to the Form Criticism Seminar, Society of Biblical Literature, New York, 1970. [Knierim, "Form Criticism: Present State"]

———. "Old Testament Form Criticism Reconsidered." *Int* 27 (1973): 435–68. [Knierim, "Form Criticism Reconsidered"]

Koch, K. "Gibt es ein Vergeltungsdogma im Alten Testament?" *ZThK* 52 (1955): 1–42. [Koch, "Vergeltungsdogma"]

———. *The Growth of the Biblical Tradition,* translated by S. M. Cupitt. New York: Charles Scribner's Sons, 1969. [Koch, *Biblical Tradition*]

———. "Sühne und Sündenvergebung: Um die Wende von der exilischen zur nachexilischen Zeit." *EvTh* 26 (1966): 217–39. [Koch, "Sündenvergebung"]

Lindblom, J. "Gibt es eine Eschatologie bei den alttestamentlichen Propheten?" *Studia Theologica* 4 (1950): 79–114. [Lindblom, "Eschatologie"]

———. *Prophecy in Ancient Israel.* Philadelphia: Fortress, 1962. [Lindblom, *Prophecy*]

May, H. G. "Introduction, Exegesis," *Ezekiel. IB* 6. New York: Abingdon, 1956. [May, *Ezekiel*]

Miller, J. W. *Das Verhältnis Jeremias und Hesekiels sprachlich und theologisch untersucht.* Assen, Netherlands: Royal VanGorcum, 1955. [Miller, *Verhältnis Jeremias und Hesekiels*]

Mowinckel, S. *Zur Komposition des Buches Jeremia.* Videnskapsselskapets Skrifter II Hist.-Filos. Klasse. 1913, no. 5. Kristiania: Jacob Dybwad, 1914. [Mowinckel, *Jeremia*]

Noth, M. *The History of Israel,* translated by S. Godman, New York: Harper & Brothers, 1958. [Noth, *History of Israel*]

Pfeiffer, R. H. *Introduction to the Old Testament.* New York: Harper & Brothers, 1958. [Pfeiffer, *Introduction*]

Raitt, T. "The Concept of Forgiveness in the Pre-exilic Prophets in Relation to Its Form-Historical Setting." Ph.D. dissertation, Vanderbilt University, 1964. [Raitt, "Concept of Forgiveness"]

———. "The Prophetic Summons to Repentance." *ZAW* 83 (1971): 30–49. [Raitt, "Summons to Repentance"]

Reventlow, H. G. *Wächter über Israel: Ezechiel und Seine Tradition.* BZAW 82. Berlin: Alfred Töpelmann, 1962. [Reventlow, *Wächter*]

Rohland, E. "Die Bedeutung der Erwählungstraditionen Israels für die Echatologie der alttestamentlichen Propheten." Inaugural dissertation, Heidelberg, 1956. [Rohland, "Erwählungstraditionen"]

Rudolph, W. *Jeremia.* HAT 12. Tübingen: J. C. B. Mohr (Paul Siebeck), 1958. [Rudolph, *Jeremia*]

Scharbert, J. "Formgeschichte und Exegese von Ex. 34:6f und seiner Parallelen." *Biblica* 38 (1957): 130–50. [Scharbert, "Exegese von Ex. 34:6f"]

Smend, R. *Die Bundesformel,* Theologische Studien #68, edited by K. Barth and M. Geiger. Zurich: EVZ, 1963. [Smend, *Bundesformel*]

Stamm, J. J. *Erlösen und Vergeben im Alten Testament: Eine Begriffs-Geschichtliche Untersuchung.* Bern: A. Francke A.-G., 1940. [Stamm, *Erlösen und Vergeben*]

Tucker, G. M. *Form Criticism of the Old Testament.* Philadelphia: Fortress, 1971. [Tucker, *Form Criticism*]

Volz, P. *Der Prophet Jeremia.* KAT 10. Leipzig: A. Deichertsche, 1922. [Volz, *Jeremia*]

Von Rad, G. *Old Testament Theology* II, translated by D. M. G. Stalker. New York: Harper & Row, 1965. [Von Rad, *Theology* II]

Von Waldow, H. E. "Anlass und Hintergrund der Verkündigung des Deuterojesaja." Inaugural dissertation, Bonn, 1953. [Von Waldow, "Deuterojesaja"]

Vriezen, T. C. *An Outline of Old Testament Theology,* translated by S. Neuijen, Boston: Charles T. Brandford, 1960 [Vriezen, *Theology*]

Weiser, A. *Das Buch des Propheten Jeremia.* ATD 20/21. Göttingen: Vandenhoeck & Ruprecht, 1960. [Weiser, *Jeremia*]

Westermann, C. *Basic Forms of Prophetic Speech,* translated by H. C. White. Philadelphia: Westminster, 1967. [Westermann, *Basic Forms*]

———. *Isaiah 40–66: A Commentary,* translated by D. M. G. Stalker. OTL. Philadelphia: Westminster, 1969. [Westermann, *Isaiah 40–66*]

———. "Sprach und Struktur der Prophetie Deuterojesajas." *Forschung am Alten Testament,* TB 24. Munich: Chr. Kaiser, 1964. [Westermann, "Sprach . . . Deuterojesajas"]

Whitley, C. F. *The Exilic Age.* Philadelphia: Westminster, 1957. [Whitley, *Exilic Age*]

Wolff, H. W. "Dei Begründungen der prophetischen Heils- und Unheilssprüche." *ZAW* 52 (1934): 1–22 [Wolff, "Die Bergründungen"]

Zimmerli, W. *Ezechiel* I–II, BKAT 13. Neukirchen-Vlyun: Neukirchener, 1969. [Zimmerli, *Ezechiel* I–II]

———. "The Message of the Prophet Ezekiel." *Int* 23 (1969): 131–57. [Zimmerli, "Message of . . . Ezekiel"]

NOTES

INTRODUCTION

1. The two waves of deportation to Babylon took place in 597 B.C. and 587 B.C. Hereafter we refer to this as the "Exile." For the reader who wishes to review the history of the Exile we suggest consulting J. Bright, *A History of Israel,* pp. 302–31. To date the most useful, broadly based, scholarly monograph on the sources and developments of this period is P. R. Ackroyd's *Exile and Restoration.*

2. As stated, this point is made without qualification. However, with all of his splendid and rather recent work on Ezekiel, W. Zimmerli has dealt to some extent with the doom/salvation shift in at least that prophet. But as is clear in his most recent book of published essays, *Studien zur alttestamentlichen Theologie und Prophetie: Gesammelte Aufsätze* II, TB 51 (Munich: Chr. Kaiser, 1974), Zimmerli does not think of Jeremiah when he thinks of prophets who deal with the Exile. In the volume just mentioned he has an article "Der Wahrheitserweis Jahwes nach der Botschaft der beiden Exilspropheten" (pp. 192–212). "The Two Prophets of the Exile" mentioned at the end of this title, and considered within the essay, are not Jeremiah and Ezekiel, but Ezekiel and Second Isaiah. When Zimmerli writes on the topic "Plannungen für den Wiederaufbau nach der Katastrophe von 587" (pp. 165–91) elsewhere in the same volume, he has nothing to say about Jeremiah. It is even true in his earlier, semi-popular article "Gericht und Heil im Alttestamentlichen Prophetenwort" (*Der Anfang* 11 [1949]: 21–46) that he does not deal with the doom/salvation tension in Jeremiah. It is all too typical of Old Testament scholarship generally that Jeremiah is not dealt with as the first of the sixth century prophets, the first of the "prophets of the Exile." Unless Jeremiah and Ezekiel are studied *together,* it is not possible to see in full dimension the radical character of the judgment preaching of those who worked under the shadow of the Exile (Jeremiah) or among the first wave of deportees (Ezekiel). And then it is not possible to analyze in detail how these two prophets moved from radical judgment to radical deliverance as the political and cultic life of Judah collapsed around them. To my knowledge, ours is the first book which sets for itself that task.

3. Even to the present day, German scholars tend to cast a value judgment on types of prophets by the very terms used to designate them. *Unheilspropheten* are "prophets-of-doom," while *Heilspropheten* are

"prophets-of-salvation." Since the genuine prophets often denounced false prophets, and false prophets were noted for currying favor through groundless optimism, the deduction has too often followed that before the Exile true prophets equal doom prophets. It is a caricature and a needless truncation of the diversity and polarities within a prophet's message to call any prophet like Amos, Hosea, Isaiah, Micah, Jeremiah, or Ezekiel a "doom-prophet." Erroneous and anachronistic, this kind of terminology should be dropped.

4. It is mostly looking at the whole of classical Israelite prophecy in hindsight and seeing that it turned toward an emphasis on salvation around 587 and after, plus the perspective one obtains on the Old Testament by looking at it through the New Testament which lead toward an exaggerated emphasis on what is promised in the various, largely authentic, words of hope in pre-exilic prophets. What needs to be seen, and almost never is, is that Amos, Hosea, Jeremiah, and Ezekiel got to the point where they saw *nothing* but disaster ahead. This is a profoundly important point for any understanding of prophetic theology to deal with, even though that point may not have been the last episode in their ministries, and even though final doom was always spoken in tension with some authentic (earlier or later) perceptions of God's desire for the people to repent, God's desire to show the people mercy.

5. This position was first advocated by H. Gressmann in *Der Ursprung der israelitisch-jüdischen Eschatologie* (Göttingen: Vandenhoeck & Ruprecht, 1905) and then later in *Der Messias* (Göttingen: Vandenhoeck & Ruprecht, 1929). At a later stage it was taken up by S. Mowinckel in *Psalmenstudien* II—"Der Ursprung der Israelitischen Eschatologie" (Amsterdam: P. Schippers, 1966 edition). The main points are accessible in English in Mowinckel's *He That Cometh,* trans. G. W. Anderson (New York: Abingdon, 1954), pp. 125–54. The most recent expression of this view comes from I. Engnell; see in the recent translation of his essays by J. Willis, *A Rigid Scrutiny: Critical Essays on the Old Testament by Ivan Engnell* (Nashville: Vanderbilt University Press, 1969), especially pp. 123–79.

6. The best overall criticism of the position of Gressmann, Mowinckel, and Engnell is found in J. Lindblom, *Prophecy in Ancient Israel,* pp. 316–19.

7. C. F. Whitley, *The Exilic Age* (Philadelphia: Westminster, 1957), pp. 58ff.; H. Renckens, *The Religion of Israel,* trans. N. B. Smith (New York: Sheed & Ward, 1966), pp. 238ff.

8. The Jewish scholar Y. Kaufmann has discerned that Christian scholars have a bias toward interpreting the prophecies of the destruction of Judah as a divine precedent within biblical history for God's subsequent alleged rejection of Judaism and his election of the Church to replace Israel as his vehicle for history's redemption. There could be no clearer justification for Kaufmann's suspicion than the statement Renckens makes on pp. 249–50 of his book *Religion of Israel.* For Kaufmann's view see his *The Religion of Israel,* pp. 403ff.

9. Renckens, *Religion of Israel,* p. 239.

10. Ibid., p. 240.
11. Lindblom, *Prophecy,* p. 313.
12. Ibid., p. 321.
13. Ibid., p. 337.
14. Ibid., p. 339.
15. Among those who have dealt with it too schematically and simplistically are: T. C. Vriezen, *The Religion of Ancient Israel*, trans. H. Hoskins (Philadelphia: Westminster, 1967), pp. 247–48; Ackroyd, *Exile and Restoration,* pp. 61–62; N. K. Gottwald, *Studies in the Book of Lamentations,* pp. 93–94.
16. W. E. March, "Prophecy," *Old Testament Form Criticism,* ed. J. H. Hayes (San Antonio: Trinity University Press, 1974), p. 162.
17. H. W. Wolff, "Die Begründungen der prophetischen Heils- und Unheilssprüche," pp. 1ff. K. Koch, *The Growth of the Biblical Tradition,* p. 218. H. G. Reventlow, *Wächter über Israel,* pp. 42–44, 65–68.
18. A good, readable review of form-critical assumptions, methods, and goals is available in G. M. Tucker's *Form Criticism of the Old Testament.* The general principles are set forth on pp. 1–21, and the application to the prophetic literature is made on pp. 54–77.
19. This criticism extends to J. Lindblom, *Prophecy* and G. von Rad, *Old Testament Theology* II, who are excellent form critics, but who do not apply a consistent form-critical methodology to deal with this issue.
20. W. Brueggemann moves toward providing a basis for seeing this point in Hosea in his *Tradition for Crisis: A Study in Hosea.* And C. Westermann deals with both forms in Second Isaiah in his "Sprache und Struktur der Prophetie Deuterojesajas," see pp. 117ff. in his *Forschung am Alten Testament.* Reventlow, *Wächter,* also deals with both genres in Ezekiel, although I think he badly misunderstands the setting and function of each genre—so much so, that the present study is quite independent of his. We should note that in none of these three studies do the authors seem to have been primarily motivated by a desire to understand the doom/salvation shift, as is the case in the present study.

CHAPTER I

1. I use the word "Oracle" because it is a time-honored, well-recognized term in connection with this speech-genre, because it acknowledges the importance of the "Messenger Formula" ("Thus says the Lord" often coming at the beginning or middle of the speech), and because it denotes that the speech itself is represented as God's declaration. I prefer to use the word "Judgment" over "Doom" or "Disaster" because God is not just foretelling bad times; God is bringing bad times for a very specific reason: to punish his people. On this point we agree with C. Westermann in his important book *Basic Forms of Prophetic Speech,* pp. 169ff.
2. This genre is sometimes called "Oracle of Salvation." "Salvation" says more than it means by having Christian connotations of saving from death, hell, satan. "Deliverance" is more descriptive of the dimensions

of what actually is promised; it is closer to the Hebrew language and mentality.

3. This is an untranslated article, whose German title is "Die Begründungen der prophetischen Heils- und Unheilssprüche," pp. 1–22. "Begründung" seems to be a hard word to render into English. In H. W. Wolff's sense it means "reason," "basis," "foundation," or "motivation." And it refers to the first major portion of the Oracle of Judgment, which other scholars have called "Accusation," "Diatribe," "Indictment."

4. An excellent survey of the history of the study of this form is found in Westermann's *Basic Forms,* pp. 13–89.

5. Wolff, "Die Begründungen," first designates the two parts in footnote 1 of page 1 of his article; there he is assuming that the two parts describe both Oracles of Deliverance and Oracles of Judgment; his description of the function of the two parts is primarily from pp. 11ff.

6. Ibid., pp. 7, 10, 12, 15, 19, 20.

7. Ibid., p. 7 for the quotation; he refers to the "pastoral" role on pp. 8, 9, 10, 17, 19, 20, 21.

8. Ibid., p. 12.

9. Ibid.

10. Ibid.

11. Ibid., p. 2; in Hebrew *lākēn, ʿal-kēn, kî,* and *hinnēh.*

12. Ibid., p. 1–2.

13. Westermann, *Basic Forms,* sees the following parts developing what he insists is fundamentally a two-member speech structure (see his statement on pp. 86–87, where he concludes his analysis of Wolff by saying, "Further efforts . . . must . . . begin with this definition of the prophetic judgment-speech as a messenger's speech consisting of two parts, the reason and the announcement").

		Introduction
Reason	–	Accusation
		Development
		Messenger Formula
Announcement	–	Intervention of God
		Results of Intervention

We will have more to say about Westermann's very helpful study on the Oracle of Judgment under our section on "Setting" where it becomes clear how much he has done with "Announcement of Judgment to Individuals" and "Messenger Formula" as feeding into this genre.

14. K. Koch, in his *The Growth of the Biblical Tradition* labels the parts as follows: I. "Indication of the Situation, or Diatribe"; II. "Prediction of Disaster, or Threat"; III. "The Concluding Characterization" (pp. 211–12). His first two segments are really the same as the two basic parts seen by Wolff; however Koch's comments mark a notable regression from the understanding of the "Reason-Accusation" obtained by Wolff and Westermann (partly seen in the weak label he gives to *I,* and also by his notion that part *II* is so much more important than *I*

that it can stand alone and independent of it, pp. 211–12). Koch makes an unconvincing case for adding the section "Concluding Characterization" (pp. 212–13).

15. See in G. M. Tucker, *Form Criticism of the Old Testament,* pp. 62–65, and especially the footnote on p. 64 where he states his disagreements with Westermann's subdivisions of the two basic parts. W. Brueggemann, *Tradition for Crisis,* calls the two fundamental components "Indictment" and "Sentence" (see pp. 56ff.); Brueggemann tends toward some subdivisions within those headings, but that is largely in exegetical application to specific texts in Hosea.

16. Westermann, *Basic Forms,* pp. 174–75.

17. "Theophany" refers to God's Self-revelation. For more on this see the discussion in the latter part of Chapter VII and the book by Kuntz footnoted and discussed there.

18. *"Sitz im Leben"* means "seat," "place," or "setting" "in life." The quotation comes from E. March, "Prophecy," *Old Testament Form Criticism,* ed. J. Hayes, p. 162.

19. This is the direction suggested by D. Knight, in his paper "The Understanding of 'SITZ IM LEBEN' in Form Criticism," *The Society of Biblical Literature, One Hundred Tenth Annual Meeting: Seminar Papers,* vol. I, pp. 105–25.

20. See p. 446 and other parts of R. Knierim's article "Old Testament Form Criticism Reconsidered," pp. 435–68.

21. Westermann, *Basic Forms,* especially pp. 98–128, but applications of this are seen in pp. 129ff.

22. See ibid., pp. 146ff.

23. See B. Gemser, "The *rîb* or controversy-pattern in Hebrew mentality," *Wisdom in Israel and in the Ancient Near East,* ed. M. Noth, Supplements to *Vetus Testamentum,* vol. III (Leiden: E. J. Brill, 1955), pp. 120–37.

24. H. Huffmon, "The Covenant Lawsuit in the Prophets," *JBL* 78 (1959): 285–95. G. E. Wright, "The Lawsuit of God: A Form-Critical Study of Deut. 32," *Israel's Prophetic Heritage: Essays in Honor of James Muilenburg,* ed. B. W. Anderson and W. Harrelson (New York: Harper, 1962), pp. 26–67. J. Limburg, "The Root *rîb* and the Prophetic Lawsuit Speeches," *JBL* 88 (1969): 291–304.

25. This is discussed in a very valuable way in H. E. von Waldow's *Der traditionsgeschichtliche Hintergrund der prophetischen Gerichtsreden,* BZAW, no. 85 (Berlin: Alfred Töpelmann, 1963).

26. E. Würthwein, "Der Ursprung der prophetischen Gerichtsrede," *ZThK* 49 (1952): 1–16.

27. *Law and Covenant in Israel and the Ancient Near East* (Pittsburgh: Presbyterian Board of Colportage, 1955 [reprinted from *Biblical Archaeologist*]), p. 46.

28. The references are both in Genesis.

29. See in R. Clements, *Abraham and David,* pp. 15–34.

30. See in J. H. Hayes, "The Tradition of Zion's Inviolability," *JBL* 82 (1963): 419–26.

31. See in L. Perlitt, *Bundestheologie im Alten Testament,* WMANT 36, ed. G. Bornkamm and G. von Rad (Neukirchen-Vluyn: Neukirchener, 1969). G. Fohrer, *History of Israelite Religion,* pp. 262ff. and 298ff.

32. R. Smend, *Die Bundesformel.* He presents a historical analysis of the phrase "I will be your God and you will be my people" and its variations.

33. H. Huffmon, "The Treaty Background of Hebrew *YADA,*" *Bulletin of the American Schools of Oriental Research,* 181 (1966): 31–37.

34. One should compare Brueggemann's *Tradition* where he argues at length about the covenantal basis for Hosea's preaching, pp. 26–105.

35. On this point it is interesting and important to note that two scholars, D. Hillers and H. G. Reventlow, have written studies which give some evidence of a correspondence of theme and wording between what is found in covenant curse liturgies and what we see in the Proclamation sections of prophetic Oracles of Judgment. Hillers does this with special emphasis on Deuteronomy 28, *Treaty Curses and the Old Testament Prophets,* Biblica et Orientalia 16 (Rome: Pontifical Biblical Institute, 1964), pp. 31ff., while Reventlow does it with a primary interest in Leviticus 26, *Wächter über Israel,* pp. 42–43 and 157–58.

36. Tucker, *Form Criticism,* pp. 65 and 69 says that prophecy is the setting for this genre.

37. In his *Suffering as Divine Discipline* (Colgate Rochester Divinity School Bulletin, 28, Special Issue, 1955), J. A. Sanders makes out that chastisement is a central teaching in Jeremiah, devoting a whole chapter to it, pp. 46–78. Actually, Sanders's idea that the plan of punishment and renewal in Jeremiah is chastisement and repentance hangs by a few verses. 2:19 is probably the only authentic use of *yāsar* in Jeremiah's doom message. That is hardly enough evidence on which to base a doctrine.

38. The bi-polar formulas are discussed in detail on pp. 174–229 of my doctoral dissertation, "The Concept of Forgiveness in the Pre-exilic Prophets in Relation to Its Form-Historical Setting." See J. Scharbert, "Formgeschichte und Exegese von Ex. 34:6f und seiner Parallelen," pp. 130–50. T. Thordarson, "The Form-Historical Problem of Exodus 34:6–7" (Ph.D. dissertation, University of Chicago, 1959).

39. Koch, "Gibt es ein Vergeltungsdogma im Alten Testament?" pp. 1ff.

40. Knierim, "Form Criticism: The Present State of an Exegetical Discipline."

41. Bright, *History of Israel,* pp. 301–2.

42. G. von Rad, *Old Testament Theology* II, pp. 192–98.

43. Bright, *History of Israel,* pp. 305–11.

44. J. P. Hyatt, "Introduction, Exegesis," *Jeremiah,* pp. 778ff. M. Noth, *The History of Israel,* pp. 279–86.

45. See below in Chapter II, pp. 40–49.

46. See in Westermann, *Basic Forms,* pp. 129ff.

47. This is discussed in Koch, *Biblical Tradition,* pp. 205–6.

CHAPTER II

1. Scholars who stress the continual accessibility of repentance are: T. C. Vriezen, *An Outline of Old Testament Theology,* p. 274; J. Lindblom, *Prophecy in Ancient Israel,* pp. 320, 383; Y. Kaufmann, *The Religion of Israel,* pp. 423–27.

2. What follows is a condensation of the main points of my article "The Prophetic Summons to Repentance," pp. 30–48.

3. The most direct support for the function of repentance in covenant renewal liturgies comes from G. von Rad, "The Form-Critical Problem of the Hexateuch" in *The Problem of the Hexateuch and Other Essays,* trans. E. W. T. Dicken (London: Oliver & Boyd, 1966), pp. 27–36 (see especially p. 33). See also R. E. Clements, *Prophecy and Covenant,* pp. 86–102. K. Baltzer, *The Covenant Formulary,* pp. 39–62, devotes a chapter to covenant renewal texts, and in them repentance has a predominant place. Compare what W. Brueggemann says about the relation of repentance to covenant renewal in Amos, "Amos 4:4–13 and Israel's Covenant Worship," *VT* 15 (1965): 1–15, and in Hosea (pp. 80–86 of *Tradition for Crisis*).

4. For further discussion of the evidence for this speech-form, its origin, and implications, see my article "Summons to Repentance," pp. 30–48.

5. S. Mowinckel, *Zur Komposition des Buches Jeremia,* pp. 20ff.; J. P. Hyatt, "Introduction, Exegesis," *Jeremiah,* p. 787, et al. accept the passage as genuine.

6. On Jeremiah's imagery for repentance see W. Holladay, *The Root Šûbh in the Old Testament* (Leiden: E. J. Brill, 1958), pp. 128–39 and 152–53. His study is good on the grammatical aspects of this key verb for repentance, and on source analysis, but does not concern itself with the failure of repentance as such.

7. There is a textual problem at the end of 9:5 so that the MT does not make sense as it stands. J. Bright, *Jeremiah,* p. 72 and Hyatt, *Jeremiah,* pp. 889–90 redivide the consonants at the end of the verse, follow the LXX reading, to concur with the RSV translation quoted above.

8. The passages on which we have specifically commented do not begin to exhaust what Jeremiah has to say about the failure of repentance, chastisement, and purgation. See also Jer. 2:22, 30; 3:1, 7, 10; 6:9–10; 7:13; 8:4–9; 11:8; 13:11; 18:11–12; 23:14; 25:3–7; 26:3; 35:15–17; 44:5.

9. Compare with W. Brueggemann's article "Amos 4:4–13 and Israel's Covenant Worship," pp. 1–15.

10. An interesting source which, unlike the present study, has as its primary purpose to *compare* Jeremiah and Ezekiel on a literary and theological level, is J. W. Miller's *Das Verhältnis Jeremias und Hesekiels Sprachlich und Theologisch Untersucht.* I came upon and read this monograph after my manuscript was all but completed. The present study and Miller's have only a few parallels, which will be noted on the

pages to follow, but these were arrived at quite independently. The most obvious differences are: Miller spends two-thirds of his space on literary and stylistic comparisons; his work is not focused on the doom/salvation shift; he does not investigate the relation between what we find in certain speech-forms and specific events in the first quarter of the sixth century.

11. W. Eichrodt, *Ezekiel,* considers 3:16–21 to be an editorial addition, dependent upon chapter 33 (p. 75). He takes the "watchman" commission in chapter 33 to be original in that context, and raises the possibility of dependence on chapter 18 in the following words about retribution for the individual without resolving the matter (pp. 442–56).

12. Both Eichrodt, *Ezekiel,* p. 240, and W. Zimmerli, "The Message of the Prophet Ezekiel," p. 157, accept the basic structure that the word of repentance to the individual and the succeeding generations comes after the ultimate word of judgment on Jerusalem, and before the encompassing turn toward salvation, as a pastorally motivated word of encouragement to the despondent survivors in Exile.

13. Compare what Miller, *Verhältnis Jeremias und Hesekiels,* says about the "radicalization of the view of history [with regard to the people's sin and God's judgment]" in Ezekiel on pp. 143–47. The passages which he selects give evidence of this. But he does not find this "radicalization" in Jeremiah; and in Ezekiel he does not probe either the causes or the consequences of the "radicalization."

14. Zimmerli, "Message of . . . Ezekiel," p. 142.

15. In Volume II of his *Theology of the Old Testament,* Eichrodt devotes a substantial section to forgiveness (pp. 443–83) and does not deal with this phenomenon. In his whole treatment of forgiveness he does not bring to attention the problematic character of OT forgiveness, or the limited extent of its consequences—merely mitigated punishment ordinarily—when it is granted. Although in many ways its methodology is dated, the best monograph on forgiveness remains J. J. Stamm's *Erlösen und Vergeben im Alten Testament.* He does recognize the presence of forgiveness denials in the pre-exilic prophets (pp. 112–15); but with his rather brief or piecemeal treatment of this, he does not put it into a meaningful context, or draw any general conclusions from it. A strong point of Stamm's study is his repeated recognition that what forgiveness in the OT really means and accomplishes is a reduction, but not cancellation, of the punishment (see pp. 109, 110, 127, 143, 147).

A whole different approach is taken by K. Koch in his 1966 article "Sühne und Sündenvergebung: Um die Wende von der exilischen zur nachexilischen Zeit," pp. 217–39. His main points are that "the divine forgiveness of sins plays no role in pre-exilic Israel," and that "the exilic/post-exilic time discovers God's readiness to forgive in that it sees forgiveness accomplished and experiences liberation out of sin in cultic acts and priestly formulae" (pp. 219 and 227 respectively). We should be quite clear that Koch is not talking about the denial of real forgiveness by the pre-exilic prophets; instead, he is saying that no one before the middle of the Exile had any notion of genuine forgiveness as a theological possibility. Since I am in almost complete disagreement with the first eleven pages of Koch's article (the latter part develops his interpretation of the meaning of post-exilic cultic expiation), I need to outline my points of difference with him here, even though a detailed counter-argument is inappropriate at this point. 1) By designating *kippẹr* and *sālaḥ* as "the *proper* vocables for expiation and forgiveness" (p. 225; italics mine), Koch falls into the methodological error of equating "words" with "concepts" as that fallacy has been clarified so devastatingly by James Barr in his *The Semantics of Biblical Language* (Oxford: Oxford University Press, 1961). 2) Koch shows no evidence of having done his homework on forgiveness images beyond those two "proper vocables," and thus he ignores the important pre-exilic use of a construct like *nāsā' 'āwōn.* 3) Similarly, he shows no awareness of the work done on the key pre-exilic passage, Exod. 34:6–7, and its echoes. 4) It is anachronistic to assume, as Koch does, that punishment and forgiveness are always and necessarily opposite lines of divine action. 5) Taking the statements out of their context, Koch converts prophetic denials of the possibility of the *expression* of God's forgiveness in this or that particular situation into abstract statements indicating that the prophets had no faith in God as a being who could readily forgive (see Koch, pp. 222–23). The foundation for my series of objections to Koch's position, in which the interested reader can find an extended analysis of the prophetic denials of forgiveness, is my doctoral dissertation, "The Concept of Forgiveness in the Pre-exilic Prophets in Relation to Its Form-Historical Setting."

16. See Chapter III, "Forgiveness in the Prophetic Oracle of Doom," pp. 97–229 of my "Concept of Forgiveness."

17. Three times in Jeremiah—4:27; 5:10, 18—the word of judgment is interrupted by the phrase "yet I will not make a full end" or some slight variation on that. Hyatt, *Jeremiah,* pp. 841, 847, 850, considers each of these a "mitigating gloss." The only other possible support for Jeremiah's accepting the remnant hope appears in 23:3 which Hyatt, *Jeremiah,* p. 988, and W. Rudolph, *Jeremia,* p. XVII, consider to be added to the book by a later editor. That Jeremiah, or one of his disciples, refers to those who will receive salvation as "the remnant of Israel" in 31:7 does not contradict what we have said. Judgment is qualified if it is promised that a remnant will be exempt from judgment or continue through judgment. But it is not qualified if, after the judgment, when God begins his saving activity, it is said that he will save a remnant of his people. The one passage in Ezekiel which seems to go against his repudiation of the remnant hope is 6:8: "Yet I will leave some of you alive." The verse is not accepted as genuine by Eichrodt, *Ezekiel,* p. 96 or G. Fohrer, *Introduction to the Old Testament,* p. 410. G. A. Cooke concluded that "Ezekiel holds no doctrine of a remnant," *The Book of Ezekiel,* p. 60. This point is reinforced for Ezekiel and accepted for Jeremiah by E. W. Heaton in his article "The Root *šᵉār* and the Doctrine of the Remnant," *Journal of Theological Studies,* n.s. 3 (1952): 30 and 39. E. Jenni, "Remnant," *IDB* 4, ed. G. A. Buttrick (New York: Abing-

don, 1962), p. 33 says: "Jeremiah and Ezekiel both give up any claim to the traditional remnant concept in their proclamation of a total judgment." One of the points on which I find myself in strong agreement with a conclusion reached by Miller is where he says: "It is therefore astonishing that Jeremiah and Ezekiel in common have renounced this 'remnant' conception transmitted from antiquity and proclaimed the total annihilation of Judah"; *Verhältnis Jeremias und Hesekiels,* p. 165.

18. See D. N. Freedman's insistence on remnant belief as normative in Jeremiah and Ezekiel in his "The Book of Ezekiel," p. 452. But this is moderate compared to H. Renckens, *The Religion of Israel,* p. 254, who says that "the theme of the Remnant of Israel contains a summary of the entire preaching of the prophets." Also Lindblom, *Prophecy,* pp. 366ff.

19. According to Brown, Driver, Briggs, *Hebrew and English Lexicon* (Oxford: Clarendon, 1955), pp. 299 and 328, *ḥûs* is translated "pity" most often, and *ḥāmal* usually rendered "spare." The RSV translation reverses these. For the sake of consistency and to aid the reader who does not have facility in Hebrew, we will use them just as in this line of our text.

It is interesting that as concerns their use together the commentaries say surprisingly little about this distinctive formulation. It is ignored by H. G. May, "Introduction, Exegesis," *Ezekiel.* G. A. Cooke, *Ezekiel,* p. 61, recognizes that it appears a number of times, offers the useful observation that "the repeated use of the phrase implies that the contrary is Jahveh's usual attitude," but does not designate its structure as a formula or litany as we shall below. This is the same with Eichrodt, who, although he apparently fails to recognize its repeated employment in Ezekiel, makes the following comment on the occurrence in 9:10: "The very refusal to show mercy or to mitigate the punishment now threatening them points back to the forbearance and faithfulness which has characterized all that God has done up to now" (*Ezekiel,* p. 133). On 9:5 Zimmerli comments: "In the unrelenting divine commission there echoes in leitmotiv fashion the pitilessness of the divine judgment decision of 8:18" (*Ezekiel* I, p. 228). Then with 9:10 Zimmerli speaks of "the expression of the relentlessness of Yahweh" appearing for the third time (also 8:18; 9:5), but he does not go into it beyond that passing comment (ibid., p. 229).

20. 15:1 is accepted by Mowinckel, *Jeremia,* pp. 20ff., Rudolph, *Jeremia,* p. XIV, Fohrer, *Introduction,* p. 394, but not Hyatt, *Jeremiah,* p. 788; 16:5 and 16:13 are accepted by Mowinckel, *Jeremia,* pp. 20ff., and Eissfeldt, *The Old Testament: An Introduction,* p. 352, but not Hyatt *Jeremiah,* p. 789 or Rudolph, *Jeremia,* p. XVI. 18:10 is held original by Eissfeldt, *Introduction,* p. 352, and Fohrer, *Introduction,* p. 394, but not by Mowinckel, *Jeremia,* pp. 20ff.; Rudolph, *Jeremia,* p. XVI*;* or Hyatt, *Jeremiah,* p. 789. 21:7 is held unoriginal by Mowinckel, *Jeremia,* pp. 20ff.; Hyatt, *Jeremiah,* p. 789; Rudolph, *Jeremia,* p. XVI*;* and Fohrer, *Introduction,* p. 395, and should be used for comparative purposes only. Finally supporting the originality of 25:29 are Mowinckel, *Jeremia,* pp. 20ff.;

Rudolph, *Jeremia,* p. 149; Fohrer, *Introduction,* p. 397, but rejected by Hyatt, *Jeremiah,* p. 1002.

21. So with Mowinckel, *Jeremia,* pp. 20 and 31; Rudolph, *Jeremia,* pp. XVI and 88; Hyatt, *Jeremiah,* pp. 788–89; Eissfeldt, *Introduction,* p. 351 on 13:14; Fohrer, *Introduction,* p. 395 on 21:7.

22. Here the (RSV) translations are reversed from what we find in RSV of Ezekiel, and follow the suggestions in Brown, Driver, Briggs, *Lexicon* (note 19). Clearly we have to take *ḥûs* and *ḥāmal* as virtually synonymous in meaning.

23. Gen. 45:20; 1 Sam. 24:10 may be early, but are not particularly instructive. In Joel 2:17 and Neh. 13:22 it is used without "eyes" in contexts which make it equivalent to forgiveness pleas (see also Jon. 4:10, 11; Isa. 13:18; Ps. 72:13).

24. So with H. E. W. Fosbroke, "Introduction, Exegesis," *Amos, IB* 6 (New York: Abingdon, 1956), p. 833. R. S. Cripps, *A Critical and Exegetical Commentary on the Book of Amos* (London, SPCK, 1955), p. 226.

25. Although he does not deal with *niḥam* at all, Holladay has some excellent observations on the endless artistry of Jeremiah's employment of *šûbh* (see pp. 129–39 and 152–53 of his *The Root Šûbh*).

26. It is often suggested that 18:1–12 comes from an alleged Deuteronomistic editor of Jeremiah (see note 20 above). If this is the case, and I have questions about its validity, then Jeremiah's disciples and editors continued his own use of *šûb* and *niḥam* with great faithfulness and undiminished brilliance.

27. The forgiveness or mercy pole appears alone in 1 Kgs. 8:23; Pss. 78:38; 86:5, 15; 99:8; 103:8–9; 106:45; 111:4; 145:8; Joel 2:13; Mic. 7:18; Jon. 4:2; Neh. 9:17; 2 Chr. 6:14; 30:9; Dan. 9:4. See pp. 186 to 214 of my dissertation ("Concept of Forgiveness"), where the possibility of the forgiveness pole existing earlier and separately from the bi-polar formulas is considered in detail. Scharbert ("Formgeschichte und Exegese von Ex. 34:6f und seiner Parallelen") sees various phrases of the formulation having different spheres of origin (pp. 133ff.), but he thinks of that history as having taken place before the elements were combined into their present arrangement in Exod. 34:6–7 by the "J" source (pp. 131–32). I think that he dates the present form of Exod. 34:6–7 several centuries too early.

28. I have gathered some of the evidence for the place of repentance and forgiveness in covenant renewal ceremonies on pp. 177–86 of my dissertation "Concept of Forgiveness." In this presentation I was very much helped by the excellent work of K. Baltzer, *Covenant Formulary,* who sees a definite rootage of these elements of turning and pardon in covenant renewal texts like Exodus 34 and Nehemiah 9–10 (see pp. 39–60).

29. This point emerges both with Koch's article discussed under note 15 above, and also in the arguments I have brought against his position there. A thread of agreement running through Stamm, *Erlösen und Ver-*

geben, Koch, "Sündenvergebung," and myself ("Concept of Forgiveness") is that much of the time forgiveness in the Old Testament means no more than mitigation of punishment.

30. See pp. 155–229 of my doctoral dissertation "Concept of Forgiveness" for a full discussion of the possible impact of those passages, and the traditions behind them, on the pre-exilic prophets.

CHAPTER III

1. There are questions about authorship and the type of distress which provide the background. J. P. Hyatt, "Introduction, Exegesis," *Jeremiah,* focuses on verse 22 to decide that the situation is a time of drought (p. 935); he considers the section to have a mixed, post-Jeremianic authorship (pp. 929, 936). Quite opposite, A. Weiser, *Das Buch des Propheten Jeremia,* sees 14:17–15:4 as one unit and insists that it addresses a situation "not of drought, but of war adversity" (p. 126). He apparently traces the words back to Jeremiah (p. 122), and urges a date around 597 B.C. (p. 126). J. Bright, *Jeremiah,* thinks of Jeremiah as the basic author of the unit including our section, and suggests that a piece composed for a time of drought has been expanded and adapted to a later situation of war (p. 103). Compare W. Rudolph, *Jeremia,* pp. 94–95.

2. See W. Baumgartner, *Die Klagegedichte des Jeremia,* BZAW 32 (Berlin: Alfred Töpelmann, 1917); also Weiser, *Jeremia,* p. 126.

3. With Weiser, *Jeremia,* p. 126.

4. The Infinitive Absolute construction: *mā'ōs mā'astā.*

5. Bright, *Jeremiah,* p. LXXXVIII; G. von Rad, *Old Testament Theology* II, p. 192.

6. This refers to the frequent formulation "I will be your God, and you will be my people." The origin and history of this form have been discussed by R. Smend, *Die Bundesformel.*

7. Weiser, *Jeremia,* p. 105.

8. D. N. Freedman, "The Book of Ezekiel," p. 456.

9. W. Zimmerli, "The Message of the Prophet Ezekiel," p. 142.

10. G. Fohrer, *Ezechiel,* p. 142.

11. W. Eichrodt, *Ezekiel,* p. 104. Fohrer, *Ezechiel,* p. 46. Zimmerli, *Ezechiel* I, p. 183.

12. W. Eichrodt, *Ezekiel,* p. 104.

13. Fohrer, *Ezechiel,* p. 46.

14. E. Rohland explicitly makes a connection between desecration of the temple and God's rejection of Jerusalem-Zion; he says this in relation to Ezek. 7:22; 9:4ff.; 24:21; etc. (pp. 194–95), in "Die Bedeutung der Erwählungsradionen Israels für die Eschatologie der alttestamentlichen Propheten."

15. Eichrodt, *Ezekiel,* p. 104.

16. This is the position of Hyatt, *Jeremiah,* pp. 1040 and 1052; O. Eissfeldt, *The Old Testament: An Introduction,* explicitly denies the authenticity of 31:35–37 (p. 362) and 33:24–26 (p. 349); Rudolph, *Jeremia* (pp. 199–201) and Weiser, *Jeremia* (pp. XL and 307) reject 33:24–26, but apparently accept 31:35–37. H. Cunliffe-Jones, *Jeremiah,* TBC (London:

SCM Press, 1960) denies authenticity to both 31:35–37 (p. 203) and 33:24–26 (pp. 211–12) on the basis that their content is contrary to the teaching of Jeremiah evident in the generally accepted portions of the book.

17. See H. D. Preuss, *Jahweglaube und Zukunftserwartung,* BWANT 87 (Stuttgart: W. Kohlhammer, 1968), pp. 157–58. H. H. Rowley, *The Biblical Doctrine of Election* (London: Lutterworth, 1950), pp. 51ff. Von Rad, *Old Testament Theology* II, pp. 198, 406.

Although his study is mainly concerned with the relation of election to the eschatological dimension of salvation preaching, Rohland does make some excellent passing comments about rejection teaching in Jeremiah and Ezekiel. He sees many of the same passages we have studied as clearly meaning rejection, and he talks about the "election-judgment" and its resolution in a "new election." See pp. 194–95 for this in Ezekiel in relation to the Zion tradition; pp. 69–70 for the Exodus tradition in Jeremiah; pp. 83–84 for the Exodus tradition in Ezekiel. Rohland, *Erwählungstraditionen.*

18. T. C. Vriezen, *Die Erwählung Israels nach dem Alten Testament* (Zurich: Zwingli, 1953), devotes pp. 98–108 to the topic "Erwählung und Verwerfung" ("Election and Rejection").

19. In a sense Vriezen's whole study on this topic is an attempted refutation of a comment made earlier by L. Köhler that "election stands side by side with rejection." See in Köhler's *Old Testament Theology,* trans. A. S. Todd (Philadelphia: Westminster, 1957), p. 82.

20. Vriezen, *Erwählung Israels,* pp. 102ff. One reason that he moves toward this view is that he entirely ignores the teaching of rejection in Hosea and deals with fewer passages in Jeremiah and Ezekiel than we have examined. At the same time he takes statements about annihilation in the "D" literature—passages in Deuteronomy 28, for example—as clear indications of the presence of the rejection teaching.

21. Ibid. This is best seen in the latter half of the book, pp. 104–8.

CHAPTER IV

1. Although the term "theodicy" may be new to the reader in the context of prophetic thought, we are not originating such a usage. Y. Kaufmann, *The Religion of Israel,* has quite a few references to theodicy in the general period that interests us: see pp. 292, 332–33, 402. C. F. Whitley suggests that Jeremiah was "the earliest biblical thinker to deal with the question of theodicy"; see *The Exilic Age,* p. 55. W. Eichrodt thinks he finds theodicy in Ezekiel (*Ezekiel,* see p. 237). Two valuable article-length studies which deal with theodicy in the Old Testament outside of the Book of Job as well as within that source are Eichrodt's "Vorsehungsglaube und Theodizee im Alten Testament," *Festschrift O. Procksch,* ed. A. Alt, F. Baumgartel (Leipzig: A. Deichert, 1934), pp. 45–70 and J. L. Crenshaw, "Popular Questioning of the Justice of God in Ancient Israel," *ZAW* 82 (1970): 380–95. Both the article by Eichrodt and the one by Crenshaw are more wide ranging than this chapter in that they include sections on Job and other sources in the Old Testa-

ment as well as some parts of the prophets. Neither of those studies arises as an attempt to understand prophetic judgment preaching in the context of the experience of the evil of 587. So, those studies and this one complement one another more than they clash or overlap. Several of my points of difference with Crenshaw are given below. Eichrodt gives theodicy a negative connotation, so that it is something which genuine faith avoids or overcomes. My own approach differs from Eichrodt's in being more descriptive and less abstractly theological. J. J. Stamm, "Die Theodizee in Babylon und Israel," *Jaarbericht Ex Oriente Lux: Van Het Vooraziatisch-Egyptisch,* Gezelschap 9 (1955): 99–107 and R. J. Williams, "Theodicy in the Ancient Near East," *Canadian Journal of Theology,* 2 (1956): 14–26, have in common that neither says much of relevance for studies in the prophets. Their central focus has to do with either non-Israelite material or the Book of Job.

2. W. Fulton, "Theodicy," *Encyclopedia of Religion and Ethics,* ed. J. Hastings, 12 (1921), p. 289.

3. See J. Hick, "The Problem of Evil," *The Encyclopedia of Philosophy,* ed. P. Edwards, 3 (New York: Macmillan, 1967), p. 136.

4. Crenshaw, "Questioning Justice of God," pp. 392–93, makes a good point about the need better to understand the mind and voice of the people in Israel's lived religion. See also his *Prophetic Conflict: Its Effect upon Israelite Religion,* BZAW 124 (Berlin: Walter de Gruyter, 1971), pp. 36–38.

5. S. Mowinckel, *The Psalms in Israel's Worship* I (New York: Abingdon, 1962), p. 194.

6. Dating Psalms is notoriously difficult, but my own sense that these ring true to the spirit of Lamentations, and the evidences of distress reflected in Jeremiah and Ezekiel, is corroborated by E. Janssen, *Juda in der Exilszeit, Ein Beitrag zur Frage der Entstehung des Judentums* FRLANT, n. s. 51 (Göttingen: Vandenhoeck & Ruprecht, 1956), pp. 19–20, who dates all four of them to the Exile; P. Ackroyd, *Exile and Restoration: A Study of Hebrew Thought of the Sixth Century B.C.,* p. 45, who takes Psalms 44, 74, and 79 as exilic; E. Kissane, *The Book of Psalms* (Dublin: Browne & Nolan, 1954), I, p. 192; II, pp. 10, 43, 90, who dates each of them, studied separately, to the Exile. W. S. McCullough, "Introduction, Exegesis," *Psalms, IB* 4 (New York: Abingdon, 1955), pp. 393, 479, 426, concurs on this dating for Psalms 74, 79, and 89; while H. J. Kraus agrees on the probable exilic date for Psalms 74 and 79, *Psalmen* I, BKAT (Neukirchen-Vluyn: Neukirchener, 1962), pp. 515, 551.

7. Kraus, *Klagelieder,* BKAT 20 (Neukirchen-Vlyun: Neukirchener, 1956), pp. 11–12, says that they are all exilic, and all closely related to the catastrophe of 587. Fohrer, *Introduction to the Old Testament,* feels that the date is undoubtedly exilic, after 587 (p. 298). N. Gottwald, *Studies in the Book of Lamentations,* summarizes his position on p. 42: "We have now established that the Book of Lamentations is a communal lament of mixed types from the sixth century B.C."

8. This interaction between the lament tradition and the prophets'

messages is included in the range of matters considered in H. W. Wolff's "Das Zitat im Prophetenspruch," *Gesammelte Studien zum Alten Testament,* TB 22 (Munich: Chr. Kaiser, 1964), pp. 36–129. Wolff has found more than 250 quotations (of the people's voice) within the prophetic books (p. 40). These include a huge variety of themes of which doubts or complaints concerning God's justice *are only a small part.* Our own study enables us to agree with him that *one* of the sources of the prophetic quotations is "the cultic-liturgical life of the community" (p. 88). Taken as a whole, the present study and Wolff's "Das Zitat . . ." have only a limited area of intersection, and correspondingly, a small area of agreement.

9. In his important article "Die Begründungen der prophetischen Heils- und Unheilssprüche," Wolff offers this passage as an example of the speech-form, p. 31.

10. Perhaps we should indicate what results source analysis has come to on Jer. 16:10–13. According to the judgment of W. Rudolph, *Jeremia* (p. 100), and J. P. Hyatt, "Introduction, Exegesis," *Jeremiah* (p. 946), it is from the Deuteronomistic editors of Jeremiah. Fohrer, *Introduction* (p. 400), says it was one of the late additions to the book. But there is stronger support for its genuineness. Mowinckel, *Zur Komposition des Buches Jeremia* (p. 20), usually skeptical unless there is good reason for discerning genuineness, takes it as from Jeremiah. J. Bright, *Jeremiah* (p. 112), says of 16:1–13 "its material is unquestionably authentic." O. Eissfeldt, *The Old Testament: An Introduction* (p. 352), and A. Weiser, *Das Buch des Propheten Jeremia* (pp. 139–40), concur that 16:10–13 goes back to Jeremiah himself.

11. Eichrodt, *Ezekiel,* p. 188.

12. Ibid., p. 189.

13. See G. A. Cooke, *The Book of Ezekiel,* p. 152.

14. Eichrodt comes to the same view without using the specific term "theodicy," *Ezekiel,* p. 191.

15. Kaufmann, *Religion of Israel,* p. 402. Compare A. J. Heschel, *The Prophets,* p. 13.

16. Ezekiel, chapter 18, is rich enough in implications for theodicy that it deserves a chapter-length analysis by itself. Yet, since it is concerned with the problem of justice for an innocent individual caught up in a corporate punishment, it is peripheral to the main concern of this book. For the reader who would like to do further study of this chapter, I would recommend the excellent analysis of it by Eichrodt, *Ezekiel,* pp. 234–49, with which I find myself in close agreement. His exegesis of that chapter can be compared profitably with W. Zimmerli, *Ezechiel* I, pp. 391–416, and Fohrer, *Ezechiel,* pp. 97–104.

17. I am not aware of anyone who has championed the suggestion that theodicy typically or usually comes within the speech-form of the "disputation speech." But that suggestion is at least implicity raised when Zimmerli says: "As a whole Ez. 18 shows the form of the 'Word of Disputation,' " *Ezekiel* I, p. 396; we add to that Fohrer's suggestion that Ezek. 14:12–23 is a "Diskussionswort," *Ezechiel,* p. 78. At least some of

the examples of "Disputation Speeches" in Second Isaiah given by J. Begrich (*Studien zu Deuterojesaja,* pp. 48–53) and by C. Westermann ("Sprache und Struktur der Prophetie Deuterojesajas," *Forschung am Alten Testament,* pp. 124–34) include units with theodicy-type motifs. The same can be said for the examples in Malachi given by E. Pfeiffer in his "Die Disputationsworte im Buche Maleachi," *EvTh* 19 (1959): 546–68. Crenshaw shows a special interest in "Disputations Speeches" in various kinds of literature, and the questioning of God's justice, but he does not seem ready to force that connection as being a necessary one ("Questioning Justice of God," especially pp. 388–94). My own conclusion from looking at examples given by students of the "Disputation Speech" is that this genre covers a much broader range of concerns than theodicy. Moving in the other direction, theodicy cuts across at least three speech-forms —Communal Laments, prophetic Oracles of Judgment, and prophetic Oracles of Deliverance. Therefore, however interesting the genre may be as a vehicle for this motif, the motif and the genre cannot be identified with one another.

18. W. Brueggemann's recent study, "Jeremiah's Use of Rhetorical Questions," *JBL* 92 (1973): 358–74, is a very interesting and valuable alternative approach to some of the same passages I have been considering. His interest is in tracing out the application to prophetic materials of what he feels is a wisdom-based speech structure, rather than in seeing how theodicy is used in the context of the impending Exile. Accordingly, his emphases and conclusions differ from mine, but on some points the two approaches complement one another.

19. It is with the recognition that God is doing a theodicy for himself in the pathos-filled counter-questions of Jeremiah and Ezekiel that I find myself least in agreement with Crenshaw's article, "Questioning Justice of God." He says, "In essence, the defense of God's justice prominent in prophetic disputations is an effort at self-vindication, a burning issue after the emergence of false prophets" (p. 393). How can that framework of interpretation do justice to the passages we have been examining? Early in his article he suggested that "the question of meaning is more basic than that of God, indeed . . . biblical man's point of departure was not God but self" (p. 382). Accordingly he seems to prefer to speak of the issue of unjust suffering as "anthropodicy" instead of theodicy. I can sympathize with this as a statement of our contemporary problem and outlook, but it overlooks the predictable reflex of Israel's lamenters who turn to God at the first sign of unwarranted pain and ask *him* "Why?" or "How long?" With God's compassionately questioning answers we have moved outside the realm of human excuses or rationalizations for divine action.

20. T. W. Overholt, *The Threat of Falsehood: A Study in the Theology of the Book of Jeremiah,* SBT, n.s. 16 (Naperville, Ill.: Alec R. Allenson, 1970), p. 94. In pointing out the difference between true and false prophecy he assumes that Jeremiah had 31:31–34 in mind during the judgment. We feel that this is wrong. Theodicy assumes that judgment has to be taken entirely seriously on its own terms. The creation of the

state of Israel may speak to the Holocaust, as the kingdom of heaven did to the persecuted under Antiochus, as the prophetic words of deliverance did to the Judean exiles, as God's whirlwind speeches did to Job. But it is taking the Holocaust, the Antiochian persecution, the sufferings of Job, and the impending fall of Jerusalem in 587 completely seriously *in and of themselves,* without unanticipated later reversals of fortune and acts of God's grace, which supplies the context for theodicy.

21. Crenshaw, "Questioning Justice of God," p. 384, sees eschatology as an answer to theodicy, but he takes it as a very bad answer. From whose viewpoint is it an inadequate answer?

22. A. Farrer, *Love Almighty and Ills Unlimited* (Garden City, N.Y.: Doubleday, 1961), p. 18.

23. Among the sources, two that I would recommend are: E. L. Fackenheim, *God's Presence in History* (New York: Harper & Row, 1970), and E. Berkovits, *Faith after the Holocaust* (New York: KTAV, 1973). A good survey of the issues, with much of the relevant literature cited, can be found in A. L. Eckardt, "The Holocaust: Christian and Jewish Responses," *JAAR* 42 (1974): 453–69.

24. A. Lelyveld, *Atheism Is Dead* (Cleveland: World, 1968), p. 181.

CHAPTER V

1. The pathology of this period of Ezekiel scholarship is faithfully recounted by H. H. Rowley in his exhaustively documented article, "The Book of Ezekiel in Modern Study," *Bulletin of the John Rylands Library* 36 (1953-54): 146–90.

2. W. Eichrodt, *Ezekiel*; G. Fohrer, *Ezechiel*; R. H. Pfeiffer, *Introduction to the Old Testament*; W. Zimmerli, *Ezechiel* I–II.

3. This is true of E. W. Nicholson, *Preaching to the Exiles* (New York: Schocken, 1970). J. P. Hyatt, "Introduction, Exegesis," *Jeremiah,* preceded Nicholson in stating this view. See also Hyatt's "The Deuteronomic Edition of Jeremiah," *Vanderbilt Studies in the Humanities,* 1 (1951): 71–95. This unfortunate trend of thought has been brilliantly counterbalanced and corrected by J. Bright in two articles: "The Date of the Prose Sermons of Jeremiah," *JBL* 70 (1951): 15–35; and "The Prophetic Reminiscence: Its Place and Function in the Book of Jeremiah," *Proceedings of the Ninth Meeting of "Die Ou-Testamentiese Werkgemeenskap in Suid-Afrika"* (Potchefstroom: Herald Beperk, 1966), pp. 11–30.

4. With P. Volz, *Der Prophet Jeremia,* and W. Rudolph, *Jeremia.*

5. Volz, *Jeremia,* pp. 283–85, 296–98; Rudolph, *Jeremia,* pp. 172–73, 188–89.

6. Hyatt, *Jeremiah,* pp. 1023–41 rejects all of these. G. Fohrer, *Introduction to the Old Testament,* p. 400, agrees in denying the authenticity of most: 30:8–9, 10–11; 31:7–9, 10–14, 23–25, 26–28, 38–40. My own reasons for dropping these twenty-seven verses can only be hinted at here: 30:10–11 and 31:10–14 show the influence of Second Isaiah; 31: 35–37 employs an argument from nature to history utterly unlike and contradictory to Jeremiah elsewhere. I would add to the post-Jeremianic

material 30:16–17 and probably 31:15–22: the former because, like mid-exilic pieces, it is very Zion-oriented and vindictive against Judah's enemies, the latter because it is a very broken genre not readily compared with any of the deliverance passages to be considered below.

7. The position I take is that the theologically more significant portion of chapter 29, verses 10–14, belongs together with the almost unquestionably authentic letter to the exiles in 29:4–7 as its interpretation. And 32:42–44 stands in much the same relationship to the undoubtedly factual symbolic act described in 32:6–15. This position on 29:4–7, 10–14 is supported by Rudolph, *Jeremia,* pp. 168–69; A. Weiser, *Das Buch des Propheten Jeremia,* pp. 251–55; J. Bright, *Jeremiah,* pp. 210–11; et. al. The decision on 32:6–15, 42–44 is supported by Volz, *Jeremia,* p. 302; Rudolph, *Jeremia,* p. 189; E. Leslie, *Jeremiah: Chronologically Arranged, Translated, and Interpreted* (New York: Abingdon, 1954), pp. 240–42; Bright, *Jeremiah,* pp. 297–98; et al.

8. Accepting at least a kernel of authenticity in 33:6–9 are Rudolph, *Jeremia,* p. 198, Weiser, *Jeremia,* p. 303; Bright, *Jeremiah,* p. 298; A. W. Streane, *The Book of the Prophet Jeremiah, Together with Lamentations,* CBSC (Cambridge: University Press, 1913), p. 207; and Leslie, *Jeremiah,* pp. 243–44. The famous passage 31:31–34 has been abundantly analyzed in a series of commentaries, journal articles, dissertations, and monographs. It is beyond the interests and scope of this chapter to comment on that literature (my argument actually hinges on 24:4–7; 29:4–7, 10–14; and 32:6–15, 42–44). We can say, however, that a clear majority of scholars attribute the words and/or the thoughts of 31:31–34 to Jeremiah himself. Jer. 32:36–41 has drawn less attention than it deserves. One wonders why its strong parallels with 24:4–7 (see Diagram A) and its freshness of conception have not given it a position of priority over 31:31–34, which it is often said to imitate. Supporting its authenticity are Bright, *Jeremiah,* pp. 297–98; Pfeiffer, *Introduction,* p. 503; and Streane, *Jeremiah,* p. 207.

9. S. Mowinckel, *Zur Komposition des Buches Jeremia,* p. 21 [his source "A"]; Volz, *Jeremia,* pp. 244–47; Rudolph, *Jeremia,* p. 145; Weiser, *Jeremia,* p. 213; Fohrer, *Introduction,* p. 398; Eissfeldt, *The Old Testament: An Introduction,* p. 353; Pfeiffer, *Introduction,* p. 503; Leslie, *Jeremiah,* p. 203; and Bright, *Jeremiah,* p. 194.

10. Hyatt, *Jeremiah,* pp. 996–98; "Deuteronomic Edition of Jeremiah," pp. 84–85.

11. Ibid.

12. Rudolph, *Jeremia,* pp. 172–73.

13. See in Bright, *Jeremiah,* pp. LIII–LIV; Hyatt, *Jeremiah,* p. 782; Rudolph, *Jeremia,* pp. VII–VIII; Weiser, *Jeremia,* pp. XXI–XXII.

14. Rudolph, *Jeremia,* pp. 172–73. See his explanations of the absence of any alleged conflict between chapters 24 and 29, and in what sense those who fled to Egypt should deserve inclusion in the judgment of 24:8–10, pp. 146–47.

15. Ibid., p. 146.

16. Ibid., p. 147.

17. For the uses of "good" (*ṭôb*) in Deuteronomistic sources compare W. Brueggemann's "The Kerygma of the Deuteronomistic Historian," *Int* 22 (1968): 387–402. In none of the Deuteronomy or Deuteronomistic passages which Brueggemann cites (to show that the promise of the "good" is a favorite theme of these sources) does *ṭôb* serve to characterize the quality involved in a divine plan for salvation instead of judgment. Deut. 30:5 as in 30:9, on which Brueggemann places central emphasis, reveals that *ṭôb* means that the blessing which God brought on the fathers will also be brought on the children. Brueggemann himself sees this as blessing (p. 393). What I want to ward off is a facile comparison of this employment of *ṭôb* in Deuteronomistic sources with the use of *ṭôb* in the Jeremianic deliverance passages under consideration. The idea of God as the original giver of the "good" (blessing) before 597 turning to give "good" again (Deut. 30:9) is merely a promise of blessing projected into the future. But for our purposes we must see that the restoration of fertility is not the equivalent of what the major prophets understand as the deliverance of a people after judgment.

18. These are my own translations of phrases at the beginning of Second Isaiah which are crucial for understanding the relation between punishment and deliverance.

19. The verses are put in parentheses when they manifest a partial or indirect example of the characteristic described.

20. R. Smend, *Die Bundesformel*. This is usually thought to be a formula for covenant initiation or reinitiation.

21. I have dealt with the comparison to these Deuteronomic passages in more detail in the article "Jeremiah's Deliverance Message to Judah" in *Rhetorical Criticism: Essays in Honor of James Muilenburg,* ed. J. Jackson and M. Kessler (Pittsburgh: Pickwick, 1974), see especially pp. 177–79.

22. The problem with the oracles of weal of the false prophets was that they "whitewashed" (overlooked) the sin of the people, proclaimed "peace" (*šālôm*) when the portents of history were full of "evil," and failed to read accurately the connection between the people's guilt and the forthcoming doom as God's conscious, just punishment. In the determination of the false prophetic promise from the true one it is crucial, but difficult, to know when it was spoken, when it was to take effect, and to whom the promise was directed. On false prophecy, compare T. Overholt, *The Threat of Falsehood: A Study in the Theology of the Book of Jeremiah,* pp. 86–104.

23. I have dealt with these and related passages in more detail in *Rhetorical Criticism,* pp. 179–81.

24. Beyond what is apparent on Diagram B there are other judgment elements or remembrances which do not readily fit into our two subcategories there. They include in Ezek. 34:12 ("scattered abroad"), 34:21b ("scattered them abroad"), 34:27 ("the bars of their yoke"), 36:15 ("not let you hear any more the reproach of the nations"), and 37:11 ("we are clean cut off").

25. Isa. 45:7; 49:14–15; 54:4, 7–8.

CHAPTER VI

1. J. Begrich, "Das priesterliche Heilsorakel," *ZAW* 11–12 (1935): 91.

2. Within the limitations of this chapter I am not undertaking to consider any of the following speech patterns which bear some resemblance to the Oracle of Deliverance: a) narrative descriptions of salvation or historical deliverance; b) hymnic responses to events interpreted as salvation or to divine words of promise; c) prayers entreating God's salvation; d) oracles of doom against Israel's enemies. None of these contain the three elements *1* through *3* specified on page 129 above.

3. This is most true in Jeremiah; it becomes progressively less true as one moves through this oracle from Ezekiel to Second Isaiah.

4. Compare the sayings about the gift of God's Spirit in Ezek. 37:14 and 39:29.

5. J. Begrich, *Studien zu Deuterojesaja,* p. 14; H. von Waldow, "Anlass und Hintergrund der Verkündigung des Deuterojesaja," pp. 27–28.

6. C. Stuhlmueller, *Creative Redemption in Deutero-Isaiah,* Analecta Biblica 43 (Rome: Biblical Institute Press, 1970), pp. 23–25.

7. Von Waldow, "Deuterojesaja," pp. 12ff.; Stuhlmueller, *Deutero-Isaiah,* pp. 23–26; C. Westermann, "Das Heilswort bei Deuterojesaja," *EvTh* 24 (1964): 355ff.; P. Harner, "The Salvation Oracle in Second Isaiah," *JBL* 88 (1969): 418–34; H. M. Dion, "The Patriarchal Traditions and the Literary Form of the 'Oracle of Salvation' " *CBQ* 29 (1967): 198–206; J. M. Berridge, *Prophet, People, and Word of God* (Zurich: EVZ, 1970), p. 184; W. Rast, *Tradition History and the Old Testament* (Philadelphia: Fortress, 1972), pp. 61ff. All of these sources are later than and dependent upon Begrich, "Das priesterliche Heilsorakel," who is the wellspring of this trend of thinking.

8. H. W. Wolff, "Die Bergründungen der Prophetischen Heils- und Unheilssprüche," p. 5.

9. Von Waldow, "Deuterojesaja," pp. 15–18 and 25; Westermann, "Das Heilswort," pp. 357, 362–63. Stuhlmueller, *Deutero-Isaiah,* pp. 20, 26–27; Begrich, "Das priesterliche Heilsorakel," p. 83; Wolff, "Die Begründungen," pp. 9ff.; K. Koch, *The Growth of the Biblical Tradition,* pp. 213–18.

10. Compare *ḥẹsẹd* in the entreaties of Pss. 17:7; 25:6; 36:10; 51:1; 119:149.

11. Jer. 31:2–6 is atypical of what we have generally found in that it assumes a continuity of God's love and relationship through the judgment displacements. Isa. 54:10 *protests* continuity (again) after an explicit acknowledgment of discontinuity in verses 7–8.

12. In Hos. 14:4; Jer. 24:7; 29:11; 31:34; 32:44; and 50:20 the "for" (*kî*), which often comes late in the oracle, introduces *an additional promise* piled on top of all the preceding ones. If there is any "logic" to this, it is that one promise is explained in terms of another or leads to another. The one real exception to this is the introduction of the saying about "steadfast love" in Jer. 31:3 with "therefore" (*'al—kēn*).

13. The great student of Ezekiel, W. Zimmerli, who has made an

extensive study of this expression, calls it the "word of demonstration," and considers it a speech-genre in its own right, with a history before Ezekiel gave it such massive expression. It has to do more with theophany and the kind of divine self-predication we found in Second Isaiah than with an explanation based on historical causes or precedents. For more details on this expression see the three articles in Zimmerli's *Gottes Offenbarung: Gessammelte Aufsätze,* TB 19 (Munich: Chr. Kaiser, 1969)—"Ich bin Jahwe," pp. 11–40; "Erkenntnis Gottes nach dem Buche Ezechiel," pp. 41–119; "Das Wort des göttlichen Selbsterweises (Erweiswort), eine prophetische Gattung," pp. 120–32.

14. We have to do with these considerations: a) The expression "for my name's sake," or a variation of it, also occurs both outside (20:9, 14, 22; 36:20, 21; 39:7; 43:7, 8) and inside (20:44; 36:22, 23; 39:25) the Oracles of Deliverance. b) The concern about God's name, as stated, is not rooted in Israel or in God's relation with it. The concern is with God's reputation for power and sovereignty vis-à-vis the gentile nations. The formulation that we find in Ezek. 36:22 is typical: "It is not for your sake, O house of Israel, that I am about to act, but for the sake of my holy name which you have profaned among the nations. . . ." c) In every instance where this expression comes within an Oracle of Deliverance, it is closely associated with the expression "then you shall know that I am the Lord." In Ezekiel God's acting for the sake of his name or just so that he will be known as God both point back to the essential mystery of God's holiness. Again, I claim that only states what is implicit when no explanation is given: God only does it for his own reasons. d) W. Eichrodt has an excellent statement on this expression in his commentary *Ezekiel,* pp. 496–97, in which he makes clear that it has nothing to do with human, historical, or institutional bases for a hope in God's salvation.

15. Begrich, "Das priesterliche Heilsorakel," pp. 83ff.; Wolff, "Die Begründungen," pp. 9ff.; Von Waldow, "Deuterojesaja," pp. 12–19; Westermann, "Das Heilswort," pp. 357ff.

16. Von Waldow, "Deuterojesaja," p. 19; Westermann, "Das Heilswort," pp. 364–65; Stuhlmueller, *Deutero-Isaiah,* pp. 20–21, 27–28.

17. For the last element in Second Isaiah, see above, this chapter, Diagram D, p. 137.

18. R. Knierim, "Form Criticism: The Present State of an Exegetical Discipline," pp. 10–11.

19. Ibid., p. 13.

20. These concerns are still shown as central in Koch's *The Growth of the Biblical Tradition,* pp. 26ff.; Knierim, "Form Criticism: Present State," pp. 2, 13–14; and G. M. Tucker's *Form Criticism of the Old Testament,* pp. 9, 14.

21. Tucker, *Form Criticism,* p. 9.

22. J. Muilenburg, "Form Criticism and Beyond," *JBL* 88 (1969): 5.

23. Koch, *Biblical Tradition,* p. 28.

24. Ibid., p. 27; italics mine.

25. Tucker, *Form Criticism,* p. 15; italics mine.

26. Knierim, "Form Criticism: Present State," p. 13.
27. Ibid., p. 7; italics his.
28. We have in mind here Von Waldow's dissertation, "Deuterojesaja." Westermann's work has come in the "Das Heilswort" article we have already noted; in an article entitled "Sprache und Struktur der Prophetie Deuterojesajas," pp. 92–170; in his translated commentary, *Isaiah 40–66*; and in a semi-popular article "The Way of Promise through the Old Testament," pp. 200–24, in *The Old Testament and Christian Faith*, ed. B. Anderson (New York: Harper & Row, 1963).
29. See note 7 in this chapter for a representative listing of those who follow in the Begrich orbit.
30. Begrich, "Das priesterliche Heilsorakel," p. 81.
31. Ibid., p. 84.
32. Ibid., p. 91.
33. Ibid.
34. Ibid.
35. Ibid., p. 92.
36. Begrich, *Deuterojesaja*, p. 14.
37. Ibid., p. 15.
38. Ibid.
39. Ibid., p. 16.
40. Ibid., pp. 91–92.
41. Ibid., p. 106; cf. pp. 91–94 also.
42. Ibid., pp. 106ff.
43. We can summarize the following points in Von Waldow's dissertation, "Deuterojesaja": a) He has an expanded structure of the genre (pp. 12–19). b) He gives an interesting example of this oracle in its life situation in 1 Chr. 20:15–17 (pp. 77ff). c) As opposed to Begrich, who normatively makes the speaker of this oracle a priest, Von Waldow insists: "The speaker of the oracle of salvation in the cult will thus be a prophet, better a cult prophet" (p. 85). d) He thinks of the setup as a cultic appropriation of a covenantal structure so that the cult-prophet stands as a mediator between the covenant-God and the covenant people (p. 86). e) Von Waldow claims that Second Isaiah was himself a cult-prophet whose office was an essential component of the covenant. He spoke these salvation oracles in the midst of a People's Lament Festival, and specifically as a cult-oracle answer to the people's lament (p. 174). On this latter point, one should note the critique given it by G. Fohrer, "Remarks on Modern Interpretations of the Prophets," *JBL* 80 (1961): 311. One can find portions of Von Waldow's position in English in his article, "The Message of Deutero-Isaiah," *Int* 22 (1968): 259–87.
44. The sources of Westermann's contribution have already been summarized in note 28. Primary elements in his views include the following. a) For Westermann, Begrich's shift from eight oracles in the 1934 article ("Das priesterliche Heilsorakel") to twenty-four in the 1938 monograph (*Deuterojesaja*) breaks apart. b) Westermann argues for an "Announcement of Salvation" genre which is distinctly separate from the "Assurance of Salvation" genre. The former has for its time orienta-

tion the future, the latter the present. The former lacks the "fear not" saying; the latter is virtually defined by that saying. While both speech-forms are answers to cultic laments, the former answers the entreaty of the whole people, the latter the entreaty of an individual. ("Das Heilswort" pp. 364–65) c) The "Announcement of Salvation" genre does not have so close a tie to the cult as the "Assurance of Salvation" . . . although in both cases they are adapted to their new setting. d) He holds that the distinction between the "Assurance of Salvation" is valid not only for Second Isaiah but for the Old Testament in general ("Das Heilswort," p. 373).

In my view this splitting up into two genres to carry the deliverance message in Second Isaiah just underlines the problem which Begrich began. Neither of these is *generic* if found only in Second Isaiah—in that case, generic to what? Westermann has failed to demonstrate the presence of either oracle in earlier prophets. Most of the criticisms in the text now to follow apply to Von Waldow and Westermann, although they are specifically aimed at Begrich.

45. Knierim, "Form Criticism: Present State," p. 7, talks about settings changing; also Tucker, *Form Criticism,* pp. 69–70. Von Waldow, "Deuterojesaja," pp. 91ff., deals with a change in setting for the priestly salvation oracle.

46. Begrich, *Deuterojesaja,* pp. 84, 91–93.

47. Ibid., pp. 93ff.

48. In his monograph *Wächter über Israel,* H. G. Reventlow develops the thesis that in the "Holiness Code," and especially in Leviticus 26, we have a developed form of a covenant festival ritual going back to much earlier times (pp. 157ff.). He sees Ezekiel's role and message as being quite specifically determined for him by his acting out an office in the priestly cult such as is evidenced by Leviticus 26 and related texts (pp. 157ff.). Reventlow specifically sees the prophetic word of judgment as an extrapolation from covenant curses (pp. 42 ff.), and the prophetic word of salvation as an extrapolation from covenantal blessings (pp. 65ff.).

49. See Westermann, "The Way of Promise," pp. 209–11; W. Brueggemann, *Tradition for Crisis,* pp. 72–79.

50. See above, Chapter V, pp. 119–22.

51. K. Beyer, "*eulogeō* Blessing in the Old Testament," *Theological Word Book of the New Testament,* ed. R. Kittel, vol. II, p. 757. W. Harrelson, "Blessings and Cursings," *IDB,* vol. I, pp. 446–47. M. Noth "For all those who rely on works of the law are under a curse," *The Laws in the Pentateuch and Other Studies,* trans. D. R. Ap-Thomas (Philadelphia: Fortress, 1967), pp. 119ff. J. Pedersen, *Israel: Its Life and Culture* I–II (London: Oxford University Press, 1926), pp. 182ff.

52. Noth, "Under a curse," pp. 120, 122, 123, 124, 126, 129.

53. On the historicization of the Patriarchal blessings, see Westermann, "The Way of Promise," pp. 209–11; Zimmerli, "Promise and Fulfillment," *Essays on Old Testament Hermeneutics,* ed. C. Westermann (Richmond: John Knox, 1963), pp. 91–93.

54. It is puzzling whether the promissory words in Hos. 2:18ff.; 14:4–7 are spoken before 722 but meant to apply after that, were limited and isolated words of hope before 722, or were added after 722 by later sources. The same question exists for the few words of promise in Amos and Micah, though there is more question about authenticity there.

55. As I read Tucker, *Form Criticism,* about the way that "genres arise, develop, flourish, and eventually decay, often giving rise in the process to mutations or new genres" (p. 8), toegther with what G. von Rad, *Old Testament Theology* II, says about "*ad hoc* improvisation" as a distinguishing quality of forms of prophetic speech (p. 39), both seem close to the idea of the possibility of a *sui generis* genre.

56. On this see H. H. Rowley, *The Biblical Doctrine of Election* (London: Lutterworth, 1950), pp. 19–23.

57. With Von Rad, *Genesis: A Commentary,* trans. J. H. Marks, OTL (London: SCM, 1961), pp. 280, 397; see R. E. Clements, *Abraham and David,* p. 22.

58. With Clements, *Abraham and David,* pp. 11, 34; Von Rad, *Genesis,* p. 280.

59. Dion, "Patriarchal Traditions," finds a close correlation between these oracles to the Patriarchs and Begrich's "priestly oracle of salvation." The view taken is that the structure of the latter may have been imposed on the former (pp. 203–6). But if the two types of speech are as closely related as Dion says, which is not apparent to me, then the possibility is raised of the influence going forward from Genesis to Second Isaiah.

60. The divine speech within Exod. 3:1–12 also deals with: a) the call and commissioning of Moses (3:4–5, 10, 12). J. Kenneth Kuntz, *The Self-Revelation of God* (Philadelphia: Westminster, 1967), analyzes what he calls "a prophetic call" here (p. 145); b) the effort to link the God of Moses' experience with the God of the Patriarchs (3:6); and c) the motif of God's responding to the pathetic situation of the Hebrew slaves in Egypt (3:7, 9). The divine speech is also broken by points of dialogue where Moses speaks.

61. Cf. W. Zimmerli, *The Law and the Prophets,* trans. by R. E. Clements (Oxford: Basil Blackwell, 1965), p. 57; Kuntz, *Self-Revelation,* p. 90; M. Newman, *The People of the Covenant* (New York: Abingdon, 1962), p. 31.

62. "P" even shows some tendencies to retroject this prophetic genre back into his version of the call to Abraham, although the differences between Exod. 6:2–8 and Gen. 17:2–8 are as instructive as the similarities. As in Exodus 6 the passage begins: "I am God Almighty" and ends: "I will be their God" with divine self-identifications or self-predications. Much that comes between these phrases is closely shaped to fit the Patriarchal situation and does not show strong affinities with the prophetic use of the Oracle of Deliverance. We would note on that point God's admonition to Abram in 17:2, the tenor of the covenant promise in 17:4, and the change of Abram's name in 17:5. This promise is also typically Patriarchal in that the promises center on land and posterity, as we found to be the case in the JE passages. We should bear

in mind, however, that this is where "P" locates the origination of the covenant. It is not very surprising that even in the midst of these differences from the Exodus 6 passage, his oracle in Gen. 17:2–8 should contain language closer to the prophetic Oracle of Deliverance than any of the other promises to the Patriarchs in the Book of Genesis. One should note that the promise of an "everlasting covenant," verse 7, and "everlasting possession" of the land, verse 8, is typically post-exilic in its perception, and not within the elements which reflect prophetic influence here.

63. Smend, *Die Bundesformel,* p. 27.

64. Ibid., p. 8.

65. Ibid., pp. 19 and 25.

66. Ibid., p. 26.

67. Kuntz, *Self-Revelation,* pp. 59–69.

68. As exemplified in Dion, "Patriarchal Traditions," pp. 198ff.; and Begrich, "Das priesterliche Heilsorakel," pp. 81ff.

69. Kuntz, *Self-Revelation,* p. 69; italics his.

70. Ibid., pp. 68–69, 89–91, 115, 164.

71. Ibid., pp. 68–69, 105, 150.

72. Ibid., pp. 150 and 162.

73. See above, pp. 136–39, 143–45, and notes 13 and 14 earlier in this chapter.

74. Kuntz, *Self-Revelation,* is so struck by the repetition of typical theophanic elements throughout Second Isaiah that he goes so far as to say "the *hieros logos,* Yahweh's special word of disclosure, resounds throughout these chapters. Only a few verses of the 333 in Isa. chs. 40–55, could be confidently excluded here!" (p. 164). Kuntz has developed his views to some extent under the stimulus of an earlier article by J. Muilenburg in which the latter said: "It is clear that the eschatological theophany receives its consummate and, if one may use the term, its classical formulation in Second Isaiah"; "The Speech of Theophany," *Harvard Divinity School Bulletin,* 28 (1964): 46.

CHAPTER VII

1. A. Johnson, *The Vitality of the Individual in the Thought of Ancient Israel* (Cardiff: University of Wales Press, 1949), p. 84.

2. The passages which come closest are: 1 Sam. 10:9, where God changes Saul's heart as a temporary endowment; Ps. 51:10, where the penitential request for a "new heart" and "right spirit" seems to be patterned after the deliverance proclamation in Ezek. 36:26 (following the suggestion of G. Fohrer, *Ezechiel,* p. 205), and Deut. 30:6 where the promise that "God will circumcise your heart" is set within the framework of the traditional Sinai Covenant and the customary conditionality which is an intrinsic part of it.

3. A. Weiser and W. Rudolph are typical of most commentators in not giving enough attention to the saying in 24:7, and in thereby making the whole "new covenant" speech in 31:31–34 isolated and seemingly extraordinary. Rudolph does not do justice to the newness of what God

does in 24:7, or see the pattern of the relationship between that transformation and re-election in other deliverance oracles (*Jeremia,* p. 146). Much the same can be said for Weiser. The whole issue is lost, or confused, when he talks about this passage drawing inspiration from covenant renewal traditions in the cult. He himself recognizes that we are not here under the terms of the old covenant, but under the terms of God's grace. One must be quite precise about the time, the era, the period of God's dispensation in which the promises of 24:4–7 are to take effect. It is quite inadequate to speak of it as "covenant renewal," and Weiser needs to change that in order to correct a contradiction in his own exegetical statement (*Das Buch des propheten Jeremia,* p. 215).

Compare G. von Rad, *Old Testament Theology* II, pp. 211, 212 where he says of 24:7 "here is the prophecy of the new covenant compressed into one sentence."

4. Weiser, *Jeremia,* p. 288; Rudolph, *Jeremia,* p. 185. The reader is encouraged to see what Weiser and Rudolph say about 31:31–34, and compare that with the lines of analysis and emphasis in my own statement. They are not so focused on transformation or on the relationship of that theme with the judgment message as I am; nor is their attention drawn to the relationship of the transformation motif to the promise of re-election as part of a pattern of sayings in Jeremiah and Ezekiel. But they deal with 31:31–34 much more extensively and adequately than with the theological implications in 24:4–7, and they do credit 31:31–34 with containing several significant dimensions of newness.

5. Fohrer, *Ezechiel,* has some good observations on what the transformation means for the individual, on which I think, however, he places a one-sided emphasis. I was impressed with this statement: "This new man is thus in the posture to do the will of God in the right way—neither out of unfree obedience, but himself willing the right, nor as a moral achievement, but as consequence of the act of redemption." As with Rudolph and Weiser in interpreting Jeremiah, Fohrer does not deal with the relationship between transformation and election, as I do, nor does he deal with it as a response to a reality within the judgment preaching (see p. 62).

6. Like Jer. 31:31–34, Ezek. 36:22–32 is so meaty theologically that it has attracted extended interpretations. The reader is encouraged to compare the remarks of W. Zimmerli, *Ezechiel* II, pp. 878–80; W. Eichrodt, *Ezekiel,* pp. 498–502; and Fohrer, *Ezekiel,* pp. 204–5. In general what they say enriches the overall understanding of these verses, but without either creating challenges for the line of argumentation in the preceding pages or duplicating the level or direction of our analysis.

7. The people are described as having a new condition making for responsiveness, obedience, or affinity with God in Jer. 29:12–13; Ezek. 37:14. The oracle in Ezek. 37:24–28 has an assurance of their obedience in the beginning (v. 24b), a promise of a (new) everlasting covenant in the middle (v. 26), and a Covenant Formula just before the end (v. 27). Even there we see the outline of the pattern discussed in our six focal texts, though loosened by intervening elements.

8. T. Raitt, "The Concept of Forgiveness in the Pre-exilic Prophets in Relation to Its Form-Historical Setting," p. 57.

9. K. Koch, "Sühne und Sündenvergebung: Um die Wende von der exilischen zur nachexilischen Zeit," p. 219.

10. J. J. Stamm, *Erlösen und Vergeben im Alten Testament,* p. 109.

11. See in my S.T.M. thesis "The Use of the Verb Nāsā' in the Old Testament in Relation to the Forgiveness of Sins" (Union Theological Seminary, 1960).

12. Stamm, *Erlösen und Vergeben,* pp. 142, 147.

13. Eichrodt, *Theology of the Old Testament* II, pp. 465–73.

14. We do not mean to suggest that these two types of forgiveness sayings are all that one finds in post-exilic literature. There are others like those found in 2 Chr. 7:14; Pss. 85:2, 103:3. But in these and other texts from this period it is still generally true that forgiveness is treated as an enduringly simple possibility.

15. With Koch, "Sündenvergebung," pp. 217ff.

16. Eichrodt, *Ezekiel,* p. 514 speaks here of a "new creation" and of a "covenant newly made." Zimmerli, *Ezechiel* II, p. 919, sees the "new heart" of Ezek. 36:26 presupposed here.

17. Eichrodt, *Ezekiel,* p. 283.

18. The words for "pleasing odor" here are exactly the same as in Gen. 8:21 where the text describes the aroma which went up from Noah's sacrifice and seemingly led to God's promise not to curse the earth again.

19. Zimmerli, *Ezechiel* I, p. 458.

20. Rudolph, *Jeremia,* p. 198.

21. Weiser, *Jeremia,* p. 304.

22. So in J. P. Hyatt, "Introduction, Exegesis," *Jeremiah,* pp. 786 and 1038; Rudolph, *Jeremia,* p. 185; Weiser, *Jeremia,* p. 288.

23. Rudolph, *Jeremia,* p. 185.

24. Weiser, *Jeremia,* p. 288; it is important to take this point together with an earlier comment from Weiser that Jeremiah "clearly distinguishes, even according to its content, this new covenant from the old," p. 286.

25. See the other terminology of election and relationship as discussed in Chapter VI, pp. 134–35, 141–42.

26. R. Smend, *Die Bundesformel,* p. 6.

27. Ibid.

28. Ibid., pp. 8–9.

29. In his dissertation, "Die Bedeutung der Erwählungstraditionen Israels für die Eschatologie der alttestementlichen propheten," E. Rohland centers the very definition of eschatology around election. In this he speaks repeatedly of a "new election," pp. 41, 43, 77, 78, 84, 85, 93, 258, 261, 273–74, often in a context where it is clear that he understands the repetition of the *Bundesformel* to communicate a new election.

30. Weiser, *Jeremia,* p. 287.

31. Fohrer, *Ezechiel,* p. 205; compare his comment on the *Bundesformel* in Ezek. 11:20, p. 62.

32. T. Vriezen, *An Outline of Old Testament Theology,* p. 370. J. Lindblom gives election a quite central role in eschatology: "The basic idea of the national eschatology with the prophets is that there is in conformity with the election-conception a renovated Israel of the ideal future"; Lindblom, "Gibt es eine Eschatologie bei den alttestamentlichen Propheten?" p. 111. "The motivation of the national eschatology lies in the election love of Yahweh for Israel"; "Eschatologie," p. 113. In surveying passages representative of "national eschatology" Lindblom never fails to pick out the *Bundesformel* as one of the notable features. He always refers to this in the terms: "Verwirklichung des Erwählungsgedankens" in "Eschatologie," pp. 104–12. This can be translated either "Realization" or "Actualization" "of the conception of Election." It is interesting that he places the center of meaning on the essential idea of election now at this time coming to reality and fruition, rather than on this formula as a reference to the covenant. The "I-Thou" quality of God-man relationship—in election, covenant, or on a one-to-one level—is the subject of M. Buber's little classic *I and Thou,* trans. R. G. Smith (New York: Charles Scribner's Sons, 1937).

33. The latter two passages are generally thought to be from the Deuteronomistic editors of Jeremiah.

34. See in Smend, *Die Bundesformel,* pp. 26–27, and with reference to his footnote 79a on p. 38 of his monograph.

35. H. Ortmann, "Der Alte und der Neue Bund bei Jeremia" (Dissertation, Berlin, 1940), see pp. 79–81. Compare his position on this with W. Lempp, "Bund und Bundeserneuerung bei Jeremia" (Inaugural Dissertation, Eberhard-Karls-Universität, Tübingen, 1954), pp. 105–11.

36. B. Anderson, "The New Covenant and the Old," in *The Old Testament and Christian Faith,* ed. B. Anderson (New York: Harper & Row, 1963), p. 232.

37. Von Rad, *Old Testament Theology* II, p. 212.

38. See in C. Westermann, "The Way of Promise through the Old Testament," in *The Old Testament and Christian Faith* (ed. Anderson), p. 219. B. S. Childs, *Myth and Reality in the Old Testament,* SBT 27 (London: SCM, 1960), p. 80. R. E. Clements, *Prophecy and Covenant,* p. 118 says: ". . . the pre-exilic prophets foretold that Israel would be judged and the covenant brought to an end. Yet beyond this judgment they pointed also to a new beginning when Israel would be reborn and would become once again the people of the covenant. The old election traditions were used by the prophets to portray the re-election of Israel, and the new covenant which Yahweh would make with them."

39. D. J. McCarthy, *Old Testament Covenant: A Survey of Current Opinions* (Richmond, Va.: John Knox, 1972), pp. 46–47 takes the former position, and does so with regard to the OT generally, and not in terms of a specific interpretation of Jeremiah; indeed, there is a limited validity for his position if he means it to apply to the whole of OT literature, but it misrepresents the very significant change which Jeremiah envisioned *within* the tradition of the Mosaic Covenant. The latter position is that taken by D. N. Freedman, "Divine Commitment and Human Obliga-

tion," *Int* 18 (1964): 421, 429–31. Again, he is talking in broader terms than in reference to Jeremiah, but I think that his position is incorrect inasmuch as it suggests that Jeremiah worked his way to a "new covenant" promise through the optimism of the Patriarchal-Davidic tradition.

40. Anderson, "New Covenant and the Old," p. 230.

41. Von Rad, *Theology* II, p. 213: "The content of the Sinai covenant was the revelation of the *tôrāh,* that is to say, the revelation of Israel's election and appropriation by Yahweh and his will as expressed in law. This *tôrāh* is also to stand in the center of the new covenant which Yahweh is going to make with Israel 'in these days.'" See Rohland, "Erwählungstraditionen," pp. 70ff. See also Weiser, *Jeremia,* p. 287.

42. So in Rudolph, *Jeremia,* p. 185; Weiser, *Jeremia,* p. 288; and others. It is very difficult and problematic to try to show that forgiveness had any secure role within covenant or covenant renewal ceremonies in the pre-exilic period. We mentioned that the Exod. 34:6–7 type of formulation but without the pole promising God's readiness to punish is found in a number of texts which are claimed to have been used in covenant-renewal ceremonies (see p. 190 in this chapter), but most of those texts appear to be from the time of the Exile or later. This is why we said, in our discussion of the restrictions on forgiveness in the pre-exilic period, pp. 185–89 above, that it is easier to demonstrate the denial of forgiveness or forgiveness possibility set in sharp dialectic with punishment possibility in the time before Jeremiah than anything approaching the unconditional forgiveness promised in Jer. 31:34.

43. See in Lempp, "Bundeserneuerung bei Jeremia," p. 118. Cf. Ortman, "Alte und neue Bund bei Jeremia," pp. 79–81.

44. So, for example, in Hyatt, *Jeremiah,* p. 1038; Weiser, *Jeremia,* p. 288; Childs, *Myth and Reality,* p. 80; Anderson, "New Covenant and the Old," pp. 230–32.

45. So in Weiser, *Jeremia,* p. 300. Cf. Rudolph, *Jeremia,* pp. 195–97.

46. See Weiser, *Jeremia,* p. 300; Rudolph, *Jeremia,* pp. 195–97; cf. Hyatt, *Jeremiah,* p. 1042.

47. Von Rad, *Theology* II, pp. 214–15.

48. R. Clements, *Abraham and David,* p. 71.

49. Cf. Hos. 2:19.

50. Eichrodt, *Ezekiel,* pp. 501–2.

51. Von Rad, *Theology* II, p. 235.

52. Ibid.

53. Fohrer, *Ezechiel,* pp. 211–12.

54. Zimmerli, *Ezechiel* II, p. 914.

55. Rohland, "Erwählungstraditionen," talks about the threefold election traditions present in Ezek. 37:24ff. on pp. 261–62.

56. Von Rad, *Theology* II, p. 236.

57. Eichrodt, *Ezekiel,* pp. 474–80, 511–15.

58. I enter this discussion of eschatology with some misgivings. Not a few Old Testament scholars refuse to use the term. For the first time since the Introduction we leave behind immediate and repeated demonstration of our points from the biblical text. Our rationale for discussing

eschatology at the end of this chapter is twofold: a) Some scholars relate doom to salvation in the prophets under the banner of eschatology; this is a position which I find quite unacceptable. b) Although one could conceptualize the sum of Jeremiah's and Ezekiel's deliverance preaching under some contrived banner like "The Dramatic, Qualitatively Different Era of Divine Deliverance," it makes more sense to use the term "eschatology" if a reasonable case can be made for that. This is especially so because it allows comparison with the eschatology so widely seen in Second Isaiah, Daniel, the New Testament, and in some contemporary expressions of theology. I ask the reader's understanding, therefore, in what is an exploration beyond the direct exegetical foundation of the rest of the book.

59. I am not undertaking a critical review of the history of scholarship on Old Testament eschatology. The best sources for this are in German: W. Köhler, "Prophetie und Eschatologie: in der neueren alttestamentlichen Forschung," *Bibel und Leben* 9 (1968): 57–81; G. Wanke, "'Eschatologie.' Ein Beispiel theologischer Sprachverwirrung," *Kerygma und Dogma* 16 (1970): 300–12; Rohland, "Erwählungstraditionen," pp. 1–19.

60. S. Mowinckel, *He That Cometh,* pp. 125–54; J. P. M. Van Der Ploeg, "Eschatology in the Old Testament," in *The Witness of Tradition,* Oudtestamentische Studien 17 (Leiden: E. J. Brill, 1972), pp. 89–99; and S. B. Frost, "Eschatology and Myth," *VT* 2 (1952): 70–80 are the primary mid-twentieth century proponents of this view.

61. O. Procksch, "Eschatology in the Old Testament and Judaism," in *Twentieth Century Theology in the Making* vol. I, ed. J. Pelikan (New York: Harper & Row, 1969), pp. 230–32.

62. E. Jenni, "Eschatology of the Old Testament," *IDB,* vol. II, pp. 126–27.

63. J. H. Grönbaek, "Zur Frage der Eschatologie in der Verkündigung der Gerichtspropheten," *Svensk Exegetisk Arsbok* 24 (1959): 10; the key term here in German is *"Abschluss-Aspekt."*

64. T. C. Vriezen, "Prophecy and Eschatology," Supplements to *VT: Congress Volume,* vol. I (Leiden: E. J. Brill, 1953), p. 233.

65. H. D. Preuss, *Jahweglaube und Zukunftserwartung,* pp. 154ff.

66. Lindblom, "Eschatologie," p. 80.

67. Ibid., p. 81; italics his.

68. Ibid. Although we see him apply this to specific passages in a way that helps us to avoid some of the generalizations of the studies considered in the previous section, and so that through the basic types of eschatological expectations certain additional emphases come forth, Lindblom is content with this basic standard of delineation and repeats it in at least three later points in his article; see pp. 106, 112, 113.

69. Ibid., pp. 83–88.

70. Ibid., p. 100.

71. Ibid., pp. 101–6. In his summary of the main conceptions of national eschatology, only the first out of more than twenty items has to do with judgment on the nation, p. 112. His list is considerably broader

than *transformation, forgiveness, new election, new covenant,* but it includes those along with deliverance and restoration motifs.

72. Ibid., p. 104.
73. Ibid., p. 111.
74. The singular importance of Lindblom's work is certainly underlined by the 1970 article by Wanke, "Eschatologie: Ein Beispiel theologischer Sprachverwirrung," in which Wanke undertakes to survey the work done on eschatology up until that time. It is an evaluative survey, a critique of methodologies used in studies done on eschatology. Wanke credits Lindblom as the one who has made the soundest contribution to this field of study; see pp. 304ff.
75. Rohland, "Erwählungstraditionen."
76. Ibid., p. 44.
77. Ibid.
78. Ibid., p. 46.
79. Ibid.
80. Ibid., p. 74.
81. Ibid.
82. Ibid., p. 77.
83. Ibid., p. 88.
84. Ibid., p. 250.
85. Ibid., p. 259.
86. Ibid., p. 273.
87. Ibid., pp. 78–86.
88. Von Rad, *Theology* II, p. 115.
89. Ibid., p. 212.
90. Ibid., p. 234.
91. Fohrer, "Die Struktur der alttestamentlichen Eschatologie," *Theologische Literaturzeitung,* 85 (1960), uses criteria similar to Lindblom's. But he imposes a stereotype on all prophets before Second Isaiah, calling them "the great individual prophets" (pp. 404ff.). Jeremiah and Ezekiel are lumped together with everyone from Amos onward. These prophets are characterized as having for the essential feature of their message an "Either/Or" calling for moral decision and repentance (pp. 404, 419). Second Isaiah and other late prophets misinterpreted this Either/Or into a "Before/After," and this temporal division became the basis for eschatology (pp. 404–5, 419). Fohrer is not only denying eschatology to the prophets before Second Isaiah, but also *protecting* them from this development which he sees as a degeneration of the moral integrity of Israelite religion (pp. 419–20). This value judgment would not have been possible had not Fohrer failed to see the integrity between Jeremiah's and Ezekiel's judgment preaching and their salvation preaching.
92. As is in keeping with the method of this study, everything which I have to say about the deliverance message of Ezekiel is based on his eleven genuine Oracles of Deliverance shown in Diagram C of Chapter VI. The question might be raised: How does the pattern of the salvation message there relate to the implementation of salvation in terms of

an ideally rebuilt temple expressed in the unit chapters 40–48? Since the concern of this book is the doom/salvation switch, and the relation of the Oracle of Judgment to the Oracle of Deliverance, I have not investigated or attempted to answer that question. If chapters 40–48 represent the thought of Ezekiel, even as transmitted through his earliest disciples—and that is much debated—then we have to say that Ezekiel made the following transitions within his life: a) from a priestly point of view to a prophetic point of view; b) dealing with the absolute end of Judah in the only terms by which that was understandable theologically: the Moasic Covenant tradition; c) a radical turn toward words of deliverance based on no institution, but conceived in the manner described in the last half of our Chapter VI, and in this chapter; d) a shift back to the priestly point of view, so that he was concerned with the reestablishment of the basic cultic and theocratic institutions once the survivors of the Exile were returned to Jerusalem. If Ezekiel himself made all four of these transitions, that is indeed amazing. We have already indicated some images in the deliverance oracles of chapters 34, 36, and 37 suggesting that he at least began turning toward stage *d*. *However,* as concerns Ezekiel, our study is *solely* concerned with stages *b* and *c* and the relationship between them. Whatever is elaborated in chapters 40–48 has no bearing on *how Ezekiel turned* from a message of doom to a message of salvation. Clearly he did not achieve that on the basis of some notion of the continuity of the cult, or the hopes radiating out of Zion. He made his all-important turning point from doom to salvation in the terms we have described. Anything which he or his disciples say *after* that is a *consequence* of this perception of God's change of plan. So, there is nothing about the institutionalism of chapters 40–48 which compromises the eschatology of chapters 34, 36, and 37. What apparently does happen in Ezekiel 40–48, as in Leviticus 26 and late additions to Deuteronomy, is that the forward momentum of radical early exilic eschatology becomes domesticated, and the Judahites try to normalize (once again) their relation to Yahweh.

93. Von Rad, *Theology* II, p. 115.

94. The reader should not assume that I have moved from the stated purpose of this book toward asserting general truths about eschatology in Second Isaiah or apocalyptic sources. What I say about eschatology in those settings is only an attempt to sketch general outlines of alternatives to eschatology in Jeremiah's and Ezekiel's Oracles of Deliverance for purposes of comparison, as that comparison helps us better to understand the doom/salvation shift in these two prophets.

95. J. A. Sanders, *Torah and Canon* (Philadelphia: Fortress, 1972), pp. 7–8.

INDEX

Index

Covenant
ended at onset of Exile, 59
faith-elements on which founded, 162
and forgiveness, 193
Mosaic covenant as setting for Oracle of Judgment, 20–25
new covenant, everlasting covenant part of Oracle of Deliverance promise, 200–206
relationship to cult, 161–62
"Covenant Formula," 63, 116–17, 134–35, 141, 168, 170–71, 196–200, 204
Deliverance Message
eschatology, 206–22
forgiveness, 184–94
new or everlasting covenant, 200–206
re-election, 195–200
transformation, 175–84
Doom/salvation shift
consequence of supposed different audiences addressed, 8–9
function of A.N.E. patternism, 7–8
function of split in God's nature, 9–11
Eschatology (in deliverance message of Jeremiah and Ezekiel)
continuity in the midst of discontinuity, 221–22
as defined by Lindblom, Rohland, Von Rad, 209–12
national deliverance (in Jeremiah and Ezekiel) eschatological, 212–14
national judgment *not* eschatological, 217–21
new criteria suggested for its presence, 215–17
unacceptable definitions, 207–9
Eschatology and theodicy, 101–2
Exile
catalyst to theodicy, 83–84
a good purgational experience, 228–30
as hermeneutical problem, 4–6
as time of religious renewal, 224
its changes arguing against

a closed canon, 225–28
God
the continuity between radical judgment and eschatological deliverance, 222
defends himself against accusatory questions with pathos-filled counter-questions, 94–102
his illogical love, 229
liberated by Exile, 228
mystery and freedom, 227
obtains new freedom in era of eschatology, 217
the ultimate unification of the justice/love tension, 12
wills to show mercy in the midst of judgment, 58, 107–8
Jewish-Christian relations, 104–5, 223–25
Oracle of Deliverance
answer to problems expressed in theodicy, 94–102
authenticity in Ezekiel, 108–10
authenticity in Jeremiah, 110–19, 123–27
context, 147–49
distinguished from false prophecy, 123–27
a "Goal" component lacking, 146–48
intention, 149–50
judgment era remembered and held in tension with deliverance era, 123–27
a "Reason" component lacking, 142–46
reconceptualizing the role "setting" can play in this genre, 160–63
setting as answer to cultic lament, 151–58
setting derived by analogy with divine declarations in Exodus, 165–72
setting in blessing, 158–60
setting not derived from Theophany genre, 172–73
structure in Amos through Ezekiel, 128–36
structure in Second Isaiah, 136–42
Oracle of Judgment
context, 31–33
intentions, 33–34
Mosaic covenant as setting, 20–25
prophecy as setting, 25–31
structure, 15–17
Prophetic Summons to Repentance, 37–40
Radicalization of the judgment message
failure of repentance, 39–49
God's refusal to forgive, 49–58
Rejection
God's rejection of Judah part of radicalization of

the judgment message, 59–74
presupposed in deliverance oracles, 76–78
texts which deny rejections and stress unbroken continuity, 78–80
Theodicy
answered by deliverance era, 99–102
contained in Oracle of Judgment, 90–94
definition, 85
Exile and Holocaust, 103
as God's pathos-filled counter-question, 94–99
issue raised by events of Exile, 83–84
Jeremiah and Ezekiel compared to Job's friends, 102–3
as the people's questioning, 86–89